DEVON & CORNWALL RECORD SOCIETY

New Series, vol. VI

*Issued to the members of the society
for the years 1959-60*

Frontispiece

Fos. 37v. and 38r. of "Gilling's Transactions" (see pp. 9 and 116—7)   (Original Size 6¾" x 8¼")

DEVON & CORNWALL RECORD SOCIETY

New Series, Vol. 6

THE EXETER ASSEMBLY

THE MINUTES OF THE ASSEMBLIES OF THE UNITED BRETHREN OF DEVON AND CORNWALL, 1691-1717, AS TRANSCRIBED BY THE REVEREND ISAAC GILLING

Edited with an Introduction by

ALLAN BROCKETT

Senior Sub-Librarian,
Roborough Library, Exeter University
assisted by

Roger Thomas,
Librarian and Secretary, Dr. Williams' Trust
with shorthand transcriptions by
the late R. Travers Herford

Printed for the Society by
THE DEVONSHIRE PRESS LTD.
TORQUAY

1963

New Series

1. DEVON MONASTIC LANDS: CALENDAR OF PARTICULARS FOR GRANTS, 1536-1558, edited by Joyce Youings (1955). 35s. or $5.75 post free.

2. EXETER IN THE SEVENTEENTH CENTURY: TAX AND RATE ASSESSMENTS 1602-1699, edited by W. G. Hoskins (1957). 35s. or $5.75 post free.

3. THE DIOCESE OF EXETER IN 1821: BISHOP CAREY'S REPLIES TO QUERIES BEFORE VISITATION, edited by Michael Cook. Vol. 1, Cornwall (1958). 35s. or $5.75 post free.

4. THE DIOCESE OF EXETER IN 1821; BISHOP CAREY'S REPLIES TO QUERIES BEFORE VISITATION, edited by Michael Cook. Vol. II, Devon (1960). 35s. or $5.75 post free.

5. CARTULARY OF ST. MICHAEL'S MOUNT, CORNWALL, edited by P. L. Hull (1962). 35s. or $5.75 post free.

6. THE EXETER ASSEMBLY: THE MINUTES OF THE ASSEMBLIES OF THE UNITED BRETHREN OF DEVON AND CORNWALL, 1691-1717, AS TRANSCRIBED BY THE REVEREND ISAAC GILLING, edited by Allan Brockett (1963). 45s. or $7.50 post free.

In Preparation

THE REGISTER OF EDMUND LACY, BISHOP OF EXETER 1420-1455, edited by Canon G. R. Dunstan.

A FOURTEENTH CENTURY FORMULARY OF AN ARCHDEACON OF TOTNES, edited by Dorothy Owen.

SOME EARLY SEVENTEENTH CENTURY BUILDING ACCOUNTS OF PLYMOUTH, edited by C. E. Welch.

CARTULARY OF THR DEAN AND CHAPTER OF EXETER CATHEDRAL, edited by Audrey M. Erskine.

CONTENTS

INTRODUCTION

Three hundred years have passed since the Act of Uniformity of 1662. Intended to enfold everyone within the national church it in fact achieved the exact opposite: it is from this time that the Free Churches as separate institutions came into being. An anniversary of this nature presents a suitable occasion for reconsidering the position of the Free Churches in the religious life of the country. The Minutes of the Exeter Assembly provide a glimpse of the activities of the Nonconformists of Devon and Cornwall during their period of greatest prosperity from 1691 to 1717.

THE EXETER ASSEMBLY OF MINISTERS

A county assembly of Presbyterian and Congregationalist ministers had existed in Devon from 1655 until 1659[1]. After the coming of toleration in 1689 these two denominations again set up voluntary associations of their ministers in many counties. In London a Common Fund was begun to assist smaller causes to continue their witness. John Howe, a Presbyterian, played the chief part in drawing up the " Heads of Agreement ", which led to the " Happy Union " inaugurated on 6th April, 1691. Under this agreement the two ministries dropped their dividing names and called themselves simply United Brethren, intending to work together in close co-operation.[2]

This example was followed immediately in Devon, as the minutes of the first two meetings of the new association, at Tiverton in March 1691 and at Topsham in June 1691, clearly show. If any one man was its architect in Devon this was veteran John Flavel, ejected from his living at Dartmouth in 1662. He died in the moment of success, immediately following the Topsham Assembly. Apart from these first two meetings, and one held at Plymouth in September 1695, the ministers always met at Exeter, and their organisation came to be known as the Exeter Assembly. It continued far longer than the London " Happy Union ". Whereas the latter had broken down by 1694, the Exeter Assembly continued to meet and to exert influence on the affairs of the Nonconformists of Devon and Cornwall as late as 1753, when its control over ordination came to an end. It still exists in a rudimentary form to this day, long since confined to the Unitarian descendants of the original Presbyterian ministers.[3]

The minutes of the first two meetings contain in full the Rules of Association agreed on by the ministers. They may be summarised under four headings. The Assembly existed for mutual consultation and

---

[1]For an account of its work and an edition of its Minutes see R. N. Worth, " Puritanism in Devon and the Exeter Assembly ", *Trans. Devon. Assoc.*, ix, 1877, pp. 279–88.
[2]Gordon, A., *Freedom after Ejection*, 1917, pp. 155–8.
[3]Minutes of the Exeter Assembly in MS., 1720 to date, kept at the National Provincial Bank, Exeter.

discipline, to ensure that only suitable candidates were ordained to the ministry, to encourage and assist young men to train for the ministry, and to assist financially the weaker churches in country districts. For this reason one of the first tasks was to bring into being a Fund to which all member churches should contribute according to their ability, and from which the poorer causes should receive according to their need. Potential candidates for the ministry received grants towards their education if they came from poor families. As will be seen from the minutes which follow the amounts distributed varied considerably. Generally speaking the size of the Fund decreased as time went on, and exhortations to all churches to make regular contributions suggest that income fell short many times after 1700. By far the greatest proportion of the amounts subscribed came from the Exeter Presbyterians. At the meeting in October 1691, for example, the three Exeter Presbyterian societies gave £30 2s. 6d. out of a total of £60 15s. 7d. This reflects the dominant position Exeter then held in the economic life of the South West.

" GILLING'S TRANSACTIONS "

Each Assembly was presided over by an elected Moderator, and its proceedings were written down by a Scribe. One of those in most constant attendance at Assemblies and the man who most frequently acted as scribe, was the Rev. Isaac Gilling. Born at Stogumber, Somerset, and educated in an Academy at Taunton under George Hammond, who had been ejected from his living at Dorchester in 1662, he was ordained at Lyme on August 25th, 1687. At the time the Exeter Assembly came into being he was settled with a Presbyterian Congregation at Silverton, and moved to Newton Abbot as successor to the Rev. William Yeo before October 1697. Here he remained until his death on August 21st, 1725.[1] He was scribe of the Assembly from May 1696 to September 1697; from May 1699 to May 1700, from May 1702 to May 1703, from September 1706 to September 1707, September 1708, from September 1709 to September 1713, and from September 1716 to September 1717; and Moderator in May 1701, May 1709, and May 1716.

Whether an official journal was kept of what transpired at each meeting, in the custody of the scribe for the time being, cannot now be ascertained. There must have been, at least, a list of all Rules relating to procedure, for in September 1709 Gilling was ordered to " transcribe the Rules for Regulating our Meetings and all other Rules relating to general practice; and bring in a copy to the next Assembly . . . in order to subscription ".[2] Each scribe certainly kept in his own hand a record of what transpired, and Gilling was enthusiastic enough to collect almost all of these into a notebook for his own use. It is through his diligence that we have a detailed record of the conclusions of these ministers in the period under consideration.

The notebook known as " Gilling's Transactions " is small, leather-bound, measuring $7''$ x $4\frac{1}{2}''$ externally, while its leaves are $6\frac{7}{8}''$ x $4\frac{1}{4}''$. There are 180 leaves. Gilling's writing is very clear and legible, although minutely small, and except where alterations have been made there is

[1]Gordon, *op. cit.*, p. 270.
[2]Below, p. 75.

no great difficulty in transcribing it. Problems arise over the arrange-
ment of his material. It must be remembered that this was indeed a
notebook, and not an official Minute Book. It had originally been used
for other purposes, and the first twenty leaves contain miscellaneous legal
notes which have nothing to do with the Exeter Assembly, and are in a
different hand from Gilling's. Scattered through the volume are odd
notes and copies of letters and certificates, sometimes in clear English,
sometimes in Latin, most often in shorthand, many of these last being
important for our understanding of the Minutes themselves. These have
been transcribed and placed in their proper chronological order as far
as this can be determined. Others have been calendared and printed in
appendices. The Minutes of the Assembly begin properly on folio 23
recto, and continue more or less in order from that point. Gilling's procedure, however, was to write only on the *recto* side of each folio at first.
When he reached the end of the book he turned it round and repeated
this procedure in the reverse direction. Consequently an opening of the
book at fo. 64, for example, reveals part of the Minutes for the May
1694 meeting facing the reader on fo. 64r., and the beginning of the
account of the May 1716 meeting upsidedown on fo. 63v.

Note on Editing

It will be realised from the foregoing that in the preparation of the
text for publication a considerable amount of rearrangement has been
necessary. Taking the main body of the Minutes as a basis, arranged in
chronological order as in the original, any additional material whose
date can be ascertained, and which has an important bearing on the
minutes for that date, has been added at the end of the Minutes for the
relevant meeting. The remainder, mostly of secondary importance, is
calendared in two appendices to the main sequence.

Consecutive paragraphs on the same subject in the original text
have now been grouped as one. This happens in most cases when dealing
with orders for ordinations to take place. In the original each ordinand
is normally given a separate paragraph. Personal forenames, often
written in abbreviated form, have also been printed in full. Punctuation
follows the original text, but the use of capitals is brought more into line
with modern custom, and they are therefore only retained when they are
clearly intended to emphasize the point at issue. Gilling's way of writing
details of grants to ministers and students has also been altered, in the
following manner:

In Gilling			Now		
£	s.	d.	£	s.	d.
02	06	10	2	6	10
46	01	06	46	1	6

To avoid too many footnotes in the text, a biographical index to
the ministers attending the meeting has been made, and the reader
should refer to this when in need of identifying any particular person.
Occasionally it is quite impossible to tell which of two persons of the same
name is meant. The Berrys, the Bartletts, the Woods, and the Shorts
are the most difficult in this respect.

The Shorthand

The transcript of the numerous passages in shorthand was made by the late R. Travers Herford, B.A., D.D., LITT.D. (HEB.), during the time that he was secretary and librarian of Dr. Williams's Library. Born in 1860, he came to the library in 1914 after a long ministry at Stand Chapel, Whitefield, Lancashire, He retired in 1925 and lived on until 1950. He was eminent as a Hebrew and Talmudic scholar, publishing a number of scholarly works of which perhaps the chief are *The Pharisees* (1924) and *Judaism in the New Testament Period* (1928.)[1]

In the brief note at the beginning of the note-book in which the transcripts of the shorthand are written and preserved in Dr. Willams's Library, Herford gave no indication as to the system of shorthand that Gilling employed nor how he himself had arrived at the key to it. In all probability it was the system of Edmund Willis of 1618, or a variant of it, though deviations from the system may be idiosyncrasies of Isaac Gilling's own. This was not Herford's only excursion into the deciphering of obsolete shorthands. Dr. Edith Morley in her books on H. Crabb Robinson acknowledges her indebtedness to him for transcripts and for supplying her with the key to the system used by Robinson.[2]

The transcripts of Gilling's shorthand appear to be accurate as far as it has been possible to check sample passages. In only two cases are there printed copies of any of the material given by Gilling in shorthand. These are excerpts from the "Heads of Agreement" of 1691 on fo. 161v, reversed (p. 32); and the paper agreed by London Presbyterians and Independents in 1696 on fos. 7v. and 8v. (p. 124). The former are quite accurate. The latter contains numerous differences between Herford's transcript and the printed version, but few, if any, of them can be attributed to errors on his part. Gilling's copy differed from the printed version of the paper which circulated widely in manuscript before it was printed in 1697 by Stephen Lobb in his *Report of the present State of the Differences of Doctrinals, between some Dissenting Ministers in London; in a Letter*, (London, 1697) pp. 11–15.

There are some brief passages, usually consisting of only a few words, which were overlooked by Herford. Without having access to a full and accurate key the best has been done to supply a transcript of these passages.

The Descent of the Manuscript.

Inside the cover of Gilling's notebook is written the following statement:

" This volume was in the possession of Bishop Trelawny, into whose hands I suspect it to have come from Mr. Bond of Looe who was an High Churchman, & obsequious servant of the Bishop; but whose near relative was an eminent Dissenting Minister, whose name is on the inside of the cover of the volume. I have seen a Treatise on some religious subject by this Mr. Bond, in the possession of the late Thomas Bond, Esquire, of Looe (author of an history of those Boroughs); it was

[1]H. McLachlan, *Robert Travers Herford . . . a brief sketch of his life and work*, (1951). Printed for private circulation, and available in Dr. Williams's Library.
[2]Robinson, Henry Crabb, *Blake, Coleridge, Wordsworth, Lamb, etc., being selections from the Remains . . .* ed. by Edith J. Morley. Manchester, Univ. Press, 1922, p. x.

in manuscript, & is now in the possession of Davies Gilbert Esquire of Eastbourne. Jonathan Couch, Polperro, Cornwall."

The name referred to appears simply as "Bond, Sept. 5, 6, 1710." The reference is to a censure by the Assembly meeting on those dates, passed on Cornelius Bond. Still unordained at that time he had left a Meeting at Sandwich (sic) in the Isle of Purbeck without first consulting neighbouring ministers. The following year, 1711, he was ordained, and settled at Ashburton. Here he remained until 1731. From midsummer of that year his successor John Cock began to receive the grant to Ashburton from the London Presbyterian Fund.[1] The descent of the manuscript seems therefore to have been that it passed into Cornelius Bond's hands after Gilling's death in 1725. Ashburton and Newton Abbot are only nine miles apart and there is evidence that the mid-Devon ministers formed a close group during this period.[2] The notebook remained in the Bond family, passed to Bishop Trelawny, and then to Jonathan Couch of Polperro, who finally presented it to Dr. Williams's Library in 1855.

THE BUSINESS OF THE ASSEMBLY

The following notes illustrate the kind of matters with which the Assembly concerned itself during the period 1691–1717:

The Ordination Controversy of 1696/7.

In September 1696, the Reverends Stephen Towgood, of Axminster, and John Ashwood, of Exeter, both Congregationalists, were brought to task for assisting at the ordination of a candidate trained by Towgood, Samuel Baker. This had taken place at Bridport but without the formal direction of the Dorset County Assembly, and against the custom of the United Brethren. In May 1697 Towgood brought forward a resolution embodying the strict Independent point of view that there was no authority superior to that of a particular church, that is, that it was not necessary to have all ordinations authorised by the Assembly. This was not accepted and previous resolutions were endorsed. Soon after this Ashwood left the county, but Towgood remained a frequent attender at the Assembly for many years to come.

This was part of a much wider controversy going on in Nonconformist circles in these years, some of which is revealed in the rambling discourse of John Galpine appended to the minutes for September 1696, with Ashwood's reply and Gilling's comments.[3] As has been noted, the London "Happy Union" had broken down soon after its formation. Three Congregational ministers in London rejected the Union at its beginning, and all Congregationalists were fearful of overmuch control by Synods. At the heart of the matter was the procedure relating to ordination of new ministers. To prevent unlearned, untrained, men entering the Dissenting ministry, the Presbyterians wished to place ordination under the direct control of county or district synods, of which the Exeter

[1]Minutes of the London Presbyterian Fund, 4 October, 1731. These Minutes are preserved in Dr Williams's Library.
[2]Below, pp. 56–7.
[3]Below, pp. 32–6.

Assembly became one. At the very least, they argued, neighbouring ministers should be called in, to give the ordinand their support and the right hand of fellowship.

The case of the Reverend Richard Davis clearly focused the differences in attitude between the two denominations. Davis was an extreme Congregationalist, and at his ordination at Rothwell in Northamptonshire on the 7th of March, 1690, he refused to allow the neighbouring ministers any part in the ceremony. To him the right to ordain was vested in the church which called him, and in no-one and no institution else. Davis was also an effective evangelist, seeking to make converts regardless of the rules and regulations of Assemblies. Wherever he was able to establish a group of converts he would allow one of their number to preach to them, whether they had the sanction of neighbouring ministers or county assemblies or not.[1]

Richard Davis also held extreme Calvinist beliefs, tending to Antinomianism, preaching that repentance was not necessary to salvation, that the elect were without sin, and without " spot before God ". Here, differences over ordination spread into a much wider theological controversy. In May 1692 were published posthumously the sermons of Tobias Crisp, a Puritan preacher, which could be interpreted as favouring Antinomianism. The book was publicly censured by Richard Baxter soon after its appearance, and later in the year came the publication of Dr. Daniel Williams's book, *Gospel Truth*, which gave the generally accepted Presbyterian answer to Crisp. The centre of the dispute was the knotty question whether in the order of grace, repentance or faith comes first.[2] Daniel Williams's book was prefaced by a group of London Presbyterian ministers including William Bates and John Howe. No Congregationalist would join in this preface. There were clear theological differences between Presbyterian and Congregational orders, the latter insisting on high Calvinism, the former modifying the idea of election and emphasizing the need for repentance in order to obtain grace. The feeling engendered by the Crisp-Williams debate, and by the Richard Davis affair, was quite enough to wreck the " Happy Union ".

The Congregationalists in London set up a separate Fund in 1695, and on the 20th of January, 1696, ministers of the same persuasion in the provinces were asked to report on the places in their region where Congregational churches existed, and to suggest possibilities for expansion.[3] It is this inquiry to which John Galpine took exception, and on account of which he accused John Ashwood of trying to break up the union of the Devon ministers. There can also be no doubt that Ashwood did make a report on the Congregational societies in Devon in 1696. This must have stressed their comparative weakness in contrast to the multitude of Presbyterian societies in the county. Congregationalists were only strong in Exeter, Tiverton, Bideford, Barnstaple and Axminster, and in Exeter the Presbyterian churches were by far the more influential.[4]

[1]Gordon, A., *op. cit.*, pp. 184–7.
[2]Skeats, H. S. & Miall, C. S. *History of the Free Churches*, 1891, pp. 136–45.
[3]*Trans., Congregational Hist. Soc.* v, 1911–12, p. 138.
[4]Allan Brockett, *Nonconformity in Exeter*, 1650–1875, 1962, pp. 64–73. The history of the Exeter Assembly is dealt with here at some length and the background is described against which the early Dissenting ministers worked.

The Antinomian controversy had died down amongst the Nonconformists by 1698, and the ministers of both persuasions met again on a
friendly basis in London, but no attempt was made at an organic union.
In Devon also the situation quietened down with the departure of John
Ashwood in 1698. Congregationalist ministers took part in Exeter
Assembly affairs side by side with their Presbyterian brethren throughout
Gilling's period. In practice the Congregationalists had little to complain
about. Ordination was not normally approved until a candidate had
received a call from a local church, and for the Congregationalists this
was the important factor.

Bideford.

Affairs at Bideford were discussed at some lengths at Assemblies
from April 1693 until September 1703. The present Congregational
Church in Bideford dates its foundation to 1648 when the Rev. William
Bartlett became Rector of the parish church, the previous incumbent,
Arthur Gifford, being sequestrated in that year. Bartlett had to resign
the living again to Gifford in 1660, but with his son, John Bartlett, the
ejected Vicar of Fremington, he remained active in Bideford until his
death. John had died in 1679. Father and son were locally known as
Boanerges and Barnabas, their characters being remarkably complemen-
tary, and they achieved extensive success in the town. John Bowden,
ejected Rector of Littleham near Bideford, succeeded John Bartlett, and
he was joined after William Bartlett's death in 1682 by an assistant from
Ireland, James Wood.[1] It was at this point that Bideford affairs were
brought to the cognizance of the Assembly. James Wood had formed an
attachment with an Irish girl, the nature of which was considered scandalous by a section of his congregation.[2] The difference was referred to
the Assembly in April, 1693, but a division took place in Bideford. A
minority of members remained loyal to Wood, and built a meeting house
for him in the High Street. He died about 1698. Bowden was joined in
1696 by another assistant, Jacob Bayley (often spelt " Bailies " by
Gilling). According to the Rev. Samuel Badcock, Dissenting minister at
Barnstaple in 1774, " Bayley's life was rendered perfectly unhappy, and
his character utterly contemptible by mean compliances with a capricious
and arbitrary wife . . . ".[3] He was never to enjoy the complete trust of
his congregation, and it was not surprising when those who had seceded
with James Wood refused to return after his death.

To counterbalance the " Little Meeting " of James Wood, the
parent society built in 1698 the " Great Meeting " in Bridgeland Street.
Bowden died in March 1699. Bayley stood out against any assistant
until William Bartlett II had completed his training at Edinburgh
University. He was a son of John Bartlett, and grandson of the founder
of the Bideford Independent church. He proved a man of moderate
views and an accomplished peacemaker. He was ordained on November
11th, 1702, and remained in Bideford until his early death on September

[1]Calamy, E., *Account of the Ministers Ejected* . . . revised by A. G. Matthews, 1934. The
careers of both the Bartletts and of Bowden are given here.
[2]Watkins, John, *History of Bideford*, 1792, reprinted 1883, pp. 124–41.
[3]*ibid.*, p. 135.

28th, 1720. Although he did not find it easy to work with Jacob Bayley at first, the minutes of the Assembly for September 1703 contain a "Testimonial of their Reunion",[1] and the Great Meeting pursued its way peacefully thereafter. Bayley remained until 1718.

In 1700 the members of the Little Meeting invited young Josiah Eveleigh to become their minister, and there was some consideration of the possibility of the two churches joining again, with three ministers between the two of them. Agreement could not be preserved, however, and as Eveleigh left somewhat hurriedly in the summer of 1701 to succeed Robert Carel at Crediton, the proposal was again dropped. He was followed at the Little Meeting by Samuel Short, 1701 to 1703, and then by John Norman, 1703 to 1716. In the minutes of the May Assembly of 1716 is a full account of Norman's call to Portsmouth,[2] which he accepted, and he remained there until his death in 1756. He was succeeded at the Little Meeting by Nathaniel Cock, who was ordained on the 24th October, 1716. He aligned himself with the Arian party in the disastrous Trinitarian disputes in 1718–19, but his personal sanctity and honesty retained the affection of his congregation. He died in 1760, when at last the two Bideford Congregationalist societies were reunited.

John Fox, and the Trinitarian controversy.

The two Assemblies held in 1717, with whose activities Gilling's notebook ends, contain several references to a dispute as to whether candidate John Fox of Plymouth should be allowed to preach or not. Fox came of a Dissenting family in Plymouth, and his father devoted him to preparation for the ministry from his earliest years. He was born on 10 May, 1693, and was sent in 1708 to the Academy run by Joseph Hallett II in Exeter, where he stayed until 1712. Here, in common with other students, he heard of the Arian ideas on the Trinity then becoming well-known, and as a result lost any disposition he had ever had to become a minister. Yet he respected his father and decided to persevere in order to please him. While Dr. Edmund Calamy, the historian, was in Devon in 1713[3] he spoke to Fox and assured him that his scruples over subscribing to the Thirty-Nine Articles need not cause him any difficulty, as he had never subscribed himself and no-one had questioned him about it.[4]

Fox became very friendly with Isaac Gilling, to whom he was related. (His grandmother and Gilling's mother were sisters.) He became attached to Gilling's daughter and married her on December 23rd, 1723. He spent the years 1714 to 1716 in London, where his contacts with Dissenting ministers made him even more reluctant to enter the Ministry himself.

Reluctance to commit himself to any doctrinal creed resulted in Fox developing a resentment against an Assembly which refused to allow candidates to preach until they had undergone an examination by appointed ministers. Some ministers did invite him into their pulpits, but this procedure was severely criticised at the Exeter Assembly of

[1] Below, p. 54.
[2] Below, pp. 109–10.
[3] Below, pp. 92–7.
[4] J. Brooking Rowe, Seventh Report of the Committee on Devonshire Records, "The Fox Memoirs", Trans. Devon. Assocn., xxviii, 1896, pp. 128–48, and xxix, 1897, pp. 156–9.

May 1717, the Plymouth men being especially vehement against Fox. For the sake of his father's feelings he made his peace with his critics, and submitted himself for examination at the September Assembly. In his memoirs he claims that his examination was cleverly stage-managed by his friends who were punctual in their attendance on the first day and elected a favourable Moderator and Examiners before the Plymouth ministers arrived. His examination appears to have been lenient, and with James Peirce in the chair (later to be ejected from James' Meeting, Exeter, for Arianism) he was probably not pressed strictly on the doctrine of the Trinity. In any case he was licensed to preach. This brought him little nearer to satisfying the desires of his father, as he was only once allowed to enter the pulpit of the Treville Street meeting house at Plymouth. The following year came the outbreak of the Arian controversy and as Fox sided with James Peirce, Joseph Hallett II, Isaac Gilling, and the minority who refused to subscribe to the doctrine of the Trinity, his candidature for the Presbyterian ministry was abruptly ended. On the death of his father in 1723 John Fox gave up any pretence of intending to become a minister, as by then he had acquired property sufficient to enable him to live in comfort. His contribution to the Nonconformity in which he was reared lay not in his participation in the ministry, but in his candid account of the divines with whom he was associated in his formative years. Towards the end of his life he wrote very readable and critical memoirs of them, which have since been printed.[1]

The Trinitarian disruption which occurred in the years 1718–19 falls outside the period of this volume.[2] In the May Assembly of 1719 all ministers were asked to declare their faith in the Trinity, in the general sense that " There is one living and true God, and that the Father, Word and Holy Ghost are that one God." Fifty-five ministers agreed. Thirteen ministers and six candidates refused to subscribe, and took no further part in the affairs of the Assembly. Amongst these latter was Isaac Gilling, who more than any other person had been devoted to its work. His refusal to subscribe, based mainly on his inbred Non-conformist reluctance to accept any doctrine not specifically laid down in the Scriptures, which were his rule of faith and life, led not only to his expulsion from the Exeter Assembly, but to the withdrawal of the larger part of his congregation at Newton Abbot. He died on the 21st of August, 1725. John Fox said of him, " He thought it a terrible disgrace to be deserted, and to continue his ministry was to him a matter of such consequence that he could never think of laying it aside, tho' he had little more or little better than the walls to talk to . . . This stuck close to him and broke his heart . . . which by very slow degrees put an end to his life." He was refused burial in the churchyard at Newton Abbot and was interred in his own meeting-house.[3]

Acknowledgements

I wish to thank the Devon and Cornwall Record Society for enabling the Tercentenary of Nonconformity to be commemorated in this manner.

[1]*Ibid.*
[2]For a full account of the issues involved and the events which took place, see Allan Brockett, *Nonconformity in Exeter, 1650–1875,* 1962, pp. 74–95.
[3]Brooking Rowe, *loc. cit.*

I am grateful also to the Trustees of Dr. Williams's Library for their permission to print the manuscript, and to the Friends of Dr. Williams's Library for making a small grant towards the cost of publication.

Personal thanks must go first to the Rev. Roger Thomas, Librarian and Secretary of Dr. Williams's Library, who has constantly assisted me in the preparation of the text for publication, particularly in checking R. T. Herford's shorthand transcripts, and in identifying many of the persons included in the biographical index. Valuable help has also been given by Mrs. Audrey M. Erskine, archivist at the Exeter Cathedral Library, and by Professor F. W. Clayton in the transcription of some Latin passages. Above all I wish to pay a tribute to the tireless efficiency of Dr. Joyce Youings, Hon. Joint Editor of the Society's publications, who has guided me through the unfamiliar task of editing " Gilling's Transactions ".

July, 1962   ALLAN BROCKETT.

THE MINUTES OF THE ASSEMBLIES OF THE UNITED BRETHREN OF DEVON AND CORNWALL, 1691 to 1717, AS TRANSCRIBED BY THE REVEREND ISAAC GILLING

[fo. 23r.]
TIVERTON, 17mo & 18mo Martii, 1690/1.

Present: Mr Richard Sanders, Moderator; Mr William Crompton, Robert Carel, Benjamin Hooper, Bernard Starr, Thomas Walsh, Robert Collings, Samuel Tapper, Joseph Hallet, Isaac Gilling, Samuel Bartlett, James Haderidge, John Knight, Thomas Chapman, Jacob Sandercock. John Moore, a candidate. Delegates from the Western Division of Somerset: Mr John Moore, Richard Tooel, Malachi Blake, Josiah Woodcock, Christopher Taylor.

The following Rules for regulating our Meetings consented to & subscrib'd.

We Ministers of the Gospel in the Counties of Devon & Exon, whose names are under written do agree as followeth.

1. We are persuaded that it is not only lawfull but also very expedient that we frequently hold meetings for mutual advice touching things pertaining to our Office, the right ordering of our Congregations, & the promoting of purity & unity in the Churches of Christ.

2. We declare our hearty willingness & desire that others of our Brethren in the County & City who are of godly life & sound in the Faith should join with us in this Agreement, for the fuller demonstration of universal concord.

3. That in such meetings as we shall from time to time have, there be chosen a Moderator, who is to begin & end the meeting with prayer, & keep order therein, & silence all private & impertinent discourses; and a Scribe to write such things as shall be transacted in the meetings.

4. To prevent any misconstruction that may be made of our meeting as is agreed we declare

    1. That we do not intend thereby any way to prejudice what may hereafter be done by publick authority in order to a more universal unity: but profess that [fo. 24r.] if an Act of Comprehension should be pass'd we shall be ready to close in with it, so far as we are persuaded in our consciences we may do.

    2. That we intend not in our debates to intermeddle with state affairs, but keep within the bounds of our calling.

5. That we will deal faithfully one with another in not suffering sin to rest upon each other, but freely & lovingly give & receive from one

1

another admonition as there shall be occasion, & shall labour to uphold the credit of the Ministry, & the esteem of our brethren in the Ministry.

6. That the majority of votes determine anything consulted on, in matters of order, in these our meetings.

7. That in all our consultations everyone present do, by word or sign, declare his actual assent, dissent or suspension of his judgment.

8. That if any are dissatisfy'd or dissent from what the majority have voted, they give their reasons; that satisfaction may be given or received if possible. That the Moderator take cognizance of any objection, & propose it to be debated either immediately or at another meeting as the majority shall determine.

9. That in matters of greater difficulty we crave the brotherly advice of the Ministers of any neighbouring county that are united in any such agreement as ours is.

10. That before the conclusion of each meeting the time & place of meeting next the person to preach the time to be spent in preaching & praying with delegates to prepare & ripen matters for debate in our own, & to maintain a correspondence with other Meetings be appointed. And if any new matter occur that it be propos'd [in writing to the Moderator][1] by any of the Brethren.

11. That we will endeavour in the sincerity of our hearts to promote the ends of these meetings according to the 1st Article; & therefore do intend as oft as conveniently we can to attend upon them, while the reason of them continues.

[All Devon ministers present signed this Agreement.]

[fo. 25r.] Concerning a Fund these 3 things considered & agreed.
    1. The Raising. 2. The Lodging. 3. The Distributing of it.
As to the Raising of it. Agreed.

1. That there be an endeavour to procure money for pious uses.

2. That each Minister endeavour to make his Hearers[2] & Friends sensible of the necessity of so doing, & that he desire one or more active persons to advise & assist him in collecting & receiving what shall be given.

3. That these following things be left to the discretion of Ministers:

    1. Whether they will make their whole congregations acquainted with this matter, or only impart it to such as are best able & most likely to give.

    2. Whether they will only proceed by private subscriptions & collections, or make a publick collection in their congregations provided such a collection be not made oftener than once a Quarter.

    3. Whether they will offer to those whom they would persuade to give the following paper subscrib'd by the Ministers of this Meeting to prevent misconstructions & to satisfy our friends in our reasons for raising money.

We whose names are subscribed, Ministers of the Gospel in the Counties of Devon & Exon. being assembled in Tiverton the 18th day of March, 1690,[3] to advise together touching things pertaining to our office, the

[1]Underlined.
[2]The term " Hearer " signified one who regularly attended religious worship and " heard " the sermon.
[3]1691 by our Calendar.

right ordering of our congregations, & the promoting of purity & unity in the churches of Christ, taking into consideration the readiness of the people in many places to hear the word of God, & that the [fo. 26r.] labourers are too few for the harvest, do judg that more must be done by us than to offer up our prayers to God for an increase of able ministers of the New Testament. We have therefore agreed upon mature deliberation to use our utmost endeavours in our stations among our people & acquaintance to procure what sums of money we may to promote the preaching of the Gospel, & for the education of such youths as are religiously inclin'd & capable of learning, whose parents by reason of their poverty are not wholly able to discharge the expences that are necessary to fit & qualify them for the ministerial imployment. And we shall use our best skill to place such youths with those Tutors that shall use their utmost care & diligence to bring them up in learning & ripen them for so high an imploiment. Hoping that God the giver of every good & perfect gift will so assist the endeavours of their Tutors as thereby to make them both pious & learned that when it shall please God to call them to labour for him in his Church they may by their learning be able to teach & by their holy & exemplary conversations go before & lead the flock of Christ. We do promise ourselves that those who have tasted the good word of God & do love the ministry of reconciliation will be forward to contribute something according to their ability to promote this good and pious design.

Now that there may be no misconstruction made of this our undertaking we do declare that we have no respect to our own private interest, but that the money so collected as aforesaid shall be deposited in such hands as shall from time to time dispose of it according to the order of the Assembly to the ends aforesaid. And there shall be such accounts kept of the distribution thereof as any concerned may inspect for their satisfaction. And we do purpose in our several meetings to use all the care we can to promote this good design, which we hope will be grateful to all that wish well to Zion & daily pray for the prosperity thereof.

[Signed by 13 of the 15 Devon ministers who attended the meeting.][1]

[fo. 27r.] As to the Lodging. Agreed that the Collectors bring or send every Quarter what they procure to Mr Goddard of Tiverton the General Receiver of this Division, taking his receipt.

As to the Distributing.

1. Agreed that none of the money be distributed but by order of the Ministers [of this Division][2] in their Meeting.

2. That those to be principally consider'd are poor and aged Ministers & hopeful youths to be educated for the ministry; [and if the Fund will reach it the poor widdows & orphans of Dissenting Ministers shall have a share of it.][2]

3. That a special regard be had to such youths as are most forward in grammar learning & most ingenious; and that no youths receive any part of it but such as appear to the Ministers assembled to be poor, capable of learning & well inclin'd.

[1]William Crompton and Joseph Hallett did not sign—they may have had to leave early.
[2]Underlined

Agreed that the next Meeting for this Division be at Topsham the 4th Tuesday in June. That Mr Carel preach, Mr Hooper pray, not exceeding 2 hours in the whole exercise. That Mr Starr be Scribe to the Meeting. That Mr Tapper & Mr Knight be delegates to prepare & ripen matter for debate from this Question: Q. What latitude may we take in admission to Sacraments? That Mr Gilling & Mr Sandercock go as delegates from this Meeting to the next Meeting of the Western Division of Somersett at Ilminster the Tuesday in Easter week.

[fo. 28r.]
TOPSHAM, 23rd & 24th June, 1691. Minutes of the General Meeting of the United Brethren of the City & County of Exon, & County of Devon.

Present: Mr John Flavel, Moderator; Mr Richard Sanders, Wood, Gaylard, Tapper, Stoddon, Balster, Hooper, Toogood, Hallet, Atkins, Gilling, Walsh, George Tross, Collings, Carel, Backaller, Knight, Short, Chapman, Ashwood, Goswel, Edwards, Bartlett. Starr appointed Scribe.
Unordain'd: Mr Hanmer, Moor, Symonds, Lewis, Larkham.
Of other counties: Mr Ames Short of Lyme Regis in Dorset.
Mr John Moor, Mr Malachi Blake, delegates from the Western Division of Somersett.

The Rules for regulating our Meetings agreed on at Tiverton, read, & subscrib'd by such ministers as had not done it before. The Moderator in the name & at the request of all the Brethren, returns thanks to Mr Carel for the great pains which he took in his sermon preached at the opening of this Assembly, & desir'd him to print it.
[fo. 29r.] The minutes of the Association, of the United Brethren of the Western Division of Somersett, at Ilminster the 14th of April read.
The Heads of Agreement assented to this year by the United Brethren in and about London, propos'd, consider'd, & assented to by all. The 2 following minutes drawn up by order 23tio die Junii, 1691.
We Ministers of the Gospel present at the General Assembly of the United Brethren of the City & County of Exon and County of Devon at Topsham [for mutual advice touching things pertaining to our office, the right ordering of our Congregations, & the promoting of purity & unity in the Churches of Christ,][1] do cheerfully & heartily assent to the Heads of Agreement assented to this year by the United Brethren in & about London, & do unanimously resolve as the Lord shal enable us, to practise according to them. Subscrib'd in the name & by the appointment of all the Brethren by John Flavel[2] Moderator.
Agreed that the Reverend Mr Flavel, Moderator to this Assembly, send this paper to the Reverend Mr Matthew Mead, Mr John How & Mr Increase Mather of London, & that we give them, & such other ministers as have been eminently instrumental in promoting this Union the thanks of this Assembly for the great pains they have taken therein. This is a true copy. Isaac Gilling, Scribe.
[fo. 30r.] The Model of the Fund read. Propos'd that those words in the 2nd Article about distributing such money as shall be rais'd (And if

---

[1]This passage is on fo. 28v. of MS. Its correct position was marked by asterisks on fo. 29r.
[2]Flavel died a few days after presiding at this Assembly.

the Fund will reach it the poor widdows & orphans of Dissenting Ministers shall have a share of it) be at present expung'd.

Resolv'd that Mr Thomas Wood of Exon, merchant, be desir'd to be Receiver of such money as shall be collected in the City of Exon & the western part of the County of Devon. Upon his undertaking it the following orders given him:

[A space of 2½ " blank follows.]

The several sums brought in this Quarter paid to the Receiver & by him enter'd in a Book for that purpose. The Book of Receipts reported as follows:

	£	s	d
Mr Robert Carel of Crediton	8	0	0
Mr Samuel Tapper of Lympston	6	0	0
Mr Bernard Starr of Topsham	5	3	1
Mr Isaac Gilling of Silverton	3	3	3
Mr Benjamin Hooper of Thorverton ...	2	0	0
Mr John Knight		10	0
In all ...	24	16	4

[fo. 31r.] Agreed that the Receiver pay the following sums to the persons undernamed.

	£	s	d
To Mr Flavel for Peter & Thomas Kellow ...	5	0	0
To Isaac Gilling for Joseph Gilling ...	3	8	0
To Mr Hooper for Benjamin Berry ...	1	0	0
To Mr Balster to buy books for his son ...	2	0	0
Total of what is received this Quarter	24	16	4
Total of disbursements this Quarter	11	8	0
Remains in Receiver's hands	13	8	4

Resolv'd that the Collections for the French Refugees be continu'd notwithstanding the Fund. That we do not think ourselves oblig'd to take notice of any Briefs so as to read them or collect for them in our Congregations. Whereas several cheats & vagabonds have travel'd the country & got collections for themselves in many of our congregations, by shewing Letters of Recommendation & Certificates under the hands of some eminent ministers in this & other counties, some of which appear to have been forged, & others granted without due caution & inquiry, whereby our hearers have been unnecessarily burthened, the Fund & such like real acts of charity obstructed, idle persons & rogues maintain'd & encouraged, Dissenters censur'd by some & ridicul'd by others for too great credulity & misimployed charity, to prevent such inconveniences for the future several expedients propos'd. As, That none of us give any Certificates or [fo. 32r] Letters of Recommendation to any unless the occasion be weighty & well known to him that recommends it. That we take no cognisance of any certificates or recommendations of persons who live not in this county, unless in extraordinary cases & upon good evidence that there is no forgery or imposture. That no Letters of

Recommendation of any persons whatsoever living in the county be regarded unless they be subscrib'd by two of the United Ministers of this county at least. That if any Minister suspect that the occasion is not weighty or the subscription or recommendation forged he forbear[1] collecting untill he receive satisfaction from those Ministers whose names are subscrib'd.

Two of Bow desire something out of the Fund to build a Meeting House. Resolv'd. That we can't give them any of that money, which being given for the education of poor scholars, etc., ought not to be alienated or imploy'd for any other use. Some of the ministers present gave them the sum of three pounds & two shillings towards the building their Meeting House.

Propos'd that some young men of pregnant parts & well-skill'd in the languages, after they have gone through a course of philosophy, be continu'd some years longer with some [fo. 33r.] learned Divines, untill they be well vers'd in Controversial Divinity & Church History, that they may be qualify'd for the defence of the Gospel.[2] That Mr Tross, Mr Tapper, Mr Hallett & Mr Starr endeavour to persuade Mr N. N. of Exon, who hath read over & epitomiz'd the Fathers of the 3 first centuries, to devote himself to the work of the Ministry. [I believe by N. N. is meant Mr Peter King.][3]

Whereas a complaint is made of some Church-Members who live in the ordinary neglect of family duties, & plead for their neglect. Agreed: That such be advis'd to read Mr Doolittle's sermon for Family Duty, in the Supplement to the Morning Exercise at Cripplegate: and be inform'd, that we judg the ordinary neglect of family duty to be a scandalous sin, & persons pleading for their neglect, a great aggravation of the sin.

The case of Honiton people reported by Mr Joshua Northcott. Mr Goswell desired & advised to settle among them as their Pastor.

Agreed that as many of us as conveniently can will be at Taunton the 1st Tuesday in September. That Mr Bartlett & Gilling go as Delegates to the General Meeting of the United Brethren of Somersett at Yeovil July the 7th.

[fo. 34r.] Mr Larkham of Launceston in Cornwall, Mr Lewis of Bovey, & Mr Withers of Lupton desire that they may be ordain'd. Resolv'd. That they be ordain'd at Exon, Wednesday August the 26th. That on Tuesday August the 25th, they be examin'd, preach on the following Texts, state & maintain the following Questions.
Mr Larkhams Text, 1.Tim:4.13. Give attendance to reading, to exhortation, to doctrine. His Question: An detur Ministerium Evangelicum?
Mr Lewis's Text: Prov: 11.30. He that winneth souls is wise. His Question: An satisfactio Christi [sit necessaria][4] ad expiandum peccatum?

---

[1]" forbear " has been substituted for " defer " in the MS.
[2]This probably marks the beginning of the first Exeter Academy, directed by Joseph Hallett II from about 1691 until 1720. H. McLachlan, *English Education under the Test Acts*, 1931, pp. 109–114.
[3]This note was added later, not in Gilling's hand. Peter King was the son of grocer Jerome King, an original member of the Exeter Presbyterians' Committee of Thirteen, elected in 1687. Peter King (1669–1734) became first Baron King of Ockham, and Lord Chancellor of England. MS. Minutes of the Committee of Thirteen, George's Meeting, Exeter, and *Dictionary of National Biography*.
[4]These two words were inserted by Gilling to replace " sufficiat."

Mr Withers's Text: 1.Tim:3.1. If any man desire [the office of a bishop, he desireth a good work][1] His Question: An dentur 3 personae in Divinâ Essentiâ ?

That Mr Tross preach the Ordination sermon, Mr Hopping give the Exhortation.

That the next meeting for this County be at Exon the 1st Wednesday in October, Mr Wood of Bytheford to preach. The exercise to begin by 9 a Clock at farthest. Mr Collings to begin with prayer.

[The Moderator desires advice about disposing of the sum of about £100, whether in his hands to be disposed of for charitable uses, whether it may not be a appropriated to the Fund.][2]

[fo. 12r. shorthand.] *Aug. 29, '91. Good Sir. I being not able to attend the usual Assembly at Taunton next Tuesday, respectfully beg you to propose these 3 necessary Questions to the Ministers.*
Q.1. Whether a title to a Particular congregation be previously necessary to the regular ordination of a Gospel Minister?
Q.2. Whether the minister or people be the proper judge of the fitness of a communicant in point of knowledge?
Q.3. Whether a credible profession or else the giving in of experiences from the people be necessary to qualify them for the supper of the Lord.
I pray take the answers and in due time give them to your most unworthy Brother, R.C.[3] I depend on your favourable pains. On Tuesday sen'night at a little after one of the clock in the afternoon.

[fo. 35r.]
TAUNTON, 2d & 3d of September, 1691. At the Meeting of the United Brethren of the Counties of Somersett, Devon and Dorset.

[Present:] Mr John Weeks preach'd & was chosen Moderator; Richard Sanders, Robert Collings, James Haderidge, John Bush, Immanuel Harford, John Moore,[4] Baldwin Deacon, Thomas Marshal, John Herring, John Balster, Matthew Warren, Benjamin Hooper, Malachi Blake, John Sprint, Stephen Light, John Gardner, Alexander Sinclare, Stephen Toogood, Aaron Pitts, Samuel Atkins, Henry Chandler, John Ashwood, Bernard Starr, John Goswell, Christopher Taylor, Richard Tooell, Isaac Gilling, John Edwards, Josiah Woodcock, Isaac Noble, Jacob Sandercock, Samuel Wood, William Horsham, Thomas Walsh, Samuel Bartlett, John Galpin, John Moore,[4] John Withers, John Lewis. Candidates: John Mead, John England, Simon Babb.

The Minutes of the General Meetings at Bristol & Yeovil, July 7th, read and approv'd.

Several of the Brethren whose hearers are withdrawn from them by the Anabaptists, desire that (according to the Resolution of the meeting at Yeovil) the 5 Brethren of the Western Division of Somerset, who have drawn up their thoughts about the subjects & manner of Baptism, would produce their papers, that a short plain Tract might be printed on that subject. Resolved by the majority. That tis not fit that an account

[1] Omitted in MS. The preceding four words were added by Gilling in a different ink.
[2] This was deleted in the MS. but remains legible.
[3] This was most likely Robert Carel of Crediton, whose name was not among those at the Taunton Meeting.
[4] There were two John Moores: one from Bridgwater, the other from Tiverton.

should be given to the whole Assembly what some particular [fo. 36r.] Brethren have written on that subject. That tis not expedient to write any more about that controversy at this time.

There being none of the United Brethren of the Eastern Division of Somersett at this Meeting besides Mr Taylor & Mr Chandler, resolv'd that they acquaint the Brethren of that Division that this Assembly is not well pleas'd that no more of them came hither, & that they desire more of them to attend such General Meetings, or greater Associations.

A letter from Dartmouth desiring this Assembly to second their request to Mr Hanmer to preach among them, & to recommend some other fit ministers to them in case of his refusall, read & consider'd. Ordered that a letter be drawn up to desire Mr Hanmer, if his circumstances will permit, to comply with the invitation of Dartmouth people: and another to Mrs Flavel to recommend Mr Malachi Blake & Mr Tho. Chapman to preach among them if Mr Hanmer refuse. Both which were drawn up read approv'd & order'd to be sent.[1]

Mr Flammick[2] desires this Assembly to recommend a minister to preach at Bodmin in Cornwall. The people propose to give £20 per annum & he to give a single man his diet & keeping of a horse.

Ordered that Mr Nicholas Billingsly (excommunicated at Glocester, join'd to the Dissenters, & desiring this Assembly to recommend him to some people for the exercise of his ministry) be inform'd, that the people of S. Petherton offer to give £30 per annum & Minehead £26 to a minister.

[fo. 37r.] Agreed that [3] Clark of Buckrell in the County of Devon (being propos'd as a fit person to be educated for the ministry at the expense of the Fund) be referr'd to the meeting at Exon October 7th.

That Mr Blake continue his correspondence with Mr Hammond of London, that he desire him to give an account what is done in their meetings, & send him an account what is done in ours.

That Mr Bartlett, Senior, & Mr Gardner deal with some of Mr Sprints congregation at Stalbridg; who (being offended with him for hearing in publick on the Lords Day, when incapacitated to preach himself, or hear elsewhere) have caused much disturbance in that meeting.

An answer to a letter of Mr Danson's (Moderator at the General Assembly held at Bristol[4]) proposing a National Meeting at London this year, reported, viz: that the London Ministers do not think it expedient to hold such a meeting this year.

All the Ministers present obliged themselves by promise to preach against the profanation of the Lords Day.

All the Ministers present give their hearty assent to the Heads of Agreement & resolve to practise according to them. Upon information that some give out that notwithstanding our assenting to the Heads of

[1] John Flavel, founder of the Dartmouth Meeting, died on June 28th, 1691. The members unsuccessfully invited Isaac Gilling (See Appendix A, 5) and were now extending their search further. Calamy, E., *Account of the Ministers ejected* . . . revised by A. C. Matthews, 1934, pp. 200–1.
[2] Henry Flamanck of Tavistock.
[3] A space was left here large enough for a Christian name.
[4] A space was left here for that date.

Agreement yet differences continue & we remain at as great a distance as before; and that though we [fo. 38r.] are agreed upon principles of union, the practice is yet wanting; the following questions propos'd, & the following resolutions agreed unto.

Q. What care hath been taken to inform our people of our Union?

Q. What course shall we take to acquaint them with it?

Q. Whether we ought not to rebuke our people sharply, who are guilty of backbiting, or slandering, ministers or members of other churches?

Q. Whether those ministers who receive to communion those that are ordinarily hearers of other Pastors, do not give just offence to such other Brethren, & act contrary to the design of the Union, if they do not persuade such members to hold occasional communion with those Pastors, whose ministry they ordinarily attend?

Q. May it not be expedient for the Pastors of neighbouring Churches, to persuade their Societies to communicate together twice a year at least, once in one congregation, & another time in the other?

Resolved, Nemine Contradicente, that members belonging to a Congregation at a distance from the place where they live, & ordinarily hear the word, are to be advised by their Pastors, to join occasionally in Communion, with the United Brother who is Pastor of that Congregation where they hear.[1]

[fo. 39r.] Resolv'd: That to reduce into practice our agreed Communion of Churches, & effectually to pursue the ends of the said Agreement, the Ministers at least of the several Congregations should manifest their cordial Union, by exchange of Pulpits sometimes, & by being exemplary to the people in owning their neighbouring Churches at the Lords Table. Resolv'd that the difference in consecration of the Elements, or the different administration of the Lords Supper, among the United Brethren, is no sufficient impediment to those United Brethren, for having actual Communion one with another in that Ordinance. Resolv'd that at the next General Association it be inquir'd how far we have practised according to the Heads of Agreement; particularly as to Occasional Communion.

Whereas the Heads of Agreement determine that none be ordain'd to the Ministry without a Call of some Particular Church except in extraordinary cases the following Question propos'd: Quest. Whether under our present circumstances some young men may not be ordain'd, without a solemn Call to a particular Church, who are call'd occasionally to preach the Gospel [fo. 40r.] & administer the Lords Supper in the families of the Gentry, or as Itinerants? Quest. If any Candidate desires Ordination without a Call to a Particular Church, who shall be judges whether his case be extraordinary?

Upon information that some have done nothing towards the Fund, resolv'd that all those ministers present who have not yet done any thing for the Fund, do use their utmost endeavours in their places to stir up all their people that are of ability to contribute towards it, & give in an account of what they have done to their next Associations.

Agreed that the next General Meeting of the United Brethren of Western Associated Counties be at Bristol, the first Wednesday in April,

[1] The shorthand passage below reveals that these instructions were carried out.

Mr Warren to preach. The next meeting for the Western Division of Somerset to be at Taunton the 1st Wednesday in January.

[fo. 7r. Shorthand.] *Whereas R. L. being a member of the Society whereof I am the present pastor, is willing occasionally to join in the Lord's Supper with the Church in Exon whereof Mr. J. A.*[1] *is pastor, I being a lover of the communion of Saints in all ordinances of Christ according to the late agreement of the Reverend Assembly of ministers at Taunton about communion of Churches, do give my free and full consent that the said R. L. do occasionally communicate with Mr J. A. and his Society and all other Churches that are under the conduct and oversight of the United Brethren. Given under my hand this* [2] *day of* [2] *B.H.*[3]

[fo. 41r.]
EXETER, 7th October, 1691. At the Meeting of the United Brethren of the City & County of Exon, & County of Devon.

[Present:] Mr George Tross, Moderator; Mr Richard Sanders, James Wood, Robert Collings, John Berry, Robert Gaylard, William Crompton, John Galpin Senior, Edward Parr, Samuel Tapper, James Haderidge, John Hopping, Henry Backaller, Samuel Stoddon, Edward Hunt, Thomas Palk, John Knight, John Balster, Benjamin Hooper, Stephen Toogood, Joseph Hallet, Samuel Atkins, John Ashwood, Thomas Chapman, John Goswell, Isaac Gilling, John Edwards, Jacob Sandercock, Samuel Wood, Thomas Walsh, John Galpin, Samuel Bartlett, John Moore, John Withers. Candidates: Mr Powel, Chappel, Perdue. Delegates and others from Somerset: Mr John Moore, Malachi Blake, Aaron Pitts, Richard Tooell, Josiah Woodcock, John Mead.

The difference at Honiton examined, both parties heard. Mr Edwards advis'd to leave the place. Several letters from Dartmouth to Mr Sanders, Mr Tapper, etc., desiring their sentiments concerning Mr Edwards. Agreed. That 'tis not expedient that this Assembly should give any recommendation of Mr. Edwards to Dartmouth people.[4]

[fo. 42r.] Mr Hunt gives information that some of South Molton, who had call'd him to be their Minister, have invited Mr Balster to administer Sacraments to them. That Mr Balster had without his consent administered both Sacraments among them. That some of them refuse to hear him, & choose rather to ly at home on the Lord's Day than to attend on his preaching. Mr Balster advis'd to desist from such practices for the future; & Mr Moore of Tiverton, whom they have chosen for their Pastor desir'd to deal with them as he shall see fit for their irregular practices.

Mr Chappel of [5] & Mr Matthew Perdue of Exon desire the approbation of the ministers now assembled, that they may preach the Gospel, in order to ordination. Agreed that the Moderator give Mr Perdue a

[1] John Ashwood, of the Castle Lane Independent Meeting in Exeter. *Dictionary of National Biography.*
[2] Blanks in MS.
[3] Benjamin Hooper of Thoiverton.
[4] Honiton affairs are continued in June, 1693, below, p. 16.
[5] Blank in MS.

Certificate under his hand, of the approbation of this Assembly, etc., to preach the Gospel. A copy of which follows:

October 7th, 1691. The Assembled Ministers in Exon having received a good & very credible information of the parts doctrine & manners of Mr Matthew Perdu the day abovesaid, did all concur to encourage him to preach for the exercising of his abilities in a subserviency to his ordination in due time, of which I was desired to give this information & certificate in the name of the Association. George Trosse, the Moderator.

[fo. 43r.] The Fund inquir'd into. The following sums paid in for Michaelmass Quarter by the persons undernamed.

	£	s	d
Mr Trosse & Mr Hallet ⎫	15	17	6
Mr Hopping & Mr Atkins ⎬ for Exon. ...	10	10	0
Mr Gaylard ... ... ⎪	3	15	0
Mr Goswell ... ... ⎭	4	4	0
Mr Ashwood, given by Robert Avery, Gent. ...	1	0	0
Mr Sanders & Mr Sandercock ⎫	6	18	1
Mr Bartlett ⎬ For Tiverton	4	0	0
Mr Moore ... ... ⎭	2	15	0
Mr Backaller of Shoobrook	3	5	0
Mr Hooper of Thorverton	2	0	0
I. Gilling of Silferton	3	0	0
Mr Balster	1	11	0
Mr Collings of Saint Mary Ottery	1	0	0
Mr Chapman of Okehampton	1	0	0
Total of receipts this Quarter ...	60	15	7
Remained in the Receiver's hands last Quarter	13	8	4
In all ...	74	3	11

Agreed that the Receiver or Scribe pay out of the Fund the following sums to the persons undernam'd for the poor ministers & poor scholars here mention'd.

	£	s	d
To Isaac Gilling for Joseph Gilling	3	8	0
To Mr Ames Short for Peter & Thomas Kellow	4	0	0
To Mr Hooper for Benjamin Berry	2	0	0
To Mr [1] for [1] Pook at London	2	0	0
To Mr Balster for his son	1	11	0
To Mr Cock for George Lissant	1	5	0
To Mr Galpin Junior for Mr Birdwood	3	0	0
for Mr Searle	2	0	0
[fo. 44r.] To Mr John Knight	2	10	0
To Mr Thomas Chapman	2	10	0
To Mr Thomas Hart	2	10	0

1Blank in MS.

Their proportions for Michaelmas Quarter.

To Mr Thomas Walsh to buy a Horse	5	0	0
Paid this Quarter	31	14	0
Remains in the Receiver's hands	42	9	11

Agreed that Mr. Toogood, Hallet & Gilling go as Delegates to the Meeting of the United Brethren of the Western Division of Somerset held at Taunton the first Wednesday in January. That the next Quarterly Meeting for this County be at Exon the 2d Wednesday in January Mr Tross to preach. That the next General Meeting for Exon & Devon be at Exon the first Tuesday & Wednesday after the first Lords Day in May Mr Tapper to preach, Mr Toogood to pray. Maii 3tio & 4to.

[fo. 45r.]
EXETER, 13tio January, 1691/2.[1] At the Meeting of the United Brethren of Exon and Devon.

The following sums paid in to the Fund for this Quarter by the persons undernamed.

	£	s	d
Mr Tross & Mr Hallet	15	15	9
Mr Gaylard...	3	15	0
Mr Hooper	2	0	0
Isaac Gilling		10	0
Mr Starr (Nov. 1691)	4	14	7
Mr Atkins	10	0	0
	36	15	4

Agreed that the Receiver pay the following sums to the persons undernamed:

	£	s	d
To Joseph Gilling	3	8	0
To Mr Masters son	2	0	0
To Mr Starr for Peter & Thomas Kellow ...	4	0	0
To Mr Hooper for Benjamin Berry	2	0	0
To Mr Atkins for John Clark of Buckrell ...	3	0	0
To Mr Hallet for George Lissant	1	5	0
To Mr Mortimers son		10	0
To Mr Hooper for Mr John Berry	2	10	0
To Mr Knight	2	10	0
To Mr Searle	2	0	0
To Mr Birdwood	2	10	0
To Mr Chapman	2	10	0
To Mr Hallet for Mr Hart	2	10	0
	30	13	0

Remains in the Receiver's hands £38 11s 6d.

[1] This is the only recorded case of a Quarterly Meeting being held. It was clearly capable of handling matters relating to the Fund only. The names of those attending were not written down.

Charles Hopping propos'd.
[There follow four blank pages, fos. 46r. 47r, 48r, & 49r. The Minutes for the May and September Assemblies of 1692 were never copied in this space left for them.]

[fo. 50r.]
EXETER, 18th, 19th, & 20th of April, 1693. At the meeting of the United Brethren of the Counties of Devon, Somerset & Dorset held at Exon.

[Present:] Mr George Tross of Exon,. Moderator; [1]Mr Ames Short of Lyme, [1]Richard Sanders of Tiverton, [1]Edward Par of Buckrel, [1]John Berry, [1]Henry Berry of Torrington, [1]Robert Gaylard of Exon, [1]William Crompton of Cullompton, [1]Nicholas Sherwill of Plymouth, [1]Samuel Tapper of Lympston, [1]Samuel Stoddon of Sidmouth, John Bush of Langport, John Knight, [1]John Galpin of Totness, [1]Thomas Palke of Ashburton, [1]Henry Backaller of Shoobrook, John Moore of Bridgwater, [1]Matthew Warren of Taunton, [1]Malachi Blake of Wellington, Benjamin Hooper of Thorverton, [1]Thomas Chapman of Dartmouth, Joseph Hallet of Exon, Aaron Pitts of Chard, [1]Samuel Atkins of Exon, [1]John Ashwood of Exon, [1]Bernard Starr of Topsham, John Goswell of Exon, Christopher Taylor of Bath, [1]Richard Tooell of Dulverton, [fo. 50v.] Isaac Gilling of Silferton, William Horsham of Stokeinham, John Galpin junior of Staverton, [1]Josiah Woodcock, Jacob Sandercock of Tavistock, Samuel Wood of North Molton, Thomas Walsh of Pittminster, [1]Samuel Bartlett of Tiverton, [1]Benjamin Mills of Bridport, Angel Spark of Moreton. Candidates: John Mead of Chard, [1]Matthew Perdue of Bovey-Tracy, John England of Plymouth, John Moore, Thomas Moore, Robert Darch.

Thanks were return'd to Mr Bush for his sermon & he desir'd to print it.

[fo. 51r.] The Rules for regulating our meetings read. These following to be added:
12. That none but United Ministers be present at our Debates without special leave of the Assembly.
13. That the Assembly will not for the future meddle with, or have the hearing of any differences, untill such time as those who desire their advice shew a disposedness to regard it & receive it peaceably.
14. That for the quicker dispatch of business, the preventing heats and animosities, and that our votes may be more free & impartial, no differences[2] be debated before the parties concern'd: but that after the case is stated & the evidence heard, all persons concern'd whether ministers or people, be desired to withdraw while their case is consider'd: and that the Moderator acquaint the parties concern'd with the sense, advice, & determination of the Assembly.[3]

---

[1]Asterisks were placed before these names in the MS. with no explanation.
[2]The words " matters of weight " were written above " no differences", but the latter were not deleted.
[3]These rules are repeated on fo. 23v. with the addition: " That none of the Brethren withdraw from the Assembly, before the conclusion of each session, without leave first obtain'd from the Assembly".

Mr Matthew Perdue formerly approv'd of by the United Brethren of Devon as a person duly qualify'd to preach as a Probationer, being about to settle at Bovey-Tracy, desir'd the Reverend Moderator of this Assembly with Mr Galpin, Senior, Mr Palk and others to assist at his Ordination, and appoint a time for it. Agreed that Mr Perdue be ordain'd at Bovey Tracey the 10th of May next. The Assembly leave it to the United Brethren of Somerset to appoint time and place for Mr John Meads Ordination.

[fo. 52r.] Approbation of Candidates. A Certificate of the Assemblies approbation of Mr Chappels preaching, & encourageing him to continue so to do in order to Ordination read approv'd & subscrib'd by the Moderator, a copy of which follows:

Exon, 19th April, 1693. The Ministers of the Provincial Assembly having had good information of the parts & abilities of Mr Christopher Chappel, as also of his good acceptance & approbation of his work in preaching by those people among whom he now labours, do declare their allowance of the same, and do encourage and intreat him to persevere in the same as a candidate for the ministry till a fit opportunity may present itself for his regular ordination, which to testify this instrument is subscribed in the name & by the consent of the whole Assembly by George Trosse, Moderator.

The following Testimonial for Mr John and Mr Thomas Moore & Mr Robert Darch propos'd, agreed to and subscrib'd:

Exon, 19th April, 1693. The Ministers in the Provincial Assembly having been well informed, & sufficiently convinced of the learning & preparatory abilities, the good conversation, & the orthodox judgments of Mr Moore (of Bridgwater) his two sons and Mr Robert Darch do earnestly desire them (considering the present exigencies of several congregations) to set speedily upon the work of preaching to, & praying with such congregations [fo. 53r.] and give them all the encouragement we can thereunto, as preliminary to their regular admission into the Ministerial function, in testimony whereof this is in the names and with the unanimous consent of the whole Assembly subscribed by George Trosse, Moderator.

Differences heard. A Petition signed by 29 members of the Church at Bydeford, desiring that some of the United Brethren may have a hearing of the difference between them and the Reverend Mr James Wood, at Bydeford. The following letter to Mr Wood read, approv'd and order'd to be sent:

To our Reverend Brother Mr James Wood, minister of the Gospel in Bydeford.[1] Revd. Brother: Some of the Church of Bydeford having made a motion to us the associated ministers met in a Provincial Assembly at Exon this 19th day of April 1693, for the hearing of a difference between your self & them, and having nominated to us 6 ministers on their part to hear the said difference, namely Mr Henry Berry, Mr Peard, Mr Hanmer, Mr Ashwood, Mr Toogood, and Mr Harding, we being willing as much as lies in us to heal breaches in the Church of Christ do desire you to pitch on the like number to hear the cause on your side, and with the other six to make determination of the said affair if it may be. And

---

[1]The affairs of Bideford Independents were prolonged and intricate, and have been explained in the Introduction, pp. xiii–xiv.

if (which God forbid) they should not be able to compose the differences, we the associated ministers of the County [fo. 54r.] of Devon shall not be wanting in our next Assembly for this County, which is to be on the 1st Tuesday and Wednesday in June next to give our best advice towards an happy end of it.

A Petition subscrib'd by 9 members of the Church at Lyme desiring the Assembly to consider the difference between them & their Reverend & aged Pastor, Mr Ames Short, was read. The Assembly advised the petitioners that passing by all that is past they continue to sit under Mr Short as their pastor: but if they cannot be persuaded so to do, that they depart in love and peace. And desired Mr Short to give a charitable licence to those dissatisfied members of his to hear & join elsewhere for some time occasionally, though not to fix as members of another society.

Mr Samuel Wood gives a large account of his difference with Mr Hunt. Mr Hunt not being present the Assembly desired Mr John Berry & Mr Hanmer once more to meet at South Molton in order to the reconciling this difference.[1]

Some of the Brethren reported the desire of many of Honiton (who are dissatisfy'd to sit under Mr Edwards as their Pastor) that the Assembly would approve of their getting another Pastor. But neither they nor Mr Edwards being present nothing was determined.

[fo. 55r.] Those of Moreton who refuse to accept of Mr Spark as their Pastor, having formerly slighted & acted directly contrary to the advice of the Assembly, adding reflections and reproaches to their contempt: and now instead of promising peaceably to receive their advice, endeavouring to get the Assembly to acquiesce in their determinations, behaving themselves with great rudeness & clamour before the Assembly, & threatening Mr Spark to keep away the Meeting place from him; were severely reprimanded, their Paper of Determinations not permitted to be read, & they order'd to withdraw.[2]

Settling and Maintaining Ministers & poor Scholars. A Petition of Hatherly people desiring a Pastor in the room of Mr Bartholomew Yeo lately deceased, & some help for his maintenance out of the Fund, was read. Mr John Knight promised to go thither in a short time, & preach among them if desired, & if he finds conveniencies for lodgings, etc., knows not but he may settle among them. A Petition of Monsieur Violet in behalf of himself & his society in Exon, who follow the discipline of the Reformed Churches in France, desiring some assistance out of the Fund, seeing they can get nothing from the Committee at London, was read & an expedient propos'd for their relief. [fo. 56r.] Ordered that if Monsieur Violet, Calvet, Lions, Pentecost, or any of them come to our Assembly & desire it, we shall be ready to receive & own them as United Brethren, & members of our Assembly upon their assent to the Heads of Agreement & Rules of Association.

[1]Wood was at this time settled at North Molton and Hunt at South Molton. The dispute dragged on for many years.
[2]Spark had succeeded Robert Woolcombe in 1692, and a division in the congregation took place, a new meeting-house being built. But he succeeded in reuniting the two parties before his death in 1721. Murch, J., History of the Presbyterians and General Baptists in the West of England, 1835, pp. 472-3.

Resolved that Joseph Gilling[1] & John Clark have their arrears paid them to Lady Day, & that John Clark have 50s. more to pay for books, & then that both be struck out of the Receivers Book. That Peter Kellow & all the rest be continu'd according to their former proportions till further order. That Mrs Cruse's son (Samuel Grigg) have 40s. per annum & 15s. now.

Assemblies appointed. Agreed that tis expedient under our present circumstances, that there be held a General Assembly of the United Brethren in the Western Counties once every year, either at Bristol Taunton or Exon: which meeting may swallow up one of the 2 yearly meetings for the County in which tis held. That a letter be sent to Mr Halsey in the name of this Assembly, by him to be communicated to the Ministers in Cornwall, to invite them to unite, & associate themselves. That the next General Assembly be at Bristol the Wednesday & Thursday in Whitsun-week, 1694. That Mr Moore of Bridgwater in the name of this Assembly desire Mr Forbes of Gloucester to preach.

[fo. 57r.]

EXETER, June 6, 1693. At the Meeting of the United Brethren of Exon & Devon.

[Present:] Mr Samuel Tapper, Moderator; Ames Short, Edward Parr, Michael Taylor, James Wood, Robert Gaylard, Robert Collings, Samuel Stoddon, Henry Backaller, John Knight, John Galpin, George Tross, John Balster, Benjamin Hooper, John Hanmer, Stephen Toogood, Joseph Hallet, Thomas Hart, Samuel Atkins, scribe, John Ashwood, Bernard Starr, John Goswell, Isaac Gilling, Samuel Bartlett, Nathaniel Harding, Samuel Hall, John Moor, John Withers, Angel Spark, John Powel, Matthew Perdu. Candidates: Penuel Symonds, Christopher Chappel, John England. Delegate from Somerset: Malachi Blake.

The difference at Honiton consider'd. The Assembly advis'd that Mr Edwards should fully consent to share the work equally with Mr Parr at Honiton, & have equal pay with him. And declar'd in case of his refusal their resolution to incourage another Meeting in that town. Ordered that Mr Stoddon desire Mr Clark to set open again the doors of the Meeting house in that place.[2]

[fo. 58r.] Some of Bydeford being desirous to have Mr Bowden for their Pastor. The Assembly advis'd Mr Bowden to administer the Lords Supper to them by way of tryal before he accept of their Call to him as fixed pastor. That Mr Wood administer the Lords Supper in the same place with Mr Bowden.

Three French Ministers, viz. Monsieur Violet of Exon [3] having assented to the Heads of Agreement were admitted as Members of the Assembly.

[1]The son of Isaac Gilling. He greatly disappointed his father, who wanted him to enter the ministry. *Trans. Devonshire Assoc.*, xxviii, 1896, p. 157.

[2]The Meeting House was in the dwelling of William Clarke, a chandler. John Edwards was the first regular minister, but he proved to have a violent temper and, as will appear later, his sexual morals were not above criticism. He was expelled but for several years continued a small separate society in Honiton. Murch, *op. cit.*, p. 315.

[3]Blank space in MS.

Junii 7mo. Mr Thomas Chapman minister of Dartmouth being charged by some of his Hearers with false doctrine. His sermon notes were read. Agreed. That this expression in his sermon, viz: that sanctifying grace, & glory, are not by purchase, is not safe or expedient to be used before a Congregation. That Mr Tross write to Mr Chapman concerning it, & give an account of the result next Assembly. That Mr Galpine Senior acquaint the people of Dartmouth that the Assembly are satisfied that their Minister is perfectly free from Arminianism & Socinianism.

[fo. 59r.] The Fund inquir'd into. Upon inquiry it was found that several of the United Brethren in this County had brought in nothing. Those Congregations who were thought capable to afford their assistance towards it, but had not, mentioned.[1] Ordered that Mr Symonds be struck out of the Fund. That George Bowcher of Silferton have £6 per annum, if the Fund will hold out. That Bovey people have £5 per annum towards the maintenance of their minister. That Nicholas Gillard have £12 per annum. John Slowly of Barnstaple & Humphrey Berry of Torrington recommended by Mr Wood & Mr Hanmer to be consider'd out of the Fund in due time.

Mr Stoddon promis'd to print his Sermon. The next meeting appointed October 3 & 4th, Mr Galpine Senior to preach Mr Moore of Tiverton to pray.

[fo. 60r.]
EXETER, 3tio & 4to 8bris [Oct.], 1693. At the Meeting of the United Brethren of Exon & Devon.

[Present:] Mr Edward Par, Moderator; Robert Gaylard, Robert Collings, Robert Carel, Samuel Stoddon, John Galpin, senior, George Tross, Joseph Hallet, John Ashwood, scribe, Isaac Gilling, William Horsham, John Galpin, junior. Malachi Blake, delegate from Somerset. John England, a candidate.

Mr Chapman's letter to Mr Tross read, in which he grants, that God gives Christ as his reward the sanctification & eternal salvation of innumerable sinners, & Christ is worthy of that reward. Isa. 53, 10–12. And by that worthiness (saith he) I mean not such as was in Abraham & David whose posterity are blessed for their sakes: that were an infinite dishonour to the blessed Jesus; His obedience & sufferings being infinitely greater, more for the glory of God, without the least defect, His person being infinitely above them, & infinitely condescending to yield that obedience & to suffer. And if Christ's so deserving our grace & glory be (as you say) his purchasing them, I heartily acknowledge it. The Assembly gave it as their opinion that Mr Thomas Chapman late of Dartmouth was orthodox in his judgment as to the merits of Christ, tho he differed in his expressions.

Mr Tross propos'd the case of Honiton, informing the Assembly that some Ministers did assist Mr Edwards in his separate Meeting. Agreed, nemine contradicente, that none of the associated ministers of this County

[1] A space was left here for the names of the defaulting congregations.

assist Mr Edwards [fo. 61r.] in his present work, whilst he carries it so contemptuously towards this Assembly.

Mr Carel informs the Assembly that since Mr Balster's departure from Ufculm, the people had laid down their Meeting, & went to hear the Anabaptists & Quakers, whereupon Mr Blake was desir'd to perswade the people to set up a meeting again.

Order'd that Mr Warren or Mr Moor of Somersett be desir'd to use their endeavours to procure a Minister for Hatherly. The people offer to raise £24 per annum.

A letter from Dartmouth people to the Assembly desiring their approbation of Mr John Galpin, junior, to be their Minister, & their call to Mr Galpin to the Pastoral Office, read. Order'd that Mr Symonds be desired to preach at Staverton for 3 or 4 Lords days that Mr Galpin may supply Dartmouth, & be acquainted that if he think fit to fix at Staverton the Assembly will give him £5 out of the Fund. Or if the people of Staverton pitch on any other of the United Brethren, he shall have the same contribution.

The Fund inquir'd into. An account given of several Congregations that had contributed nothing to it, & of some that had withdrawn their contributions, particularly Tiverton. Mrs Palk[1] presented her 2 sons to the Assembly, desiring some supply out of the Fund towards their education. [fo. 62r.] Resolv'd that the Assembly will make up what is wanting in the contributions of Newton & Ashburton people to the maintenance of Mrs Palks 2 sons. Order'd that Mr Toogood receive £5 out of the Fund for Samuel Baker, £3 of which he brought to the Fund. That Mr Nicholas Gillet be placed with Mr Hallet for his education.[2] Mr Hallet offer'd to teach him for 40s. per annum. That Monsieur Violet have 40s. per annum.

That the next Meeting of this Assembly be the 1st Tuesday in May, Mr John Berry to preach, Mr Samuel Hall to pray.

Collected out of Mr Ashwood's minutes.

[fo. 63r.]
EXETER, 8vo. & 9o. May, 1694. At the Meeting of the UnitedB rethren of Devon & Exon. Mr Benjamin Hooper, Moderator, Mr William Horsham, scribe.[3]

Agreed that no Candidate be ordain'd by any of the United Brethren of this County but by order of the Assembly. That Mr John Mede & Mr Richard Evans be ordain'd in the Congregation at Ashburton, Mr Hallet to begin with prayer, Mr Galpine, senior, to preach, Mr Tross to pray over Mr Mede, Mr Hooper to give the Exhortation. That Mr Evans state & defend the following Question: Quomodo Fides se habet ad justificationem? That Mr Martin be ordain'd at Hatherly, & tha the state & defend the following Question: An Foedus gratiae sit conditionatum? To hold it affirmatively.

Mr Edwards his case consider'd. A paper containing his apology read. The following Minute drawn up, & a copy of it subscrib'd by the

[1]Thomas Palk of Ashburton had died on 18th June, 1693. MS., fo. 24v.
[2]This is probably the Nicholas Gillard who was given a grant at the previous Assembly.
[3]The names of those other ministers attending are not given, although a space was left.

Moderator given him. Viz: Forasmuch as Mr Edwards hath given satisfaction to this Assembly touching some contempt cast upon it, & hath declar'd his willingness to be reconcil'd, promising to behave [fo. 64r.] himself as a member of this Association, we unanimously retract the Vote formerly pass'd against any of our members assisting him in preaching at Honiton.

The following sums brought in for the Fund:

						£	s	d
Mr Stoddon	...	...	...	...	...	5	0	0
Mr Carel	...	...	...	...	...	7	1	0
Mr Galpine, senior...		...	...	...	...	3	11	1
Mr Wood of Bytheford	...	...	...	...	3	0	0
Mr Starr	...	...	...	...	...	3	1	6
Mr Tross	...	...	...	...	...	2	0	0
Mr Hooper ...	...	...	...	...	...	1	15	0
Mr John Berry	...	...	...	...	...	1	10	0
						26	18	7

[I sent mine two months ago.][1]

Order'd that Mrs Palks 2 sons be maintain'd out of the Fund as to their diet & schooling for one year. That the Meeting at Hatherly have £5, Kings Kerswell £6 for one year. That if the Fund will reach it John Slowly & Humphry Berry shall have a contribution towards their maintenance.

The Assembly taking into their serious consideration the very poor condition of the French Protestants, following the discipline of the Churches of France, being excluded from having any interest in the Publick Charity; do earnestly recommend them as very proper objects of the pity & compassion of all well disposed Christians in our respective congregations.

Order'd that the next Assembly be September the 4th, that Mr Sanders be desir'd to preach, or if he fail Mr Backaller, Mr Moor to pray.

[fo. 65r.]
Bristol, May 30, 1694.[2] Articles agreed on by the Association at Bristol, May 30, 1694, when several Ministers were present from many counties of England and Wales, and which were then resolved to be put in practice immediately.

1. It is believed by us to be very necessary for the advancement of the interest of Religion that there be a General Correspondency betwixt all the United Ministers throughout the Kingdom: the head of which Correspondency is to be fixed in London, or some such place where a select number of Ministers shall be appointed to receive all the accounts that shall be given in from time to time that they may digest them methodically; which Register shall contain a general idea of the whole Non-Conformist interest in the Kingdom.

[1]This was a shorthand note by Gilling.
[2]The following passage consists of resolutions passed at a Bristol Provincial Assembly, submitted to London, and now referred back to all Divisions of the country for consideration in detail and further comments.

2. That for this end the Nation be divided into several parts according to the number of Congregations, all which shall meet provincially (much after the manner of our meeting at Bristol) by Delegates (together with such as are willing to give their attendance) twice every year.

3. That there be an exact account given to the Scribe of each Provincial Association of all the Congregations in that Province or Division, the names of each Minister, the number of the people of each Congregation, Communicants & Hearers as near as can be calculated. The state of it as to its increase or decrease, encouragement or opposition, as also what schisms factions or disputes have arisen or are likely to arise in each Congregation, or with those who are of a different persuasion, whether Churchmen, Anabaptists, etc., to give a character of every such [fo. 66r.] opposer, schismatick or factious person, according to the most free candid ingenious & prying observation, & also if there be any probable way of reconciling these disturbances.

4. That every one of us be carefull to observe, and faithfull to relate, to every such Provincial Meeting, and to that select number thereunto appointed in London or elsewhere, the confusions, disorders & scandals that have arisen, not only in their own congregations, but also in those that differ from them; and especially if any new Sects arise, to give a speedy & true account to those who are appointed to maintain the Correspondency with them.

5. That upon all occasions relative to the publick good, there be no clashings allowed, either with moderate Churchmen or men of other Communions, but that as far as possible we cultivate all endeavours towards a Union upon those common principles notwithstanding any little differences between us on other accounts.

6. That all possible care be taken to suppress & ease if possible all heats scandals slanders etc., that may be laid on any of the body. That we be so far from emulating each other, that rather we mutually assist each other, to vindicate each other's just quarrels or injured reputations, as far as fairly we may, & procure such needfull assistance for any in distress or under opposition, that it may in effect ingage us all to support the cause of every such distressed individual, & this not only with our counsel, interest & advice, but also with our purses too, if need require.

7. That the first work done at all such Associations as these shall be to appoint a select number of our brethren who are men of the most solid judgments, of greatest experience & largest intelligence to inspect the progress of this Correspondency in all its several parts according to Article 3.

[fo. 67r.] 8. That before this present Meeting break up there be an account required of each of us particularly (according to the above-named instructions) of the present state of every one of the Congregations to which we belong, that so this matter which hath been so long delayed may now commence.

9. That one person in each Division be chosen to manage this correspondency for his own Division with either the whole when formed in London or elsewhere, or with any other part till that can be obtained.

10. That care be taken in each Division for a Common Stock, that if any particular member or members shall fall into distress by the malice

of any whatsoever that such may be relieved thereby, as also to defray the charges of the Correspondency.

11. That no controversial book or sermon be printed without the approbation of the Provincial Association, or such select numbers of Ministers as shall be appointed in each Division for that end.

Mr James Forbes of Gloucester, Moderator.

Sir, Whereas the United Brethren at Bristol have agreed to several articles, & sent them up to London (a copy of which is herewith sent) some of the Brethren here about London (having considered of their expediency, & highly approving their design as necessary to promote a mutual correspondence & union in order to a furtherance of the Gospel) have resolved to write to their respective friends in the country to know the sentiments of our Brethren there. I do accordingly desire you to communicate them to as many of the Brethren in your parts as you can, and at as General a [fo. 68r.] meeting as may be had, or by some other way, to know the sense of your Brethren, & if they agree to this or any such method, that you would signify it with the names of such ministers with you as desire it, that it may be further considered & promoted.[1]

[fo. 69r.]
EXETER, Sept. 4, 5, 1694. At the Meeting of the United Brethren of Exon & Devon.

[Present:] Mr Robert Collins, Moderator; Mr Par, Gaylard, Berry, Stoddon, Galpin, Backaller, Knight, Tapper, Carel, Tross, Balster, Hooper, Hallet, Atkins, Ashwood, Star, Goswell, Gilling, Sandercock, Horsham, Moor, Withers, Mead. From Somerset: Mr Moor of Bridgwater, Mr Blake of Wellington.

Mr Moor of Tiverton prayed, Mr Backaller preach'd.

A letter from Mr James Wood of Bitheford to Mr Tross, desiring the advice of the Assembly by what means he may repair the credit of the Gospel & Ministry to which he hath been so great a scandal. Agreed, that considering our present circumstances tis not convenient for him to preach a Penitential Sermon at Exon. A letter to the Church of Bitheford desiring them to entertain a Christian tenderness & compassion towards Mr Wood as one of whose repentance we have very great hopes, and that they would not obstruct his removal to any people if call'd by them by publishing his miscarriage or sending reports of his scandal before him, drawn up by Mr Galpin & Mr Hooper, read, approv'd & order'd to be sent. A letter to Bristol ministers recommending Mr Wood to them (if there be any vacancy in those parts) as one of whose repentance this Assembly hath great hope, drawn up by Mr Ashwood, read, approv'd & order'd to be sent.

[fo. 21v. Shorthand.] *Exon, September 5th, 1694. Sirs, The report of Mr Wood's foul miscarriage has been brought to the ears of this Assembly before we met together; which indeed ought to be bewailed with tears of blood, considering how much hereby God has been displeased, the Gospel and ministry reproached and what numbers are hereby scandalised, and without true repentance his soul gravely endangered; but that which doth somewhat alleviate our sorrow is this, that we*

[1] The rest of fo. 68r. was left blank.

have great trust that God hath made him sensible of his sin, and truly humbled for it. Here was a letter of his read in our Assembly this day, in which he declared such broken-ness of heart for his folly, and takes the shame of it to himself, and is ready to take any further course we shall advise him to, for manifestation of the truth of his penitence, and removal of the scandal as far as in him lies. We hear he has preached a penitential sermon at Bytheford, and the Assembly has received great satisfaction by the atonement made, and appointed me to certify it to you, desiring you to carry it with all kindness and meekness towards him as to one, who, though he has fallen deeply by sin has risen again by penitence. And, seeing upon penitence God will pardon the offence committed against him we should also the offence committed against us. Also, that you would not obstruct his removal to any other place to which he may be called by making his miscarriage more public than it is. We trust the sense of his fall will make him more humble and watchful and circumspect for the time to come that he will both preach and live much better than yet he has done, by which means the Church of Christ and the souls of men may reap benefit by his gifts and labours. Subscribed in the name and by order of the Assembly by me, Robert Collins, Moderator. To Bitheford.

[fo. 70r.] A letter to Mr Tross from Mr Chappel desiring the concurrence of this Assembly that he may be ordain'd at Exon, read & consider'd. Agreed, that it is most proper & convenient that Mr Chappel be ordain'd at the Congregation at North-Molton. And that Mr Berry, Hunt, Cudmore, & Hanmer, the adjoining ministers, be desir'd to ordain him there.

Mr Symonds who preaches to those of Moreton who are dissatisfied with Mr Spark applied himself to the Assembly desiring ordination. Agreed, that his ordination be differ'd[1] untill the next Assembly. That he preach a sermon for trial on 1. Tim:4-ult. at Mrs Lawrences the 1st Tuesday in October before some ministers who are to judg of his abilities & report accordingly to the next Assembly.

That Mr Carel write a letter in the name of this Assembly to Mr Joseph Gilling to invite him down to take the charge of the Congregation at Bow.

	£	s	d
Brought into the Fund by Mr Tross	2	0	0
Mr Mead from Ashburton & Newton Bushel ...	6	10	0
Mr Galpin Senior	2	15	6
Mr Collins		10	0
Mr Star	4	3	7½

Out of his deducted £2 15s. for Samuel Rabjent.

	£	s	d
Agreed that Mr Balster's son have this Quarter	3	10	0
That Samuel Grigg have an addition of per annum	4	0	0
That John Slowly of Barnstaple have	10	0	0
& Mr Berry's son of Torrington yearly out of the Fund while they continue students at Edinburgh	6	0	0

The next Assembly to be at Exon the 1st Tuesday & Wednesday in

[1] Sic. This should be " deferred ".

April, Mr Sherwill to preach or if he fail Mr Collins. Mr Sandercock to pray.

[fo. 71r.]
EXETER, 1695, April 2, 3. At the Meeting of the United Brethren of Exon & Devon.

Mr Robert Carel Moderator; Mr Samuel Hall Scribe.[1]

The Fund inquir'd into.

	£	s	d
Brought in by Mr Hooper	2	5	0
Mr Galpin, Senior ...	2	14	9
Mr Gaylard	2	10	0
Mr Stoddon	8	0	0
Mr Carel	7	0	0
Mr Hall	5	0	0
Mr Collins		10	0
	27	19	9

Ordered that the Receiver pay

To Daniel Wilcox	8	0	0 per annum
To Mr Balster's son from Ladyday last	8	0	0 ,, ,,
To Mr John Berrys son after he goes for Edinburgh	16	0	0 ,, ,,
To Short	6	0	0 ,, ,,
To Plimtree meeting	4	0	0 ,, ,,

That the £10 allow'd to John Slowly be continu'd till the next meeting & no longer unless Tavistock people will lay their contribution to the Fund or give an account what they advance for him, that it may be registered in the accounts of the Fund.

[fo. 72r.] A Petition from Plimtree & another from South Molton desiring the advice of the Assembly as to a Pastor for the latter & for somewhat out of the Fund for the former.

An information given that many of Mr Balsters hearers & several members of his society at Uf-Culm are turned Anabaptists & dipt, & that when there is any vacancy Anabaptists preach at Plimtree & Ufculm. Ufculm people promise to keep up their meeting if they can get £5 per annum out of the Fund. The use which some Anabaptists educated in learning under Mr Toogood & Mr Warren make of what learning they have gained propos'd to consideration. Murch of Plymouth, Knotwood of Bovey, brought as instances. Resolved that private tutors among us be caution'd against educating for the Ministry those who professedly oppose the Heads of Agreement assented to by the United Brethren. The following letter to Mr Warren read, approv'd & order'd to be sent. Reverend Sir: Upon several complaints which we have receiv'd that the reputation of learning among some preachers of the Anabaptists hath been improv'd by them to stumble some & seduce others of our hearers

[1]No further names are given, although a space was left.

it is the unanimous opinion of the Ministers now assembled that it is inconvenient for any United Brethren who are concerned for educating any young men for the Ministry to assist those who are fixed in that opinion & design for the Ministry by instructing them in languages or sciences [fo. 73r.] or to receive or continue any others under their tuition who professedly oppose the Heads of Agreement assented to by us. This their opinion is recommended to your serious consideration in their name & by their order by, Sir, your unworthy Brother & fellow Labourer Robert Carel, Moderator, Exon, 3 April 1695. To the Rev. Mr Matthew Warren, Minister of the Gospel in Taunton.

The following letter to Mr Harding of Plymouth read, approv'd and order'd to be sent. Reverend Sir, It being a principal end of our associating to resolve on such methods as may tend to the support & encouragement of young students in order to their being hereafter useful in the Ministry & finding this our design to be much obstructed by the great diminutions of our publick Fund occasioned by the withdrawing of several contributions which were formerly brought in for its support: it is the desire of this Assembly that as you have formerly procur'd the commendable & charitable assistance of your Congregation so you would stir them up to the continuation thereof. And they unanimously resolve that the money so raised by you shall be imploy'd in the behalf of such persons whom you shall recommend to receive it. Since we greatly fear that the private disposal of such sums as are collected for the promoting so publick a good will be greatly prejudicial to the common interest which we all have espoused and to that coalition which is necessary to be preserved among the United Brethren, which is recommended to your serious consideration in the name [fo. 74r.] of the whole Assembly by, Sir, your unworthy Brother & fellow Labourer, R. Carel, Moderator. Exon, April 3, 1695. To the Rev. Mr Nathaniel Harding, Minister of the Gospel in Plymouth.

Question, whether this Assembly should not clear themselves by suspending Mr Wood from publick preaching in the town of Biddeford for some time upon the account of his former miscarriage. Mr Ashwood and the Moderator were for the affirmative, but after long debates it being put to the vote all but 3 or 4 were for the negative.

Mr Jellinger Symonds proposed himself to the Assembly for Ordination, having received a Call from Bow. This Question given him to state & defend. An gratia conversionis sit irresistibilis? This text to preach upon[1]: Apollos was an eloquent man & mighty in the Scriptures. The time for these exercises May 14th, being the Tuesday in Whitsun week at Mrs. Lawrences. At the same time Mr Hallet to be Respondent on this Question, An Coltus fratrum unitorum sint schismatici? & Mr Gilling on this An Paedobaptismus sit licitus? Mr Carel, Backaller, Tapper, Balster, Hooper to ordain Mr Symonds at Bow the last Tuesday in July next.

[fo. 75r.] The next Meeting to be the 1st Tuesday in September Mr Sherwil to be Moderator, Mr Collings to preach, Mr Horsham to pray, Mr Star to be Scribe.

---

[1]A space was left here for the reference.

Cases of Conscience propos'd to the Assembly.

Q. Is pronouncing the Blessing a prayer or an act of ministerial power & authority? If it be an act of authority how can candidates pronounce it?

Q. Is it lawful to administer the Lords Supper at any other time than in the evening? One declares he can be a sufferer rather than receive at any other time than in the evening.

Q. A womans husband marries another woman upon whose decease she would know whether she ought to respect him as her husband, & whether she may return unto him without adultry? By Mr John Galpin, junior.

Q. Whether a man who hath buried his Wife may lawfully marry her Sisters daughter? Propos'd by Mr Sandercock as a case now depending in the West of Cornwall. Lev:18,14. Thou shalt not uncover the nakedness of thy fathers brother; thou shalt not approach to his wife, she is thine aunt. The nephew must not marry his aunt, whether may the uncle marry his wifes niece? Doth the line of affinity & consanguinity run equal? [fo. 76r.] Resolv'd that many casuists having been consulted, who do account it unlawfull for a man to marry his wife's sister's daughter, and as we conceive it being against the laws of the land so to do, this Assembly cannot approve it.

Q. Seeing the Assembly disapprove the marriage what shall be done in case there be any contract between them? Doth that rule hold here, Quod fieri non debet factum valet?[1]

[fo. 77r.]
PLYMOUTH, 1695, Sept. 3, 4. At the meeting of the United Brethren of Devon. Mr Sherwill, Moderator; Mr Mead, Scribe; Mr Galpine, Horsham, Collings, Sandercock, Young, Harding.

Moneys brought in to the Fund.

	£	s	d
By Mr Sherwill	10	18	6
Mr Harding	11	5	0
Mr Sandercock	3	3	6
Mr Mead	3	1	0
Mr Galpine	2	12	4
Mr Young	2	10	0
	33	10	4

Mr Sandercock gives an account that Tavistock people advance £4 per annum towards the maintenance of Mr Slowly, which was included in the account his friends gave of what they could do for him. Agreed that the former sum allotted him out of the Fund be continued untill the next Assembly. Upon presumption that the Fund is sufficient agreed that Mr Force's son shall have £15 for his better education, viz. £5 at Michaelmas, £5 at Christmas, & £5 at Lady Day next. [fo. 78r.] That Mr George Bowcher shall have an addition of £8 for one year, to begin

[1]The remainder of fo. 76r. is blank.

immediately after the death of Mr Balster's son. That the usual pay to Mrs Palk's sons be continued until the next Assembly. That Ufculm Meeting have £2 10s. between this and next Assembly. That £8 per annum be allowed toward the maintenance of an assistant to Mr Touching of Foy.[1] That £5 be given to Mr Hancock of Loo.

Mr Peter and Thomas Kellow apply'd themselves to the Assembly for Ordination. Agreed that a letter be sent to Mr Taylor, Berry, Bowden, Balster, Peard, & Hanmer desiring that they or any 3 of them will give Mr Peter Kellow a Theological Question, & a Text to preach a probation sermon upon before them or any 3 of them; & that they ordain him, if they approve him. That a letter be sent to Mr Touching, Flamanck, Hancock, Halsey, Tingcomb, Facy, desiring that they or any 3 of them will give Mr Thomas Kellow a Theological Question, & a Text on which to preach a probation sermon before them or any 3 of them, & that if they approve him they will ordain him.

[fo. 79r.] The next meeting to be at Exon on the first Tuesday & Wednesday in May, 1696. Mr Tingcomb to preach or if he fail Mr Toogood, Mr Ashwood to pray, Mr Stoddon to be Moderator.[2]

[fo. 80r.]
EXETER, 1696, May 5 & 6. At the Meeting of the United Brethren of Exon and Devon.

[Present:] Mr Samuel Stoddon, Moderator; Isaac Gilling, Scribe. Mr James Wood, Edward Parr, Robert Collings, Robert Carel, Samuel Tapper, John Knight, George Tross, Henry Backaller, Benjamin Hooper, Stephen Toogood, Joseph Hallet, John Ball, William Horsham, Samuel Hall, Jacob Sandercock, Baily, Thomas Walsh. From Cornwall: Mr Tingcomb, Deliverance Larkham, Thomas Kellow. From Somersett: Mr John Moor, John Moor, junior, Thomas Moor, Edmond Badson. Candidates: Samuel Broadmead, William Symonds.

Mr Tingcomb preach'd, Mr Ball pray'd. The Minutes of the last meeting at Plymouth read. Mr Thomas Kellow ordain'd according to the order of that Assembly.

A letter from a Provincial Meeting at Bradford near Bath in Wilts., to desire the sentiments of this Assembly whether tis convenient to endeavour to get an Act of Parliament in favour of our private Academies, & to desire Delegates to a meeting at Sherburn the 1st Tuesday & Wednesday in September. [fo. 81r.] An answer drawn up by Mr Ball, that we think it not convenient to make any such motion as yet. Sent by Mr Badson.

Concerning the Fund. The Fund inquir'd into. Twas found to be charg'd very highly. A probability that it would decrease by reason of the scarcity of money. Resolved, that seeing the younger of Mrs Palks sons is not so fit for learning, & seeing the Fund is design'd for such as are most capable of it, & inclin'd to it, his contribution be continued no longer than Midsummer next. A young person of Cornwall, & the Meeting of Chulmleigh recommended to the Fund. Resolv'd, that they

[1]Fowey, Cornwall.
[2]The remainder of fo. 79r. was used otherwise.

be considered next Meeting if the Fund will bear it. Great objections being made against sending money out of the County to maintain meetings in other counties, it being fear'd that it might be very prejudicial to the Fund, resolv'd that the £8 per annum given by the Assembly at Plymouth to Foy meeting in Cornwall for the maintaining an assistant to Mr Touching during his life, be paid out of the money brought in to the Fund from Plymouth & Tavistock. Resolv'd that Mr John Berry & Mr John Balster have but £8 per annum, & Ufculm Meeting but £6 per annum (at Midsummer) for the future. [fo. 82r.] A letter of thanks & a receipt for Mrs Harvey, of Totness, for a legacy of £25 given by her husband to the Fund drawn up by Mr Hallet, read approv'd subscrib'd & order'd to be sent.

[p. 14v. Shorthand.] *To Mrs Harvey in Totness, 6th May 1696. Mrs Harvey, We the United Ministers of the Congregations of the Counties of Exon and Devon, being associated, cannot but express the grateful sense we have of the kind legacy which Mr Harvey by Will was pleased to leave to the Fund destined to the education of young Scholars to the ministry. We look upon it as a very charitable and pious deed, and seems a strong evidence of his great affection for Religion and his zeal for the promotion of it after his decease. May so excellent and singular an instance of love to religion and the Gospel Ministry be a [1] inducement to others to write after so fair a copy. We readily and thankfully own the receipt of his large and charitable legacy, being the sum of £25 for the use afore mentioned. Subscribed in the name and by the order of the Assembly by Samuel Stoddon, Moderator, Isaac Gilling, scribe.*

[fo. 82r.] The charge of the Fund, 1696.

Scholars	Per annum £		Meetings & Ministers	Per annum £
Mr Hopping	20		Mr Searle	8
Bowcher	14		Berry	8
Wilcox	14		Balster	8
B. Berry	16		Pardew	5
Torrington Berry	6		Martyn	5
Slowly	4	& £4 from Tavistock	Walsh	6
Lissant	5		Plimtree	4
Grigg	6		Ufculm	6
Short	8		Foy	8
Masters	8			___
Palk	12			58
	___			113
	113			___
				171

Thanks were given to Mr Thomas Wood of Exon for his great care & diligence about the Fund, & for his generous refusing a salary for his pains & trouble. And it was ordered that this should be inserted among the Minutes of this Meeting.

[1]indecipherable in MS.

[fo. 83r.] The Assembly was informed that Mr John Edwards of Honiton's wife was deliver'd of a child in 20 weeks after they were married; that he did at first for a considerable time deny that he ever lay with her before marriage, offering to call God to wittness, & take the Sacrament upon it. But now owns it & endeavours to justify it, behaving himself proudly & impudently, discovering no signs of repentance for his foul miscarriage & the great scandal he hath brought upon the United Brethren. The following minute drawn up by order of the Assembly [*by Mr Tross & Mr Horsham*][1], to certify the people of Honiton of our sense of this matter.

Whereas Mr John Edwards of Honiton a member of this Assembly hath lately fallen into a notorious scandal & doth manifest no reparation in way of humiliation & repentance, but rather seems to vindicate his actions & carries it as tho he were guiltless: we judge it our duty to declare our utter abhorrence of such scandalous actions & resolve till he hath made some due and satisfactory amends for the great offence which he hath committed against and reproach cast upon God, Religion, and the United Brethren that we will not [fo. 84r.] give him the right hand of fellowship, nor own him as a Member of our Assembly. Subscribed by Order of the Assembly by the Moderator. The Moderator was desired to make an Exchange with Mr Ball on some Lords Day, & then to publish the foregoing Paper in the meeting at Honiton.

Mr James Wood of Bytheford who voluntarily absented from our Assemblies for the space of 2 years, now appears, declaring his unfeigned repentance for his sin; certifying the Assembly of the extraordinary assistance and signal presence of God attending his labours in Bytheford, but withal the unchristian & incompassionate carriage of some of that town towards him. The Assembly declar'd that they judged it his duty to continue at Bytheford untill he hath a clear call to remove from thence.

The Ministers present (except Mr Tross & Mr Symonds a Candidate) subscrib'd the Parliaments Association with this Inscription: To the Kings most excellent Majesty, the Association of several Ministers of the Gospel in some things dissenting from the Establish'd Church now assembled together in your Majesties City of Exon.[2]

[fo. 85r.] Resolved that the next meeting be at Exon the 2d Tuesday & Wednesday in September, viz. September 8th & 9th, Mr Taylor of Holsworthy to preach or if he fail Mr Hooper, Mr Baily to pray or if he fail Mr Gilling, Mr Knight to be Moderator.

EXETER, 1696, Sept. 8th & 9th. At the Meeting of the United Brethren of Exon and Devon.

[Present:] Mr John Berry, Moderator; Isaac Gilling, scribe; Mr Parr, Tapper, Collings, Mortimer, Stoddon, Tross, Backaller, Balster, Carel, Hooper, Hallet, Ball, Atkins, Withers, Pardew, Star, Goswill, Sandercock, Horsham, Hall, S. Wood, Walsh, Galpin junior, Moor, Mead, Evans, Peter Kellow, T. Kellow, Jellinger Symonds. Candidates: Mr John

[1]This was written in shorthand.
[2]The shorthand passage giving the text of this Association is mentioned in the Appendix, below, pp. 125-6.

Walrond, Edward Grove, Josiah Eveleigh, Wm. Symonds. From Somerset: Mr Malachi Blake.

Mr Knight sent a letter to excuse himself from being Moderator, proposing Mr John Berry. Mr Taylor of Holsworthy & Mr Baily of Bytheford failing, Mr Hooper preach'd, Mr Gilling pray'd.

Mr Ball gave an account that the Paper against Mr Edwards had not been published in his congregation for fear of causing a new disturbance at Honiton.

[fo. 86r.] Brought into the Fund.

					£	s	d
By Mr Hooper	...	...	...	...	...	5	1	0
Mr Starr	...	...	...	...	...	3	16	2
Mr Berry	...	...	...	...	...	1	0	0
Mr Stoddon, a legacy from William Acleigh of Sidbury	...	...	...	...	5	0	0
					14	17	2

Mr Harding promises (by Mr Grove) £14 per annum for Mr Barron who is at Mr Warrens. An order given to the Receiver to pay to Mr Thomas Kellow £4 for Foy Meeting for Michaelmas Quarter. To Mrs Palks younger son £3 at Michaelmas, no more after. To Mr Berry & Mr Balster 10s apiece more for Midsummer Quarter. To Mr Star for Samuel Rabient 30s. To Mr Barron or order £14 per annum out of Mr Hardings money of Plymouth. And to continue the former payments. A letter to Mrs Palk drawn up by Mr Sandercock & Mr Ball to let her know that the contribution to her younger son will be continued no longer than Michaelmas next.

The following letter from the Association at Sherburn read.[1] To the Reverend the United Brethren of the County of Devon to be assembled at Exon. Reverend Brethren We understand that some who are of your association, to wit, Mr Toogood, Mr Ashwood etc., have [fo. 87r.] join'd in the Ordination of persons for the Ministry, who have not addressed themselves for Ordination to the Associated Brethren in the Ministry, when they might have so done. We doubt not but you are as sensible as we of the mischiefs that may in process of time follow such irregular ordinations, therefore we humbly intreat you to admonish the forementioned Brethren to forbear such practices for the future. We commend you Brethren & your consultations to the blessing of our Lord in whom we are yours. Subscribed in the name of the Assembled Ministers, Matthew Warren, Moderator, Sherborne, Sept. 2nd, 1696.

Mr Ashwood sent for, who came & gave the Assembly an account that being desir'd he had join'd in ordaining Mr Samuel Baker at Bridport, who had been some time with Mr Toogood, & besides his proficiency in the tongues, had read some part of Burgersdicius's Logick.[2] That the

[1] The controversy between Independents and Presbyterians over Ordinations, to which this refers, has been dealt with in the Introduction, pp. xi–xiii.
[2] Francis Burgerdyck (1590–1629). His *Logic* was reprinted many times and was a popular manual in Nonconformist Academies. McLachlan, *op. cit.*, p. 301.

neighbouring Ministers particularly Mr John Pinney had been sent to
& desir'd to assist at the Ordination but came not. That he had done
nothing herein contrary to the Heads of Union, manifesting himself
against an imposing spirit, & desiring to be left to his liberty in things
of [fo. 89r.] this nature, & not to be oblig'd to acquaint Associations
with such matters. Mr Galpine junior inform'd the Assembly that Mr
Ashwood had received a letter or letters from London (which he supposed
might have a tendency towards breaking the Union, & might be the
encouragement to such practices as this complain'd of by the Association
at Sherburn) wherein were several questions propos'd concerning the
state of the Congregational interest in these parts, who there were that
were of that Faith, what was to be done in order to their encouragement,
and where there were convenient places to fix persons of that Faith, with
several other things, of which he gave no particular account. That Mr
Ashwood returned an answer with an account of the state of the Congregations in Exon. Mr Ashwood was earnestly importun'd for peace sake for
the future not to proceed to ordain persons without the order of the
Assembly according to our Agreement. [(May 8th 1694. p.63). That no
candidate be ordain'd by any of the United Brethren of this County but
by order of the Assembly.]¹

The next Assembly to be the first Tuesday and Wednesday in May
1697, Mr Taylor of Holsworthy to preach or if he fail Mr Ball of Honiton,
Mr Withers to pray or if he fail Mr Mead, Mr Balster to be Moderator.

[fo. 86v.] Heads of Agreement.² Tit. 6. Of Occasional Meetings of
Ministers, p.13.
1. We agree that in order to concord & in any other weighty & difficult
cases, it is needfull & according to the mind of Christ, that the Ministers
of several Churches be consulted, & advised with about such matters.
3. That particular Churches, their respective Elders, & members, ought
to have a reverential regard to their judgment so given, & not dissent
therefrom without apparent grounds from the word of God.
Vide Tit. 2. par. 5., & 7, p.7, 8. Tit. 4, par. 1, p. 10.

[fo. 162r., reversed, shorthand.]³ *We whose names are hereunto subscribed,
ministers of the Gospel of the County of Devon, being assembled at Exon this [9th]
day of [Sept.] in the year of our Lord [1696] for mutual advice touching things
pertaining to our cause or the ordering of our congregations and the promoting of
purity and unity in the Church of Christ, having received a complaint from the
United Brethren of some neighbour counties against some of the United Brethren in
this county for their joining in the ordination of persons for the ministry who did
not address themselves for it to the associated Brethren in the ministry when they
might have so done: and this, notwithstanding the former agreement of the Assembly
at Exon May 8 1694 (That no candidate be ordained by any of the United Brethren
of this county but by order of the Assembly) to whose judgment they were obliged
to have a very reverential regard, and not dissent therefrom without grounds from
the word of God, according to the Heads of Union to which they have assented,*

¹Underlined.
²This quotation from relevant parts of the " Heads of Agreement " of 1691 was written
 on fo. 86v., facing the letter received from Sherborne. See Introduction, pp. xi–xiii.
³This may only be Gilling's draft and never adopted. He was the Scribe to this Assembly.

Tit. 6.3.[1] *Taking into our serious consideration how greatly God is displeased, religion discredited and the ministry brought into contempt by unqualified ministers, and being apprehensive that if 2 or 3 of the United Brethren should, without the advice and consent of their Brethren in the ministry engage in so weighty an affair as ordination, if 1, 2 or 3 unlearned persons should thus get into the ministry and they, after the same example without the advice of their ordainers or any other ministers, should proceed to ordain others like themselves, hereby a door will be opened for illiterate, conceited, persons to invade the sacred office, to vent crude notions and erroneous opinions, by which means the progress of the Gospel and edification of souls will be obstructed, the peace of our Churches destroyed, and great discredit is like to redound to the whole body of the United Brethren, of which Mr Davies*[2] *in Northamptonshire is a very sad instance. That we may, as much as in us lies, prevent and obviate this and the like inconveniences and prosecute the ends of our assembling together, viz: the glory of God, the credit of a Gospel ministry and the purity and uniformity of the Church of Christ, we agree and resolve as followeth:*

1. That we will not for the future own any of this county as United Brethren nor admit them to vote in our assembly until they have consented to the Heads of Agreement and the rules for regulating our meetings or have shown satisfactory reasons for their refusal.

2. That those scholars and students in Philosophy and Divinity who have contributions from our Fund and are educated in this county or Somerset, shall once a year [*pass*][3] *under an examination before the Assembly or such as they shall appoint, as to their proficiency in learning.*

3. That no Grammar scholar shall receive any contribution from the Fund in order to his reading logic, philosophy or divinity until he has given satisfaction to the Assembly or some deputed by them, of his skill in the Latin and Greek tongues.

4. That we will not encourage any students in divinity to preach until they have been examined by the Assembly, or some deputed by them, concerning their knowledge in the Scripture, aptness to teach, and other qualifications for so great a work, and have a Testimonial of their satisfaction.

5. That we will for the future carefully observe and act according to the agreement of the Assembly May 8, 1694, touching the Ordination of Candidates, unless there be a real and evident necessity for speedier ordination than the meetings of the Assembly permit.

6. In case of such a real and evident necessity we will not proceed to ordination or approbation without the advice of at least 6 of the next adjoining United Brethren.

[fo. 161v., reversed] *7. We will not without the advice of the Assembly approve or ordain any until they have stated and defended a Theological question in Latine, and preached a practical*[4] *sermon before at least 5 of the United Brethren of the neighbourhood to their satisfaction.*

8. That we will not refuse to approve of or ordain any person who appears to have scriptural qualifications, upon the account of his sentiments as to the modes of ecclesiastical government, formerly distinguished by the names of Synodical and Congregational.

[1]The reference is to the relevant section of the 1691 *Heads of Agreement*, quoted above, p. 30 (fo. 86v. of MS.) The most convenient reprint of, and commentary upon, the "Heads of Agreement" is that contained in Alexander Gordon's *Cheshire Classis*, 1919, pp. 111 ff.
[2]Richard Davis. See Introduction, p. xii.
[3]The Manuscript reads "against" but this does not make sense.
[4]The exact wording here is doubtful. The meaning is quite clear however.

We desire all our Brethren to join with us in this agreement, or to give their reasons in writing why they refuse; beseeching them to consider what an ill aspect the practice of private ordination in a time of peace and liberty has upon our Union; and as for those who shall slight our agreement and permit in the contrary practice, we enter our protest against their proceedings, as having a tendency to [1] the credit and reputation of the ministry and to dissolve the Union.

Art. 2, § 5.[2] 'Tis ordinarily requisite that the pastors of neighbouring congregations concur with the preaching elder or elders, if such there be, of the Church over which the ordained person is to be set.

Art. 2, § 7, p.7.[2] It is expedient that they who enter on the work of preaching the Gospel be not only qualified for communion of saints but also that, except in cases extraordinary, they give proof of their gifts and fitness for the said work unto the pastors of the churches of known abilities to discern and judge of their qualifications, that they may be sent forth with solemn approbation and prayer; which we judge needful, that no doubt may remain concerning their being called to the work, and for preventing as much as in us lieth ignorant and rash intruders.

[fo. 163v., reversed.[3]] Reverend Sir, The unbrotherly way of worrying me with a public charge before the Assembly having not discoursed me 1st privately, gives me just ground to suspect not only your friendliness towards me but the sincerity of your respect to the Union you have talked of so much. But when I consider what falsities you have whispered against me to your friends to the breaking of my reputation, I am confirmed there is a bitter though unobserved rancour in your heart against me; and I wonder with what peace and satisfaction you can address yourself to God in duty under so much guilt. Sir, you declared before the Assembly that a letter was sent me from London that had a tendency to dissolve our Union. I deny it and expect that you will prove it. You asserted that my letter was dropt and perused by your friend. I am assured there was no such thing, and therefore it concerns you to clear up yourself in this matter. You have pretended to know the contents of my letter, and have intimated to some that I had this ill expression in it, that there was no hope of dissolving the Union here and advancing the Congregational interest in these parts while Mr Tross was alive; but if he was dead, something might be done. I call the God of Truth and the avenger of lies to witness that there was no such passage in my letter nor anything like it. Mr Tross's name was not mentioned by me at all in the letter nor the name of any other man as obstructing such a design. You would do well to consider how such a reflection suits with your words that I had answered like a Christian. If I have so done I am sure you have not acted like a Christian in casting on me such a false and ill expression. This untruth has not wanted agents to spread it in the country. I am wrongfully censured by many, but I have my innocence to support me and the gracious word of the ever blessed God. I have in some measure learned to support bad report as well as good, yet am obliged in a due method to vindicate my reputation. I desire you therefore to acquaint me with the author of this information or to admit that you have knowingly wronged me. Which concludes all from your abused friend J. Ashwood. Exon. 8br 8th, 1696.

[1]Indecipherable. " Undermine " would make sense.
[2]These are citations of passages in the 1691 " Heads of Agreement ". The second number is that of the paragraph quoted, and Gilling has actually supplied the page number from his copy for the second reference.
[3]The following letters, in shorthand, do not form part of the Minutes, but relate directly to the Ordination Controversy, and are therefore printed at this point. The first letter is addressed to Mr John Galpine, junior, by John Ashwood.

[fo. 163v., reversed. Shorthand.] *Dartmouth, 8br 13th, 1696. Reverend Sir, If your resolved opposition to the desire of all the Brethren extorted from me the discovery of what wheels your policies seemed to move, you may rather thank yourself than call it unbrotherly in me. For I had not mentioned what you call a charge against you (being wholly ignorant of the complaint sent by the Eastern ministers till it was publicly produced) had not your strange behaviour before the Assembly compelled me thereunto. And truly Sir, your great opinion of your private sentiments and your strong censure of the whole fraternity was too nauseous and notorious: it ill becomes you to tax them as ' busy Bishops ' when you yourself act a metropolitan. Now, Sir, notwithstanding all this, I shall with the greatest sincerity profess that what I spoke was wholly free from personal [prejudice]*[1]* it flowing purely from a sincere zeal against those principles which tend directly to diminish and divide the best interests and for which we have suffered so much already both from God and man. But you pretend to have the key of man(s) heart and will call it bitterness and rancour, and wonder how I can address myself to God under such guilt. But Sir, I shall leave this to your second thoughts to consider how much you have exceeded the bounds not only of discretion but also of charity and modesty herein. For where you censure me as a hater you prove yourself a false accuser of the Brethren, and so may take back the guilt which you would injuriously fasten on me. I now proceed to consider your imputation of falsity and self-contradiction. You say you received no letter from London which had a tendency to wreck the Union, which (you say) I asserted. I say you received a letter of Queries concerning the Congregational Interest, viz: Who they be who be of the Faith in your country? What was necessary for their support? What places were convenient for the finding of persons of such faith? I think there were six enquiries of this nature, so my friend told me. Now Sir, though you may say this has no tendency to wreck the Union, yet, it being done in a seperating way, it has no good aspect on the Union, and whatever might be the design of the writer, whom I will by no means condemn, yet your following proceedings do sufficiently declare what interpretation you put on it. You say you are assured your letter was not dropt. I answer here your intelligence fails you, for it was so dropt that the contents came to the cognizance of my friend, who had a sight thereof. You say Mr Tross's name was not mentioned in that letter. I suppose you may have written several on that same subject. However, my friend told me that Mr Tross's name was mentioned in that letter which he saw, and I am verily persuaded that whether your memory fails, or your words were unfortunately inexpressive of your thoughts in the matter, or else 'tis some other letter that you spoke of, for it seems impossible that he should mention Mr Tross to me whose name I believe was never observed in your lines. [fo. 163r., reversed] But the great difficulty is, how such a passage should correspond with the account I gave of your letter that you answered like a Christian. I answer, all the parts of your letter were not of the same complection, and I was willing that it should have its denomination from the best, giving it in charity the most favourable and encouraging character, to win you to a compliance with the advices of the Assembly,*[2]* and to show that I had a respect to your reputation. But since you left us in such a hopeless state concerning the agreement of your [temper]*[3]*, notwithstanding I again addressed myself to you at the head of the stairs with Mr Star and others, renewing our request. I thought fit to communicate the passage that all might know on what point you were resolved to steer. And now,*

---

[1] This word is a little doubtful.
[2] This refers to the preceding shorthand passage on pp. 30–2.
[3] This word is a little doubtful.

Sir, though you so accuse me of falsity, I do with the greatest sincerity declare that I have not added or altered the passage which I have spoken [of] in this affair from what was imparted me by an eye witness of your letter, for whom also I ought to retain a charity, since he could have no sinister end in declaring it. You must excuse me from gratifying your expectation in discovering his name, since it is not at all necessary to your vindication; it being better for you, since you are innocent, to repair your self by producing all the letters, having 1st expunged the name, it being not necessary that we should bring any of our London friends on the stage. I shall gladly find my friend to be under a mistake, and rectify his misapprehension concerning you. Thus, Sir, having fully though perhaps not satisfactorily answered all your charges, give me leave in a brotherly way to mention a few passages of yours which perhaps have occasioned the Brethren to call your sincerity to the Union in question. When you made a motion in one of the Assemblies concerning Mr Wood that he might be publicly censured by the Brethren for his late scandal after he had manifested so great a remorse and penitence that the Christians in Bytheford did again sit down under his ministry, the ministers judging it unseasonable and inexpedient wholly to cut him off from his ministerial work, you replied that then it might justly be reported that the Assembly were friends to such proceedings and (if I am not mistaken) we had no more of your company at the meeting. Another time, when you proposed Mr Audley as a Candidate for the ministry and to be encouraged by the Fund (who, if he had not a spice of distraction, deserves a worse character) and the ministers thinking they might expend their moneys to better purpose, you replied you saw the Assembly resolved to oppose whatever you did approve, and that if he had been proposed by any others the motion might have been accepted, and hinted that it was done out of design and not in this last occasion what occasioned the complaint abovesaid [was] your saying that the Assembly were unnecessarily curious in what did not concern them, and that you did it as you would not be imposed on, or fearing that the Assembly might impose on you; for that you saw they were of an imposing spirit according to the best recollection that I can make. Now sir though I am as much against the invading the liberties of [1] churches as yourself, yet you will have leisure to think what miserable provision you make for such poor souls who (being perhaps actuated by some partial recommendation) may desire it to set over them such guides whose great abilities in learning may be to scramble over a Distich of Ovid or recite the Predicaments. Sir, we impart matter for our enemies' triumphs and insults, and render ourselves the deserved scorn of the world if we could prefer our private and many times ungrounded humours to the interests of our great Lord and Master. It would be an effectual Bar to such proceedings. And I verily believe there had been no room to complain that you have so many enemies, were your converses more sincere and free, and if you would plainly express your thoughts and not under such disguises that a person can hardly interpret your meaning, and not use such an offensive method of couching sharp reflections under seemingly smooth expressions and words. I might charge you also with unfairness in sending up such an ambiguous account of this transaction at the Assembly that I had received a charge from London, that I mentioned Mr [2] name which though you might not press them now, Sir; yet there were such dark hints which it seems did impose upon the apprehension of my friend. Sir, for my part I love as near as I can to keep the center of truth, for if we satisfy ourselves in being merely within

---

[1]This word is indecipherable, but should probably read " particular ". The grammar of the preceding passage is obscure, but the shorthand has been checked carefully, and appears to be correct.

[2]Blank in MS.

the circumference thereof there may some times be an intersection. Thus, Sir, I have used a brotherly freedom with you, that I declare to be without the least tincture of bitterness or rancour, being always ready to give you the right hand of fellowship when you do not wrest yourself from the brotherhood by such extra-regular proceedings; and if you could accept my counsel I could. I desire you to abstain from such expressions which show how unnecessary and frivolous you think the Assembly of the ministers to be, since you will be as far from obtaining your end thereby, that you will indeed diminsih yourself. Thus I have acquitted myself to be, Your non-abusive plain-hearted though unjustly condemned friend, John Galpine.

[fo. 163v., reversed.[1]] *Reverend Father, You may see what advantage I have obtained by plucking a thorn out of your foot. I question not but you could have furnished me with better materials than any I have made use of in my defence. However, I have thought fit to communicate the following letter that when I am again assailed you may instruct me to guard the part best which you shall find to be the weaker. You may communicate it when you think it will be for the advantage of truth; for I find that it is the design with a full cry to run down your poor J. Galpine. Dartmouth 8br. 14, 1696. To the Reverend Mr Gilling in Newton, these.*

[fo. 162v., reversed.] *Reverend Sir, Yours dated 8br (I suppose by mistake for 9br) 14th received the 19th instant, by your neighbour Mr Joyce. I am heartily sorry for the hard dealing you have met with for my sake and for giving so notorious a proof of my assertion. But this affords me some consolation that you have made a vigorous defence and will I trust come off from the combat with credit and comfort. Tis peace and truth for which you appear; and I doubt not that at last those little arts by which both have been assaulted, will be exposed to deserved contempt and shame. However we may have our satisfaction in our endeavours to prevent what others by being too mealy mouthed too much promote. I had no account of this hurricane. The too well known temper of $\delta \tau \iota \xi$[2] made me expect no less than what has happened. Sic notus Ulysses. I was on Tuesday last in company with Mr Mead, Pardew and Evans to whom I communicated yours. They all rejoiced that so just a cause had so good a Patron, and were extremely satisfied in the matter and manner of your defence. I wish there were more of your spirit to be found among those that are well-willers to these Mathematicks. When others appear so barefaced in their assaults, I cannot understand the reason of so gentle a treatment as they have met with. Plain dealing is necessary too with such underhand dealers. Why should we encourage others to play their old game, and teach them to undermine us? 'Tis time to improve our method. We have strength if we had wit to imploy it. Fas est et ab hoste doceri. Let us act by consent. We have 5 to 1. We must beware of false Brethren. Grove and Peter Kellow are suspected. I think it has been a great blunder in politicks to make some folly popular. 'Tis pity they should be set on the stage who declaim afore the curtain. We have too many of them already in this county. 'Tis every one's interest for the future as there shall be occasion, to take care what answers be approved to the 3d Query. Had Mr W.[3] been removed from B.[3] and a brisk man sent thither as assistant to Mr Bowden or successor to Mr W. the frontiers might have been recovered; but now 'tis too late. They are building a Church for Mr Baily there, which as I am informed, will cost near a £1000. I would recommend to your consideration a few anti-queries, to be considered, improved,*

---

[1]This was a covering letter to a copy of that sent to Ashwood.
[2]The meaning of this is " a certain person ", i.e. John Ashwood.
[3]Mr. Wood from Bideford.

enlarged and if it seem requisite made more public in due time, viz. Query, How much money have the Brethren of the Faith or Interest (which I take for synonyms) brought into or received out of our Fund? What advantage has it been to the common cause that some have united with us, whose faces we seldom see for 2 hours together in the convocation? Whether some brethren meeting the 1st day somewhere for private work, their frequent withdrawing into the Lobby, their clubbing and caballing, their hindering all freedom of debates in our Assembly about Church government and discipline, their frequent outcries, impositions and reflections when any little tricks are mentioned, do not deserve highly of us all? Whether we are not concerned to promote the education of Taylors etc and the sending out of Tools in 2 or 3 years time after they are taken from the Plough or shop to do jobs for Anabaptists etc.? And whether those who imploy their gifts that way do not deserve the thanks of the house? When you are bound for Exon, if you please to honour me with your company one night we might talk over some of these things, and [1] each other in review on our common proceeding. 'Tis a comfort there are no more of those politic ecclesiasticks among us. If you have not done it already, or think it not inexpedient, I will upon advice communicate yours to Mr Tross, Atkins, Hallet, Hooper or any others whom you shall propose if it would be encouraging. I trust to see you before Christmas. In the mean time, macte tua virtute puer is the counsel of your dutiful father, I. Gilling. 9bri 30, 1696. If this be considered a heretick or schismatick let it expiate such crimes in purgatory-hole, and not fall into the hands of the Church whose censure it dreads. To the Reverend Mr John Galpine, Minister of the Gospel in Dartmouth.

[fo. 90r.]
EXETER, 1697, 5th and 6th May. At the Meeting of the United Brethren of Exon and Devon.

[Present:] Mr John Balster, moderator, Isaac Gilling, scribe; Mr James Wood, Hallet, Galpin, Tapper, Atkins, Harding, Stoddon, Ashwood, Withers, Tross, Star, Mead, Hooper, Goswell, Walsh, Toogood, Baily, Evans, Moor, Peter Kellow. Candidates: Walrond, Eveleigh, Gatchel, Broadmead. From Somerset: Moor, Pitts, Blake. Candidates: John and Thomas Moore, Edgley.

Money brought into the Fund.

	£	s
Mr Harding from Plimouth	16	0
Mr Hooper from Silferton & Thorverton ...	5	0
Mr Tross from Mrs Arscot	4	0
Mr Ball	4	0
Mr Stoddon	4	10
Mr Balster, a legacy from Mrs Gear of Oke-hampton	3	0
Mr Tapper	4	0
Mr John Galpin	1	2
Mr Wood from Puddington	1	0

[1]Indecipherable. " Consult " would make sense.

[fo. 91r.] Upon the failure of the Fund agreed that a fifth part be deducted from the yearly payments to Ministers and Meetings.

	£	£	s	£	s
Mr Searle ...	8	6	8	1	12
Berry ...	8	6	8	1	12
Balster ...	8	6	8	1	12
Pardew ...	5	4	0	1	0
Martyn ...	5	4	0	1	0
Walsh ...	6	4	16	1	4
Plimtree ...	4 to continue	4	0	1	0
Ufculme ...	6	4	16	1	4
Foy ...	8	6	8	1	12
	58	47	4	11	16 per quarter

Ordered that Mr Brinly's son have £6 per annum, the first Quarterly payment to commence at Midsummer. That Mr Grigg have £5 per annum added to the £6 per annum which he hath already the 1st payment likewise to commence at Midsummer.

The present payments to young scholars:

	£	Quarterly	
Mr John Hopping	20	5	0
George Bowcher	14	3	10
Wilcox	14	3	10
Barron (out of Mr Harding's money) ...	14	3	10
Palk	12	3	0
Grigg	11	2	15
Short	8	2	0
Ben. Berry	16	4	0
Torrington Berry	6	1	10
Slowly	4	1	0
Lissant	5	1	5
Brinsly	6	1	10
Masters	8	2	0
	138	34	10

Quarterly Payments	£	s		Yearly payments	£	s
To Ministers ...	11	10		To Ministers ...	47	4
To Scholars ...	34	10		To Scholars ...	138	0
In all ...	46	6		In all ...	185	4

[fo. 92r.] Upon Mr Tross's motion, agreed that it is expedient & convenient that the Scriptures be publickly read in our Assemblies every Lords Day, by the Minister and not by a private person.

That no ministers be ordain'd for the future by any of the members of this Assembly before the matter hath been propounded to the Assembly unless in case of necessity & that the necessity be communicated to the next Assembly.

Mr Baily of Bytheford represents the ill consequences of Mr James Woods continuing in that town. That hereby a schism is made in that church of which he is Pastor 4 of his members withdrawing from him. Mr Bowden's petition to the Assembly read, & Mr Baily's request that the hearing & deciding the differences between Mr Wood & them be adjourn'd until the next Assembly, agreed to.

Thanks given to Mr Ball for preaching & Mr Withers for praying. Resolved that tis requisite for the future that the Exon ministers take their turns in preaching & praying at the Assemblies here.

Mr Gatchel declar'd that he could not continue with Cullompton people.

Mr Toogood & Mr Ashwood shewing much unwillingness to bring Ordinations to the Assembly & not being satisfy'd with the Declaration of the Brethren that they did not confine the power of Ordination [fo. 93r.] to Synods & that they would not reject any person duly qualify'd from Ordination, merely upon the account of his opinion about the modes of ecclesiastical government, whether he held it to be Synodical or Congregational. Mr Toogood deliver'd in the following paper desiring the Assemblies assent unto it, viz: "Agreed, that it is utterly unlawfull for any minister of the Gospel or Assembly of Ministers to deny Ordination unto the ministerial office to any person for this reason because he doth not own & will not submit unto any power or jurisdiction in ecclesiastical matters which any may suppose to be lodged in any minister or ministers superior to that in a Particular Church." After much debate upon this paper the majority of the Assembly rejected it, judging it sufficient to declare their own purpose & oblige themselves as to their future practice without condemning most of the Reformed Churches who are of the contrary opinion. The following Questions were propos'd but not fully debated:

Q. Whether it be not convenient that Candidates for the Ministry be examined before the Assembly before they have an approbation to preach; the better to prevent ignorant & unlearned intruders into the Ministry.

Q. What exercises shall be given to such candidates.

[fo. 94r.] Q. What preachers are there of this county who continue unordained and what are their reasons.

Resolved that the next meeting be the 1st Tuesday & Wednesday in September. Mr Hanmer to preach or if he fail Mr Balster, Mr Baily to pray or if he fail Mr Mead, Mr Ball to be Moderator.

[fo. 16r., Shorthand.] *Benjamin Berry to Mr Hooper, Edinburgh, July, 1697.*

In Scotland, in every 20 parishes or thereabout, a Presbytery is held in which the affairs of the several Churches are adjusted, scandalous sinners summoned before it, Calls given by parishes to ministers brought before it. The moderator with his brethren dispute whether they will give it him or no. When any young man is brought to preach, his name is given to the moderator by his Professor of Divinity, he having been with him 3 or 4 years, never less, besides 3 years with his Philosophy Regent. They never admit of any [sinners[1].] The 1st thing he doth is a Latine

[1]This word is not certain.

exegesis on any Divinity head which the moderator gives him. Next that he preaches in English on a text given him. This he doth twice. After this the ministers impugn and he defends the Divinity Thesis of which he had his exegesis. Then he is try'd in the Greek and Hebrew tongues. After this he is licensed to preach.

[fo. 97r.]
EXETER, 1698, May 3.[1] At the Meeting of the United Brethren of Exon and Devon.

[Present:] Mr Samuel Tapper, moderator, Mr Richard Evans, scribe; Mr George Tross, Edward Par, Joseph Hallet, John Ball, Christopher Chappel, Samuel Hall, Samuel Atkins, Bernard Star, Benjamin Hooper, Jacob Sandercock, Samuel Wood, John Goswell, Monsieur de Lion, William Horsham, Petter Kellow, Jelinger Symonds, John Moor, Monsieur Violet. Delegates from Somerset: Mr John Moore, John Moore junior, John Smith, Thomas Moore, Malachi Blake. Candidates: Mr John Walrond, Josiah Eveleigh, Thomas Edgly, William Peard, John Enty.

Money brought into the Fund.

	£	s	d
Mr Carel by Mr Peter Kellow	8	18	6
Mr Tross from Mr Arscot	4	0	0
Mr Ball	4	0	0
Mr Benjamin Hooper	3	5	6
Mr Bernard Star	5	0	0

Mr Star had 20/- of it for Samuel Rabient.

Taken off from the charge of the Fund.

	£	s	d
From Mr Wilcox	14	0	0
Mr Short	2	0	0
Mr Bowcher	2	0	0
Mr Grigg	3	0	0

[fo. 98r.] Agreed that 40s per annum be given to Mr Thomas Berry's son of Torrington. That £6 per annum be added to Mr Brinly's son. Mr Hardings money was sent to Mr Warren's to the young man to whom tis appropriated. Order'd. That the Exon ministers shall inspect the Fund and as they find the Fund will bear, dispose of it for the education of young men.

That Exon ministers examine Mr Wilcox and if they find him fit give him a Licence to preach. Mr Walrond proposes himself to Ordination. Agreed that Mr Tapper, Mr Par, Mr Stoddon & Mr Ball ordain him. The week & day to be refer'd to his own determination.

The next meeting to be the Tuesday after the first Lords Day in September. Mr Balster to preach, Mr Mead to pray, Mr Ball to be Moderator.

---

[1] No minutes are extant for the meeting in September 1697. Part of fo. 94r. and the whole of fos. 95r. and 96r. were left blank.

[fo. 99r.]
EXETER, 1698, Sept. 7th & 8th.

[Present:] Mr Ball, moderator, Mr Larkham, scribe; Mr Carel, Tapper,
Tross, Par, Balster, Berry, Hooper, Toogood, Hallet, Star, Goswell,
Horsham, Wood, Withers, Hall, Rosewill, Evans, Bartlett.

Money brought into the Fund.

						£	s	d
Mr Berry	...	...	...	...	...	1	0	0
Mr Hooper ...	...	...	...	...	...	3	5	0
Mr Star	...	...	...	...	...	4	15	0
Mr Ball	...	...	...	...	...	2	0	0
Paid Samuel Rabient . . . 20s.								

Mr Carel propos'd this case. Question: Whether a capital crime
confess'd to a minister, by a penitent under horrour of conscience, ought
to be reveal'd to the magistrate by the minister in order to punishment?
Negative.

Tis the general opinion of the Assembly that any member thereof
pitch'd on to be Moderator, to preach or pray, shall if possible attend to
officiate as order'd by the Assembly, or send timely to an Exon minister
his reason why he cannot, or otherwise it shall be look'd upon as a contempt of the Assembly.

Agreed Nemine Contradicente that no minister settled in any
Congregation shall settle in another Congregation without offering his
reasons to the Assembly for so doing.

Mr Humphry Berry and Mr Joseph Manston allowed to preach as
Candidates.

Tis the opinion of the Assembly after consideration of debates
betwixt Mr Thomas Edgly & some of Tottness people, that tho there
may have been some imprudences in him yet nothing of scandal hath
been prov'd against him by that people.

[fo. 3r., Shorthand.] *Tis ordered after Mr Thomas Edgly's year at Totness
is out, he shall retire from Totness for a Quarter or more and the place be supplied
by ministers settled. John Ball, moderator.*[1]

Next meeting May 9th, 1699, Mr Toogood to preach, Larkham to
pray, Mr Backaller to be Moderator.

[fo. 100r.]
EXETER, 1699, May 9 & 10th. At the Meeting of the United Brethren
of Devon.

[Present:] Mr Henry Backaller, Moderator; Isaac Gilling, scribe; Mr
John Berry, Stoddon, Tapper, Tross, Carel, Balster, Hooper, Hallet,
Toogood, Atkins, Galpine, Horsham, Sandercock, Ball, Hall, Larkham,
Pardew, Evans, Peter Kellow, Walrond. Candidates: Edgly, Manson,
Eveleigh, Broadmead. [Visitors:] Mr Quick of London, Mr John
Moore, Senior, Thomas Moore, Darch, of Somerset.

[1]This shorthand passage is preceded on fo. 3r. by a repetition of the immediately preceding
    paragraph, taken from fo. 99r.

Brought into the Fund.

	£	s	d
By Mr Stoddon	8	11	0
Mr Hooper	3	6	0
Mr Tross	3	0	0
Mr Tapper	3	0	0
Mr Ball	3	0	0
Mr Berry from Puddington	1	10	0
Mr Backaller	1	0	0
Mr Evans	1	15	3
	25	2	3
From Exon	18	3	0
	43	5	3

	£	s	d
Paid to Mr Stoddon for Natthaniel Loveridge at Ottery School	1	0	0
To Mr Ball for Robert Wood at Mr Moore's at Bridgwater	1	10	0

Mr Hall propos'd John Stoddon at Mr Warren's who hath made good progress in Grammar Learning. The present charge of the Fund out of Mr Wood's accounts:

Ladyday Quarter last paid:

	£	s		£	s
To Mr Hopping ...	5	0	Mr Brinly's son ...	3	0
Bennet's son ...		10	Hody[1] ...	1	10
Lissant ...	1	5	Slowly ...	1	0
Grigg ...	2	0	Mr Berry & son ...	5	12
Short ...	1	10	Mr Pardew ...	1	0
Bowcher ...	3	0	Mr Walsh ...	1	4
Palk ...	3	0	Mr Serle ...	1	12
			Mr Martin ...	1	0
	16	5		15	18

	£	s
Mr Balster	1	12
Ufculm	1	4
	2	16
	15	18
	16	5
	34	19

Due to Mr Wood ... £14 13s 4d

[fo. 101r.] Three of Bytheford in behalf of Mr Woods congregation manifested their desires to have Mr Powel now at Blandford for their Pastor. Mr Powels letter to Mr Tross read, in which he declares that he had receiv'd an invitation from that congregation to settle

[1]This is the first appearance of Matthew Huddy, often spelt as it is here, Hody.

among them as their pastor: & refers himself to the Assembly for their advice & direction. It appeared to the Assembly that all attempts for union & accommodation between this congregation & Mr Baily's have been fruitless. That Mr Powel hath a very great interest in the affections of the people of the town. That many of Mr Woods congregation are so dissatisfy'd in Mr Baily that they declare their resolution not to accept of him as sole pastor: but they profess their desire of union with Mr Baily & his congregation upon any reasonable terms to which Mr Powel shall consent. That Mr Powel hath endeavour'd after union & made fair proposals in order to it: but Mr Baily refus'd his offers of joining with him, declaring his resolution to stand by himself at present, & to wait for the assistance of Mr Bartlett,[1] now a student at Edinburgh. No other person could at present be thought of who was like to be acceptable to both congregations. It appear'd that Mr Powel hath not undertaken the pastoral charge of the people at Blandford. [fo. 102r.] After large debates with Mr Carel & Mr Peter Kellow who oppos'd Mr Powels removal from Blandford where he had done much good, & pleaded that the prejudices against Mr Baily were groundless, & opposed the settling another minister in the room of Mr Wood deceased, at length the following paper was drawn up & sign'd by the order & approbation of the whole Assembly except only Mr Carel, Mr Toogood, Mr John Berry, & Mr Peter Kellow.

May 10, 1699. The Ministers of the Gospel now assembled at Exon after much debate & deliberation declare it as their opinion & advice that Mr John Powel should accept of the call of Mr Woods congregation in Bytheford to settle among them as their pastor: provided Blandford people be supply'd before he leave them, & consent to his removal, and that he do what in him lies in order to union with Mr Baily & his congregation: and have ordered us in their names to signify it. Wittness our hands, Henry Backaller, Moderator, Isaac Gilling, Scribe.

Mr Lyon's letter to the Assembly & Mr Violets to the Consistory of Plymouth, read. Order'd that Mr Ball write to Mr Lyon to assure him that there was no contempt shown him or anything he writ: & to exhort them to peace & endeavour to convince him how scandalous their differences about small matters one with another are when they are exiles on the account of Religion.[2]

[fo. 103r.] Thanks given to Mr Larkham for praying. Agreed that Mr [Toogood having continu'd above two hours in sermon][3] all future preachers have warning given them to keep to their hour: and that the Clark turn the glass when the text is nam'd & take it away as soon as tis run out.

Mr Broadmead having a call from Beer people to be their pastor, proposes himself to ordination. Order'd that Mr Broadmead preach at Ottery the 17th of June on this text: Take heed to thyself. That at the same time he state & defend this Question: An Christus sit Mediator

[1]William Bartlett II. A space was left for his Christian name.
[2]The exact nature of the dispute is not known. J. L. Violet was minister to Nonconforming Huguenots in Exeter from c.1686 until c.1699. Lyon (or De Lion) must have occupied a similar position in Plymouth. Violet was succeeded by Andre Majendie in 1761. Trans. Devon. Assoc., LXVIII, 1936, p. 275.
[3]This is underlined in red ink, not necessarily by Gilling.

secundum utramque naturam? That the ministers examine him as to his skill in languages, arts, sciences, & other ministerial qualifications, and if they approve him, that he be ordain'd at Culliton, by Mr Kersage, Mr Stoddon, Mr Tapper, Mr Star, Mr Ball, who are to fix the time for his ordination, & divide the work between them, as they shall think fit.

Next meeting to be the 1st Tuesday & Wednesday in September. Mr Hallet to preach, Mr Walrond to pray, Mr Toogood to be Moderator.

A paper from Mr Whinnel & his church against Mr Edgly read in which he is accused of lasciviousness, lying & railing. Mr Toogood gives an account of a journey of his to Culmstock, that he there said Mr Whinnel had sent him thither to preach whereas Mr Whinnel had charg'd him not to preach. A letter of Mr Pitts of Chard with a accusation against him. Mr Edgly endeavours to excuse himself. [fo. 102v.] Mr Edgly produces the following certificate: We whose names are underwritten do certify for Mr Thomas Edgly that during the time of his residence in his Tutor's family we know nothing in his conversation[1] but what did agree with his profession. And we judg him competently qualify'd for the ministerial work, witness our hands, Immanuel Harford, Matthew Warren, Malachi Blake, Bartholomew Nowel.

[fo. 103r. cont.] Mr Samuel Mullins desires ordination but is at present deny'd.

[fo. 104r.]
EXETER, 1699, 5th & 6th September. At the Meeting of the United Brethren of Devon.

[Present:] Mr Toogood, moderator, Gilling, scribe; Tross, Carel, Backaller, Hooper, Hallet, Atkins, Ball, Horsham, Galpin, Sandercock, Larkham, Wood, Bartlett, Evans, Rosewell, Martyn, Peter Kellow, Walrond, Enty, Moor, Par. Candidates: Powel, Eveleigh, Cox, Edgly, Mullins, Marshal, Short, Berry, Slowly, Clifford, Grigg. Somersett: Pitts, Knight.

Brought in to the Fund.

	£	s	d
Mr Hooper, Silferton	3	8	0
Mr Ayers	1	0	0
Mr Ball	2	10	0
Mr Rosewell	1	13	0
	8	11	0

Order'd that Mr Short, Mr Bowcher, Mr Slowly & Mr Berry's son of Torrington be struck out of the Fund.

The next Assembly to be the 1st Tuesday & Wednesday after the 1st Lords Day in May. Mr Atkins to preach, Mr Enty to pray, Mr Hallet to be Moderator.

That the Exon Ministers examine Mr Short & Mr Bowcher & if the[y][2] approve of them that they give them licences to preach.

Exon, Sept. 6th, 1699. Tis the desire of the Ministers now assembled that Mr John Berry & Mr John Hanmer examine Mr Slowly & if they

[1]This is the old use of the word " conversation ", meaning the way in which he behaved.
[2]The final y omitted in the MS.

be satisfy'd in his qualifications that they give him a Certificate of their approbation of him as fit to preach & have ordered us to signify it. Stephen Towgood, moderator, Issaac Gilling, scribe.

[fo. 105r.] Resolved that Mr John Cox who hath obtain'd a Certificate under the hands of Mr Harford and Mr Warren of Taunton of their approbation of him as a person duly qualify'd to preach the Gospel be reputed as sufficiently licenced.

Mr Samuel Mullins of Tottness again desires Ordination. Order'd that on Tuesday October 3, he preach at the new Meeting in Exon on this Text: Who is sufficient for these things. That at the same time he state & defend this question: Utrum Lex Moralis sit fidelibus obligatoria ?[1] That he be then examin'd as to his other ministerial qualifications. That he be ordain'd at Tottness on Wednesday the 11th of October. Mr Hooper to preach, Mr Tross to give the exhortation, Mr Hallet, Tucker, Horsham, Withers to be present.

A letter from Mr Balster intimating that he had received an invitation from Bytheford. Mr Lovering, Lendon, Carter of Bytheford, on behalf of Mr Woods congregation, declaring that several of that congregation cannot coalesce with Mr Baily & desiring the Assembly to provide them a minister. The Assembly was inform'd that while the Anabaptist had preach'd among them since the last Assembly because they could not get a Minister, that he offer'd to admit them to the Lords Supper without rebaptizing. A letter from Mr Baily & some of his congregation desiring that Mr William Bartlett now in [fo. 106r.] London may be proposed as the person to be called & try'd with all convenient speed. Question: Whether to prevent the inconveniences that are growing at Bytheford tis not highly expedient speedily to recommend a Minister to Mr Woods Congregation ? All present except Mr Kellow & Mr Bartlett[2] were for it. Question: Whether Mr Bartlett or Mr Wilcox be recommended ? Agreed that Mr Wilcox go & preach some time to Mr Woods congregation in Bytheford. Question: Whether the Assembly shall in compliance with the request of Mr Baily & his people advise the 2 congregations in Bytheford to chuse 3 ministers apiece to hear their differences, & to endeavour to heal the breach among them ? This was consented to, & that each congregation choose ministers themselves. It being propos'd to Mr Lovering he declares that he hath no commission about it, and thinks that at present it may not be convenient.

Mr Edgly's friends appear desiring that he may be ordain'd. A letter of Mr Warren & Mr Harford. Mr Warren declares that whilst Mr Edgly was a member of his family which was about a year or more he never observed any gross immorality in him. That his great weakness lay in being addicted to vain boasting, etc. A letter from Mr Edglys Hearers to Mr Tross, in which they declare that for many weighty reasons tis the sentiment of the whole congregation consisting of more than 400 souls, that [fo. 107r.] if Mr Edgly do wilfully depart or be cut off by sickness or death that then they will choose another minister if he be to be gotten within the bounds of 3 kingdoms rather than they will join with the other

[1]This was an Antinomian tenet opposed.
[2]This would be Samuel Bartlett, the Tiverton Independent, and an ordained minister, not to be confused with William Bartlett II, still at this time a candidate.

congregation. That they resolve to sit down quietly in a distinct congregation and to carry it as inoffensively as they can, both to them & others. Mr Whinnell, Webb, & Eliot at the request of those of Tottness people who are dissatisfy'd with Mr Edgly being come to Town to make good their charge against Mr Edgly. Question: Whether the Assembly shall admit Mr Whinnel and his friends to give in their testimony as to those things which they have to charge Mr Edgly with? Affirmative. Question: Whether it be consistent with the deference we ought to give to Mr Warren & Mr Harford to admit Mr Whinnel to give in his evidence against Mr Edgly? Affirmative. Question: Whether the Assembly will consult their own credit or the reputation of the Ministry if they should refuse to hear their evidence & should not expose themselves to censure for endeavouring to stifle those things which they have to charge him with. Agreed that Mr Whinnel shall be heard. Pro. 11. Contra 5. [fo. 108r.] Mr Whinnel, Webb & Elliot heard. They charge Mr Edgly with many lies & some indecent carriages towards women. Most of which he positively deny'd appealing to God for his innocency. Afterwards Tottness people bring in their charge against him. Mr Pitts of Chard likewise charges him with deliberate lying. Some of these charges he deny'd, as to other he said that he was under a mistake. After Mr Edgly & his friends with those of Tottness who appear'd against him were withdrawn. The Assembly debated the matter; and the majority judging Mr Edgly not to have clear'd himself as to some of those matters of which he stood accused they order'd the Moderator to give him their sentiments in the following words: Mr Thomas Edgly, we look upon some of those accusations and charges that are brought against you to be of force for our present delay of your ordination, & therefore we desire you to be more cautious and circumspect of your words & carriage for the future.

[fo. 109r.]
EXETER, 1700, May 7th & 8th. At the meeting of the United Brethren of Devon & Exon.

[Present:] Mr Hallet, moderator, Mr Gilling, scribe: Mr John Berry, Tapper, Stoddon, Tross, Balster, Hooper, Ball, Atkins, Sandercock, Walsh, Hall, Withers, Larkham, Evans, Martyn, Enty, Daniel Kellow, Thomas Kellow, Broadmead, Mullins. Candidates: Mr Eveleigh, Powel, Wilcox, Baron, Short, Edgly, Bartlet. From Somerset: Mr Moor, senior, Mr Pitts, Mr Moor, Mr Norman.

Brought in to the Fund.

	£	s	d
Mr Carel	9	13	8
Mr Stoddon	5	1	6
Mr Hooper	3	3	0½
Mr Berry from Barnstaple...	3	0	0
from Puddington	1	19	3
Mr Tapper	2	3	0
Mr Ball	2	0	0
Mr Arscott	2	0	0
	29	0	5½

Mr Bond & Wills proposed to the Fund. Order'd: that if the Fund will bear it they shall have each of them £5 per annum.

[fo. 110r.] Mr Josiah Eveleighs call from the people to whom he preaches in Bideford, read. The Assembly was satisfy'd that neither Mr Eveleigh nor Mr Wood's people had acted contrary to the order of the last Assembly with respect to the reference of their differences to Ministers. Resolv'd nemine contradicente that Mr Eveleigh is obliged to accept of the call given him by that congregation in Bideford among whom he hath bestow'd his labours. At Mr Eveleighs request as well as at the former request of Mr Baily the Assembly once more advises the two congregations in Bideford to choose three or more ministers apiece to meet them between this and the 1st of June next to hear their differences & endeavour to compose them, and unite the two congregations. Resolv'd that if there be not such a meeting of ministers, or if after such a meeting a union between the two congregations cannot be obtained between this and the 1st of June, that Mr Eveleigh be ordain'd at Bideford before Midsummer by Mr Berry, Balster, Hanmer, Atkins, Hallet, Pardew, who are to share the work between them. That before his Ordination he be examin'd as to his qualifications, & state & defend the [fo. 111r.] following question: An S. Scriptura sit perspicua et perfecta fidei et morum regula? Resolv'd that when another person can be found in which both congregations will unite rather than in Mr Eveleigh, then the Assembly advise Mr Eveleigh to remove from Bideford. At the request of the Assembly Mr Balster consented to join in Mr Eveleigh's Ordination.

A petition from Launceston people desiring Mr Berry's speedy ordination read. Resolv'd that Mr Berry be ordain'd sometime the 1st fortnight in August by Mr Michael Taylor, Mr Tross & Mr Tingcomb, Mr Hanmer, Mr Ball, Mr Sandercock. His Question: An Christus sit essentialiter Deus?

Mr Balster Mr Ball & Mr Withers examin'd Mr Short & reported their great satisfaction in his ministerial qualifications upon which he had the approbation of the Assembly to preach for some time.

A letter from some of Dartmouth informing, that being unaccountably deserted by their Pastor Mr Galpine, & understanding that Mr Horsham had some inclination to settle among them, they desire the Assemblies advice. [fo. 112r.] Exon, May 8th, 1700: The Assembly at the petition of Dartmouth people left it to Mr Horsham to propose his removal to Dartmouth to his people at Stoke in Ham. And to consent to his removal thither provided they can be prevail'd with to part with him, and be otherwise provided with a Minister to their satisfaction. This is certify'd in their name & by their order by Joseph Hallet, moderator, Isaac Gilling, scribe.

Plympton people desire the Assembly to recommend a Minister to them. They say there are about 200 hearers. They have from London £6 per annum & can raise £25 per annum themselves. Resolv'd that Mr Bowcher be advised by the Assembly to go to Plympton & preach there some time.

Mr Colton, Shepheard & others of Tottness presented their petition desiring that Mr Thomas Edgley might be ordain'd. A petition from Mr Mullins's people desiring the Assembly not to proceed to his ordination. Mr Harris, Cockey, Farwell, & Bowden gave an account before the Assembly why they oppos'd Mr Edgly's ordination. The following question propos'd: Q. Whether Mr Edgly's Ordination shall be advis'd. Pro: Mr. Tross, Tapper, Hooper, Withers, Hall, Star, Martyn, Broadmead. Contra: Hallet, Larkham, Rosewell, Enty. [fo. 113r.] Mr John Berry suspended his judgment. Mr Stoddon whose occasions call'd him away desir'd Mr Atkins to declare that he was against it. Mr Evans who also went away before it was put to the vote was against it. Mr Sandercock after he had spoken much in Mr Edgly's behalf voted against his ordination. Some others who were against his ordination withdrew. Resolv'd. That Mr Edgly be ordain'd at Topsham the 3rd Thursday in June, by Mr Tapper, Hooper, Starr, Hall. His Question: An gratia regenerans sit irresistibiliter efficax? The Moderator gave the sense of the Assembly to Mr Edgly in these words: Mr Edgly, We declare that we are willing of your Ordination: but it is our earnest advice to you that you use your interest with the people you preach to in Tottness that they would be contented with your withdrawing from them, to some other place, and that they would unite with the other congregation in that Town.

Ministers caution'd against encouraging vagrants by recommending them under their hands as objects of charity.

Next Assembly Sept. 3, 4. Mr Star to preach, Mr Spark or Pardew to pray, Mr Atkins to be Moderator.

[fo. 114r.]
EXETER, 1700, September the 3rd & 4th. An account of what past in the Assembly of the United Brethren of Exon & Devon.

[Present:] Mr Samuel Atkins, moderator, Mr John Enty, scribe. Mr Tross, Tapper, Carel, Blackaller,[1] Balster, Hooper, Hanmer, Toogood, Violet, Hallet, Ball, Star, Gilling, Wood, Horsham, Bartlet, Harding, Evans, Baily, Peter Kellow, Jellinger Symonds, Edgly, Berry. Candidates: Mr Short, Henry Atkins, Bowcher, Eveleigh, Wilcox, Grig, Wood. From Somerset: Mr Moor of Bridgwater.

Brought in to the Fund.

	£	s	d	
By Mr Hooper ...	2	16	6	
Mr Starr	4	15	0	Paid him for Mr Rabjent.
Mr Ball	2	5	6	Paid to Mr Wood.

Ordered that Mr Benjamin Berry and Mr Charles Hopping be struck out of the Fund at Michaelmas next.

	£	s	d
That Mr Bond have per annum ...	8	0	0
Mr Bennet...	6	0	0
Mr Wills	5	0	0

The first payments to begin at Christmas.

A letter from Mr James relating to Truro. The Assembly desired Mr Bowcher to go and preach at Truro for some time, to which he con-

[1] For 'Backaller.'

sented, being unwilling to tarry at Plympton. [fo. 115r.] Mr Henry Atkins & Mr Grig by the Advice and at the request of the Assembly consented to go to Plympton to preach there for 2 months.

Mr Benjamin Berry being return'd from Edinburgh was recommended to the Assembly. Order'd. That Mr Berry his father, Mr Hanmer & Mr Peter Kellow do examine him & if they approve him that they give him a licence to preach, and that they give an account hereof to the next Assembly.

Mr Wilcox was propos'd to be ordain'd. Ordered that Mr Tross, Mr Hallet, Mr Atkins, and Mr Gilling be the persons concern'd in the ordination. The time the 23rd of October next. His Thesis: An verè sancti possint excidere a gratiâ? Order'd that Mr John Marshal of Staverton be ordain'd at the same time, & by the same persons if he consent. His Thesis, An Christus sit verè Sacerdos in Terrâ?

Resolv'd. That there be 2 ministers appointed at every meeting of the Assembly to prepare for preaching before the next Assembly, that if he who is desir'd primarily should fail the other may supply the place. That Mr Harding preach at the next Assembly, and in case he fail Mr Gilling. That Mr Spark pray. [fo. 116r.] A letter to Mr Spark to desire him to pray at the next Assembly ordered to be sent.

A letter order'd to be sent to Mr Peard to know whether he be willing to submit to ordination.

Concerning Biddeford. Propos'd whether or no for the sake of peace & union between the two congregations at Biddeford Mr Bayly and his people will agree to call Mr Josiah Eveleigh to preach among them, and that he shall be upon an equal foot with Mr William Bartlet, and that neither of them shall be ordain'd before the other, or preferr'd to the other in any ministerial office, unless it be by the consent of the majority of each congregation as they now stand, (viz.) by those of them that are members or contributors. The question being put in order to peace it was unanimously agreed on that to act according to the import of this proposal would be the most proper expedient to obtain the desired peace and union. Advice hereof was sent to the people of Biddeford, in the following words: At the advice and desire of this Assembly Mr Baily and some of his people, (viz:) Mr Daniel Darracot, Mr Johns, Mr Copplestone, did on a proposal made for peace & union between the 2 congregations now in Biddeford [fo. 117r.] consent & promise as far as it did concern them, that Mr Josiah Eveleigh should be call'd to preach, & they did farther declare that they were willing that Mr Eveleigh be upon an equal foot with Mr William Bartlet, and that neither of them should be ordain'd before the other, or preferr'd to the other in any ministerial office, unless it be by the consent of the majority of members & contributors of each congregation as they now stand, this proposal being in our apprehensions the best expedient for peace & union. The same advice is now recommended to Mr Baily's and Mr Eveleigh's congregations, with desire that they would likewise consent and promise as the abovementioned have done, and promote the proposal in order to peace and union, as Mr Baily, Mr Darracot, Mr Johns, Mr Copplestone, have before the Assembly promised to do. Subscribed in the name of the rest by Samuel Atkins, moderator, John Enty, scribe. Resolv'd. That in case this be not consented to by Mr Baily's people, Mr Eveleigh shall be ordain'd according to a former appointment of this Assembly.

[fo. 120r.][1]
EXETER, 1701, May 6th & 7th. At the Meeting of the United Brethren.

[Present:] Mr Isaac Gilling, moderator, Mr John Enty, scribe; Mr Tapper, Backaller, Tross, Balster, Hooper, Stoddon, J. Berry, Hallet, Atkins, Sandercock, Walsh, Harding, Larkham, Withers, Spark, Ball, Hall, Mead, Evans, Jelinger Symonds, Walrond. Candidates: Mr Eveleigh, Baron, Bartlet, Bowcher, H. Atkins, Short, Grigg.

Brought into the Fund.

						£	s	d
By Mr Stoddon	...	...	...	...	...	9	10	0
Mr Backaller	...	...	...	...	...	1	5	0
Mr Hooper	...	...	...	...	...	3	16	9
Mr J. Berry	...	...	...	...	...		4	0
						14	15	9

Resolution. That Kingsbridge have some provision made for it as to a Minister. That till this provision be made Mr Evans be there May the 11th, Mr Atkins the 18th, Mr Enty the 25th. Mr Cox was afterward desir'd to preach there some time. Resolv'd. That Mr Stoddon have £14 per annum for Mr Loveridge. That Mr Bennets son of Exon have £4 per annum.

That Mr Gilling preach next Assembly, if he fail Mr Sandercock, Mr Walsh pray.

Several things were discours'd on about Biddiford, as whether Mr Eveleigh should [fo. 121r.] return to the Little Meeting. Whether in leaving the Little Meeting he had comply'd with the advice of the last Assembly. Negative. Whether it was convenient that they should have a Minister. Affirmative. Somewhat was propos'd about Mr Baily's and Mr Bartlet's being desir'd to preach to the Little Meeting.

Out of Mr Enty's Minutes.[2]

[fo. 16r., Shorthand.] *May 7, 1701. In compliance with the desire of some of the people of the Little Meeting in Bideford, the Assembly make it their request and advice to Mr Baily, Eveleigh and Bartlet, that if the people of the meeting in general desire it, they supply the meeting by turns in order to the promoting love and peace. And if this be not complied with by the said ministers by the 27th of this month that they may get Mr Short or some other minister to continue to spend his labours among them.*

Mr Eveleigh's letter to Mr Hallet. If it be true what you charge me with that I have used insinuations and devices to accomplish it, I think it justifiable in our circumstances as the case stood.[3]

[1]fos. 118r., 118v., 119r., contain a list of ordained ministers and candidates in May 1701. All the information given has been included in the Biographical Index below, pp. 133–48.
[2]The remainder of fo. 121r. was left blank.
[3]This short passage is also on fo. 16r. of MS. Eveleigh was invited to Crediton shortly after the death of Robert Carel on 20th of May, 1701, and accepted. He would appear to have left Bideford some time before this date. Calamy, *op. cit.*, Carel.

[fo. 124r.][1]
EXETER, 1701, 9th & 10th of Sept. At the Meeting of the United Brethren.

[Present:] Mr Benjamin Hooper, moderator, Mr Humphry Berry, scribe; Mr Samuel Tapper, George Tross, Henry Backaller, John Balster, Joseph Hallet, Samuel Atkins, Isaac Gilling, William Horsham, Jacob Sandercock, Samuel Wood, Thomas Walsh, Samuel Bartlet, John Moore, Deliverance Larkham, John Withers, Angel Spark, Samuel Hall, Matthew Pardew, John Mead, Richard Evans, [Michael] Martyn, Jelinger Symonds, John Enty, Samuel Mullins, Thomas Edgly.
From Dorset: John Powell, William Giles.
From Somerset: John Moore, Malachi Blake. John Norman, Simon Brown, Candidates.
Candidates of Devon: Mr Henry Atkins, Samuel Short, George Bowcher, Peter Baron, Joseph Manston, John Cox, William Bartlet, John Hughes, John Grigg, Robert Wood, Mathew Clode.

Brought into the Fund.

						£	s	d
By Mr Hooper	...	...	...	...	...	3	12	6
From Crediton, Mr Carel's money			...	...		8	0

Mr Tapper, Hallet, Larkham, Evans & Enty, being appointed to examine Mr John Prew, declar'd their approbation of him as a person qualify'd to preach the Gospel.

[fo. 125r.] A professor that hath been scandalously flagitious, to the great dishonour of God, discredit of religion, and grief of good men: no less is judg'd requisite by the Ministers assembled for the reparation of such damages as the Christian religion hath sustain'd by such an abomination, and in order to his restoration to formerly enjoy'd priviledges, than such an open avowed confession of the sensibleness of his sin, with all shame & sorrow, hatred and indignation against himself with most sincere fix'd resolutions of a more Scriptural walk and life; as may give satisfaction to the Society mostly concern'd. And that he be for some considerable time afterward kept off from the Sacrament.

Bovey people desir'd to have Mr Mathew Pardew their former Pastor restor'd to them. Mr Pardew wholly referr'd himself to the determination of the Assembly. The Assembly after they had heard South Molton people, & had debated the matter, judg'd it most conducive to the glory of God, the furtherance of the Gospel, etc., that Mr Pardew should continue at South Molton.

The case of Crediton & Silferton being weigh'd, it was the earnest advice and desire of the Assembly that Mr Josiah Eveleigh would accept of and comply with [fo. 126r.] the call from the people of Crediton to be Mr Hooper's assistant, in order to the continuance of both meetings.[2]

Mr Samuel Short, Henry Atkins, and George Bowcher, apply'd themselves to the Assembly desiring Ordination. Agreed. That they be ordain'd at Crediton October 16th. The Moderator & Mr Tross to

---

[1]fos. 122r. and 123r. contain notes not in this sequence.
[2]Hooper, a neighbouring minister, was called on to supervise affairs until Eveleigh's ordination on August 6th, 1702.

ordain, Mr Hallet to preach, Mr Backaller to give the Exhortation. The Questions given them to state & defend are these:

To Mr Short: An datur Electio personarum particularium? Aff.

To Mr Atkins: An Electio sit ex Fide praevisâ? Neg.

To Mr Bowcher: An Christus perfecte satisfecit pro peccatoribus? Aff.

[fo. 127r.]

EXETER, 1702, May 5th & 6th. At the Meeting of the United Brethren.

[Present:] Mr Joseph Hallet, moderator, Isaac Gilling, scribe: Mr John Berry, Deliverance Larkham, Thomas Edgly, Samuel Tapper, Jacob Baily, Henry Atkins, Samuel Stoddon, Samuel Hall, George Tross, Richard Evans, Benjamin Hooper, Michael Martyn, Stephen Toogood, John Walrond, John Ball, Humphry Berry, John Moore, William Giles, Thomas Walsh, Samuel Short, Candidates: Josiah Eveleigh, John Cox, John Slowly, William Bartlett, William Orchard, Charles Gillingham, Jaspar Howe, Edward Bearne, Ebenezer Taylor, Norman, Baker, Lissant, Monsieur Majendie, Thompson, Wood.

Brought into the Fund.

	£	s	d	
Mr Stoddon	7	10	0	
Mr Eveleigh	6	19	0	
Mr Hooper	2	12	6	(charged Sept. 1701)
Mr Hooper now	3	0	$2\frac{3}{4}$	
Mr Walsh	3	3	6	

Orderd that Mr Lissant be struck out of the Fund. That Mr Palk have 40s per annum abated since his coming from Mr Warren's, and that Mr Alexander Bennet's son have 40s added.

[fo. 128r.] Agreed that Mr Eveleigh, Mr Cox and Mr Slowly be ordain'd at Crediton, the first Thursday in August.

Mr Eveleigh's Question: An detur Resurrectio Mortuorum?

Mr Cox's: An Christus secundum humanam naturam sit ubique?

Mr Slowly's: An detur Transsubstantiatio?

May 5th. A Committee of 6, viz. Mr Tross, Hooper, Towgood, Ball, Gilling & Larkham, appointed to consider the affairs of Biddeford this night, & report their opinion of it tomorrow morning.

May 6th, 1702, Exon. The Ministers assembled having considered the request of many of the Congregation in Biddeford to have Mr Bartlet ordain'd, and understanding that the members of the Congregation in general (providing Mr Bailies will consent thereto) are desirous thereof: are willing to comply with their request; and do unanimously desire and advise Mr Bailies for the promoting peace, union and edification in the Congregation, so to do. And they do also advise Mr Bartlet to do his utmost that all affairs may be carried with all possible unanimitie and [fo. 129r.] concord between Mr Bailies and him, and that he carry it with due deference towards Mr Bailies as his superiour in age and seniour in the Ministry. Order'd that Mr John Berry and Mr Hanmer do appoint the time, place and exercises for Mr Bartlet's Ordination, when Mr Bailies and the Congregation have given their consent. The Assembly likewise advise the people on each side to lay aside all differences, mutually to forgive one another, and live for the future in love and concord. And that a Fast Day (if so desir'd) be set apart to humble themselves before God. Subscribed in the name and by order of the Assembly by Joseph Hallet, moderator, Isaac Gilling, scribe.

Next meeting the 1st Tuesday & Wednesday after the first Lords Day in September, Mr Sandercock to preach or if he fail Mr Horsham, Mr Bailies to pray or if he fail Mr Mullins.

Cases propos'd: One who had a Base Child above 10 years ago, nam'd a false father, and was perjur'd: for which she was prosecuted and excommunicated. This person hath for several [fo. 130r.] years past seem'd very penitent, confessing her sin with a flood of tears, and is ready if requir'd, to make a publick acknowledgment of it in the Congregation to which she belongs: she also earnestly desires to be admitted to the Lords Table. The Pastor is satisfy'd of the sincerity of her repentance, yet doubtful whether he should receive her to Communion; her perjury added to her fornication very much prejudices people against her, & the communicants urge this against her admission, that thereby an odium will be drawn upon the Church. The Assembly think it advisable that the Pastor should receive this penitents confession of her sin and declaration of her repentance before the communicants and upon that receive her to Communion. As to the Excommunication, that is an Act of the Lay Chancellour, in which the Assembly cannot intermeddle.

Question: What is to be done in case a person can't drink wine. Whether Beer or Cyder may not be receiv'd by such a one in the Lords Supper? In Muscovy they have no wine, but use the drink used in that country.

[fo. 131r.]
EXETER, 1702, Sept. 8th and 9th. At the Meeting of the United Brethren.

[Present:] Mr William Horsham, moderator, Isaac Gilling, scribe; Mr Tapper, Moore, Bowcher, Backaller, Larkham, Short, Tross, Withers, Henry Atkins, Balster, Hall, Cox, Hooper, Evans, Eveleigh, Toogood, Peter Kellow, Monsieur Majendie, Hallett, Enty, Walrond, Sandercock, H. Berry, Wood, Edgly, Walsh, Giles. Candidates: Peter Baron, Edward Bearne, Glanvil, William Bartlet, Matthew Hody, How, John Hughes, Samuel Snowdon. Delegates from Somerset: Mr Norman, Mr Darch, Mr Baker.

Mr Sandercock preach'd, Mr Edgly pray'd, and kept to the time allotted them.

Brought in to the Fund.

			£	s	d
By Mr Hooper	...	...	1	0	0
Mr Tapper	...	...	1	0	0

Order'd that Mr Hody who had £6 per annum out of the Fund, be struck out. That his six pounds per annum be so divided between Mr Alexander Bennet's son, Mr Bond & Mr Wills that they have an equal sum out of the Fund yearly.

[fo. 132r.] Certificates were given to several ministers lately ordain'd subscrib'd by their Ordainers, in this form: We whose names are hereunto subscribed do certify that Mr John Cox was on the 6th of August anno 1702 solemnly set apart to the office of the Ministry, by fasting and prayer with imposition of hands, in the congregation at Crediton, according to an order of the Assembly of the United Brethren of Exon, May the 6th last past, George Trosse, etc.

Mr Hughes of Dartmouth desires to be ordain'd. Agreed that he be ordain'd at Dartmouth the 6th of October next. Mr Hallet to begin with prayer, Mr Horsham to preach, Mr Hooper to pray over him, Mr Gilling to give the Exhortation, Mr Withers to conclude with Prayer. His question: An Ordinatio Presbyterorum sit Authentica?

Exon, September 9, 1702. The United Ministers now assembled do unanimously agree that according to their agreement at their last Assembly in May last, in compliance with the request of the congregation in Bidde-ford, that Mr William Bartlet should be ordain'd, he be without further delay ordaind accordingly. And they do further advise that he be ordaind in Biddeford. And they desire Mr John Berry, Mr John Balster, and Mr John Hanmer, with such other ministers as they think fit, to ordain him, & to appoint time and exercises, and share the work between them.

[fo. 22r., Shorthand.] *Newton Abbot March 9, 1702/3. These are to certify whom it may concern that Mr Bartholomew Par late of Exon was for some years a communicant with the Reverend Mr John Hopping and my Brother Mr Samuel Atkins lately deceased. I do not understand but that he behaved himself as became a Christian and Church member, nor have I heard any thing objected against him to hinder his being received to communion by any of the United Brethren, unless his being unfortunately entangled with his for-father [sic] who has proved a bankrupt be thought of sufficient weight to bar him from the Lords Table. He has spent several weeks in my family since he was [¹] to Bideford; and, had there been any opportunity for it, I should readily have admitted him. Isaac Gilling, Minister of the Gospel in Newton Abbott and one of the United Brethren in Devon.[2]*

[fo. 133r.]
EXETER, 1703, May 4th & 5th. At the Meeting of the United Brethren.

[Present:] Mr Deliverance Larkham, moderator, Isaac Gilling, scribe; Mr John Berry, Horsham, Thomas Kellow, Tapper, Moor, Peter Kellow, Stoddon, Withers, Mullins, Tross, Ball, Edgly, Balster, Hall, Walrond, Hooper, Evans, Short, Hallet, Martyn, Henry Atkins, Giles, Eveleigh, Bowcher, John Slowly, William Bartlet.

Brought in to the Fund.

	£	s	d
Mr Stoddon	6	0	0
Mr Ball	2	7	0

Mr Ebenezer Tailor proposes himself to be ordain'd at Ashburton. A certificate from the University of Glasgo dated 1680 of his proceeding

¹Blank in MS.
²A further example of provision for intercommunion between one church and another.

Master of Arts. Resolv'd that he be ordain'd at Ashburton the first Tuesday in July (viz: July 6). To preach and perform his exercises July 1 at Exon. His Question: An Quartum Praeceptum sit morale?[1] His text: 2 Tim: 2,3. Endure hardness. Mr Ball or Hooper to pray over him, Mr Hallet to preach, Mr Gilling to give the Exhortation, Mr Withers to pray.

[fo. 134r.] Resolv'd that ordinarily before any Candidate have leave of the Assembly to be ordain'd, he produce a Testimonial under the names of some of the chief of those among whom he preaches of his diligence and labours in the Ministry, and of the unblameableness of his conversation.

Ministers wanted for Truro and Leskard[2] in Cornwall.

Next meeting to be Tuesday September 7th, Mr Walsh to preach, or if he fail Mr Moor, Mr Berry to pray, or if he fail Mr Peter Kellow.

[fo. 135r.]
EXETER, 1703, Sept. 7th & 8th. At the Meeting of the United Brethren.

[Present:] Mr Jacob Sandercock, moderator, Mr Josiah Eveleigh, scribe; Mr Stoddon, Moor, Henry Atkins, Trosse, Evans, Giles, Balster, Martyn, Bartlet, Hooper, Peter Kellow, Norman, Hallet, Jelinger Symonds, Monsieur Majendie, Gilling, Mullins, Larkham, Edgly, Withers, Berry, Horsham, Cox, Bailys, Slowly, Walsh, Bowcher, Wood, Short.
Candidates: Mr Brinly, Edward Bearne, Brett, Wills. Mr Baker from Somerset.

Brought in to the Fund from Crediton. ...   £6   9s   6d

Mr Wills read a Theologicall Essay on the Life of Timothy. Order'd that Mr Hooper, Gilling, Larkham, Enty, do examine him. He being examin'd and well approv'd order'd that he have a Testimonial and leave to preach.

Order'd that the next Meeting be Tuesday May 9th, Mr Moor to preach, or if he fail Mr Withers, Mr Giles to pray, Mr Walsh to be Moderator.

Cases propos'd and debated. Whether the Apostolical Office were essentially distinct from that of Presbyters? Whether the Office of a Deacon be Civil or Spiritual, & whether it be [fo. 136r.] a standing office?

Mr Bailys and Mr Bartlett presented a Testimonial of their reunion, with thanks to the Assembly for their endeavours towards it. Order'd that the following coppy of the said Testimonial be inserted in the Minute Book. Biddiford Sept. 4th, 1703. There having been lately an hearty reconciliation and mutual agreement between Ministers and People in the great Meeting House in this town of Biddiford, we are willing to have this known to all whom it may concern, especially to them of the Reverend Assembly. In testimony whereof we have given our names. John Darracott, Daniel Darracot, John Smith, George Davie, J. Power, etc., George Strange, etc. Subscrib'd by near 30 names of the members.

[1]The question to be debated was whether the Fourth Commandment (Remember the Sabbath Day) belongs to the moral or to the ceremonial law. Gilling put a line over the 'a' in 'quartum' but this seems to have been a slip of the pen.
[2]Liskeard.

[fo. 137r.]
EXETER, May [9th,] 1704. At the Meeting of the United Brethren.

[Present:] Mr Joseph Hallet, moderator, John Sloly, scribe; Mr John Berry, Samuel Stoddon, Samuel Tapper, George Trosse, Benjamin Hooper, Isaac Gilling, William Horsham, Jacob Sandercock, Nathaniel Harding, John Moore, Deliverance Larkham, Samuel Hall, Richard Evans, Michael Martyn, William Giles, John Walrond, Samuel Mullins, Thomas Edgly, Majendie, George Bowcher, Samuel Short, Henry Atkins, Josiah Eveleigh, John Hughes, William Bartlett, John Norman, Ebenezer Tailor. Candidates: Mr Edward Bearne, William Orchard, Samuel Grigg, Benjamin Wills, William Peard, Matthew Hody, William Palk, Peter Baron, Richard Glanvil, Henry Brett.

Brought in to the Fund by Mr Stoddon £6 0s 0d
Twas propos'd to the Assembly whether an ordain'd minister that hath liv'd in the practice of notorious and scandalous crimes for several years may be incourag'd to exercise his ministerial function amongst a people? Tis the opinion and advice of the Ministers (nemine contradicente) for the present: that he ought to desist from the exercise of his ministry for some years.

Mr Baron & Mr Hody propos'd themselves to the Assembly for ordination. Order'd that they be ordain'd at Plymouth on Wednesday July 19, by Mr Halsey, Hallett, Gilling, Sandercock, Withers. Mr Halsey to preach, Mr Hallet to give the Exhortation. [fo. 138r.] Mr Baron's Thesis: An secessio nostra ab Ecclesia Anglicana sit Schismatica? Mr Hody's: An paedo-baptismus sit validus? Order'd that Mr Hody between this and his ordination preach a probationary sermon on 2 Cor.7,1, in Mr Harding's congregation on a Lecture Day, and that the Ordainers receive a Testimonial from the Plymouth ministers.

Mr Withers to preach next Assembly, or if he fail Mr Larkham. Mr Peter Kellow to pray or if he fail Mr Bowcher.

[fo. 139r.]
EXETER, 1704, Sept. 12, 13. At the meeting of the United Brethren.

[Present:] Mr Benjamin Hooper, moderator, Mr John Cox, scribe; Mr Samuel Tapper, Deliverance Larkham, Samuel Stoddon, John Withers, George Trosse, Richard Evans, John Balster, Martyn, Benjamin Hooper, Thomas Edgly, Joseph Hallet, George Bowcher, Stephen Towgood, Samuel Short, Isaac Gilling, Henry Atkins, John Ball, Josiah Eveleigh, Jacob Sandercock, William Giles, Samuel Wood, John Cox, Samuel Bartlet, John Slowly, Horsham, John Hughes, John Moore, John Norman, Majendie, William Bartlett. Candidates: Edward Bearne, William Orchard, Samuel Grigg, Benjamin Wills.

Resolv'd that if a candidate who has a permission from the Assembly to preach by way of probation, lead a scandalous life, that permission ought to be revok'd. That it is requisite that some ministers be deputed to talk with and admonish any such candidate who has an ill fame. It is the request of this Assembly that the Ministers of Exon do talk with and admonish Mr P. Pr-w, a candidate who has an ill fame.

Brought in to the Fund by Mr Ball two pounds. Order'd that Mr Benjamin Wills and Mr Nicholas Brinly after the reception of Michaelmas Quarter be struck out of the Fund.

[fo. 140r.] Mr Cornelius Bond having been examined by Mr Ball, Mr Hallet, and Mr Larkham, was judg'd qualify'd to preach as a probationer.

Mr Larkham to preach before the Assembly next May, and if he fail Mr Wood. Mr Peter Kellow to pray & if he fail Mr Short.

Mr Hooper laid before the Assembly the state of a case about an estate given between two brothers, etc. Resolved, nemine contradicente, that it is the opinion of this Assembly, that, seeing both parties consented to the division of the estate, one moiety in right & justice devolves on the family of the brother that died intestate. It being propos'd, whether or no, seeing the Common Law devolves a right to the whole estate upon the Elder Brother, he may not manage that right for the benefit of the younger children, in case the elder son should prove refractory. Resolv'd, that seeing the Elder Brother has no right, the moiety of the Estate devolves of right on the Elder Son of the Junior Brother deceased. However, if evidence appear, that it was the Junior Brothers will to oblige the Elder Son to pay portions to the younger children, the Elder Brother may endeavour as far as he can by law to oblige the Elder Son to pay portions out of the said moiety to the younger children.

[fo. 166r., reversed. Shorthand[1]] *We whose names are hereunto subscribed being sensible of the difficulties which attend the sacred work to which we are devoted, have after solemn consideration agreed to these following Articles, in the observance of which we trust to contribute some assistance to one another in it.*

1. We will (grace assisting) preserve and cultivate brotherly love, and discover the regard we have to that Christian grace by hiding from our people the faults of all our Brethren, and by reproving mildly everything we judge unbecoming a Minister either in our Civil or Religious conduct. Under this Head we oblige ourselves to conceal all real or supposed imprudencies we condemn in each other, that the dignity of our ministry be not lessened.

2. We will meet together as often and in such towns as shall be judged convenient. Then one of us chosen by the majority shall preach in the morning, who shall confine his whole exercise to one hour and a half. In the afternoon we agree to dispute orderly some question in polemical or controversial divinity.

3. Tis agreed that during the whole disputation nothing of levity or banter be admitted, and the guilty person be sharply reproved and fined not exceeding six pence.

4. To prevent the causeless breach of these articles we oblige ourselves to a critical observance of them, under these following penalties. If either of us be not present at our stated meeting without producing a reason that the majority shall approve he shall forfeit 2s. If any person refuse to preach in his turn he shall forfeit 2s 6d, and if there be at any time reason sufficient for the appointed preachers to be absent, then another shall preach in his place, and he supply his turn for it.

5. Tis agreed that all our treats be as little costly and expensive as is convenient, viz: not above 2 dishes.

6. The several sums forfeited shall be imploied in buying books as shall be thought most conducive to our mutual advantage.

[1]This passage shows that small groups of ministers also met in fraternal gatherings at intervals, in addition to the county assemblies twice-yearly.

7. We agree that the majority determine everything that relates to the breach of these articles or any other that may be thought hereafter necessary.
8. The majority determine that we all preach by turns, and no person be obliged to preach twice to any others' once.
Newton Abbot, September 20th, 1704. Isaac Gilling, Thomas Edgly, William Giles, William Orchard, Edward Bearne, George Bowcher.[1]

[fo. 141r.]
EXETER, 1705, May 8th & 9th. At the meeting of the United Brethren.

[Present:] Mr John Moor, moderator, Samuel Short, scribe; Mr Tapper, Stoddon, Tross, Hooper, Hallet, Gilling, Horsham, Sandercock, Larkham, Hall, Wood, Ball, Balster, Evans, Toogood, Withers, Pardew, Mullins, Baylies, Edgley, Peter, Thomas [&] Daniel Kellow, Majendie, Enty, Berry, Giles, Bowcher, Atkins, Cox, Eveleigh, Norman, Bartlett, Symonds, Taylor, Sloly. Candidates: Peard, Wills, Bearn, Palk, Brett, Glanvil, Bond, Grigg, Wood.

Brought in to the Fund.

						£	s	d
By Mr Ball ...	...	...	...	...	...	2	5	0
Mr Eveleigh	...	...	...	...	...	6	0	0
Mr Stoddon	...	...	...	...	...	7	0	0

Order'd that Mr William Palk, & Mr John Bennet be struck out of the Fund after Midsummer next. That Stephen Edwards of Chard have £10 per annum out of the Fund.

That Mr Samuel Wood preach before the Assembly September next, & if he fail Mr Angel Spark: & that Mr Jelinger Symonds pray.

That Mr William Peard and Mr Samuel Grigg be ordain'd at Barnstaple the 6th of June next by Mr Hooper, Mr Hallet, Moore, & Pardew. That Mr Richard Glanvill be ordain'd the 1st Wednesday in August next at Liscard, by Mr Roger Flammick, Joseph Halsie, Theophilus Tingcomb, Jacob Sandercock, & John Entie. His thesis: An justificatio nostra sit gratuita? That Mr Robert Wood be ordain'd at Honiton by Mr Samuel Stoddon, Ball, Towgood, Walrond and [fo. 142r.] Evans, at the time they shall agree upon. His Thesis: An satisfactio Christi sit necessaria? Aff.

The case of Pensanse and St. Ives being represented by Mr Hooper: order'd that Mr Flammick, Halsie, Tingcomb, Daniel and Thomas Kellow, and Mr Jaspar How inspect (inquire) into that affair, and give an account thereof to any of the Ministers of Exon, against the next Assembly.

A case propounded concerning the marrying of two sisters. Resolv'd, 1. That the Laws concerning marriages, Lev:18, are obliging to Christians. 2. That the marrying of two sisters successively is there forbidden, and consequently is a sinful marriage. 3. That such a marriage ought to be dissolv'd.

These following questions were propos'd by some people of Exon. 1. Whether a Ministers removal from one place to another on a clear

[1]At this time Gilling was minister at Newton Abbot, Edgley at Totness, and Bowcher at Bovey Tracey, so this was a Mid-Devon group. *See App. C.*

call be not in some cases allowable? Resolv'd, N.Contrad. in the affirmative. 2. Whether there may not some circumstances occur which may make such a removal a probable dutie? Aff. 3. Whether in a call of Mr Walrond of Ottery by the citizens of Exon such circumstances do not occur as make it his probable duty to accept of this Call? This question was not debated because it appear'd to the Assembly that Mr Walrond had utterly refus'd to accept of that Call.

[fo. 142v.]
EXETER, 1705, Sept. 3, 4. At the meeting of the United Brethren.

[Present:] Mr Deliverance Larkham, moderator, Thomas Edgley, scribe; Mr Tapper, Stoddon, Tross, Hooper, Hallett, Gilling, Horsham, Sandercock, Wood, Moor, Withers, Giles, Evans, Martyn, Majendie, Symonds, Short, Taylor, Atkins, Norman, Eveleigh, Grigg, Hughes, Bowcher, Bartlett, Spark, Sloly. Candidates: Palk, Bearn, Stoddon, Bond, Orchard, Wills, Hancock, Carkeet.

Mr Hallett, Withers, Evans, appointed to examine Mr Eliezer Hancock and Mr Samuel Carkeet, declare that they find them well qualify'd; whereupon they were desir'd to preach as Candidates, and a Certificate of this approbation given them.

Ordered that Mr William Palk and Mr Benjamin Wills be ordain'd at Appledore October 17th. Mr Palks Thesis: An Gratia sit omnino gratuita? Mr Wills's: An Arbitrium sit liberum? The ordainers Mr Balster, Hallet, Bailies, Pardew, Peter Kellow.

Order'd that Mr Bond preach at Holsworthy at the request of that people.

The Assembly having heard the difference between Mr Humphrey Berry and his people at Launceston: and having read & consider'd their affectionate letter relating to him, they think his reasons not sufficient to warrant his removal. Tis also their opinion that considering Mr Berry's great aversion to return, and his declaring that it will be to his utter ruin if he should: it will be best for the people of Launceston to chuse some other Minister to supply that place. Order'd that a letter be sent to Mr Clode to desire him to go down to Launceston upon trial.

Order'd that Mr Hallett write to Mr Calamy to desire him to print his 2nd edition of Mr Baxter's Life so as that it may be no prejudice to such as have bought the first, by printing a sufficient number of distinct supplements.[1]

Next Assembly to be May 7th. Mr Angel Spark to preach, Mr Short to pray, & if he fail Mr Atkins.

[fo. 174r., reversed.[2]] *To the Reverend Mr William Palke, Reverend Sir, We whose names are hereunto subscribed who are members of the congregation of dissenting Protestants in Chudleigh having had some trial of your ministerial*

[1] The first edition of *An Abridgment of Mr Baxter's history of his life and times . . . by Edmund Calamy, 1702*, contained in Chapter IX (nearly half the book) biographical accounts of ejected ministers of the period 1660–62. A 2nd edition was at once called for, but did not appear until 1713.
[2] This shorthand passage is an example of a formal " call " to a minister to settle with a congregation. Palk's ordination had been arranged by the previous Assembly, in Sept. 1705.

abilities and being well satisfied of your good conversation, do earnestly desire you and hereby invite you to come and settle among us as our Pastor and minister to instruct us, watch for our souls and administer all the ordinances of Christ among us; and if it shall please God to incline your heart to comply with this our desire, we trust our submission to the Gospel and cheerful contribution towards your maintenance will be to your satisfaction.

[fo. 143r.]
EXETER, 1706, May 7, 8. At the Meeting of the United Brethren of Devon, Cornwall and Somerset.

[Present:] Mr John Withers, moderator, Mr Peter Baron, scribe; Mr George Tross, Samuel Tapper, John Balster, Stephen Towgood, Joseph Hallet, Isaac Gilling, William Horsham, Jacob Sandercock, John Moor, Angel Spark, John Ball, Samuel Hall, Richard Evans, Michael Martyn, Jelinger Symonds, Peter Kellow, Thomas Kellow, John Enty, Samuel Mullins, John Walrond, Thomas Edgley, William Giles, Samuel Short, Henry Atkins, John Cox, Josiah Eveleigh, John Slowly, John Norman, Ebenezer Taylor, William Peard, Samuel Grigg, Robert Wood, Jaspar How, William Palk, Benjamin Wills. Candidates of Devon: Edward Bearne, Nicholas Brinley, John Stoddon, Samuel Stoddon, Eliezer Hancock, Samuel Carkeet, Rutter, Hugh Brown, Furse, Bishop. Ministers of Somerset: Mr John Moor, Matthew Warren, James, Humphrey Berry, Charles Gillingham. Candidates: George Lissant, Samuel Baker, Short, Copplestone. [Visitors:]Mr Nicholas Jillard of Kent. 43 ordain'd ministers, 14 candidates.

Brought into the Fund.

	£	s	d
By Mr Ball ...	2	5	0
Mr Stoddon ...	2	0	0
Mr Walrond ...	6	10	0

Paid Mr Ball for Stephen Edwards, £2 10s. Order'd that Mr Loveridge who for some years has had £12 per annum be struck out of the Fund. Mr Warren being now to be paid 10s.

That Mr Evans preach before the Assembly in September next, or if he fail, Mr Walrond: Mr Atkins pray, or if he fail Mr Eveleigh.

That Mr Savage's son of Lympston have five pounds per annum out of the Fund. [fo. 144r.] Order'd that Mr Thomas Kellow have £4 yearly out of the Fund. That Plym-tree meeting have £3 yearly.

The people of Sidmouth presented a petition to the Assembly representing their case with respect to a new erected Meeting-place. The case appearing intricate, and seeming to be determin'd by law against their request, as to the said Meeting-House: the Assembly advis'd them to peace, & to join with others in erecting another Meeting-house at Sidford.[1]

[1]Sidmouth affairs occur frequently between this entry and 1709. A knowledge of local geography helps to understand the difficulty. The Meeting House at Sidmouth had been also attended by people at Sidbury, some 2 miles away, and at Sidford, halfway between the two. Their late minister Samuel Stoddon wanted them to rebuild at Sidford, as being more convenient to all. As will be seen, neither side would agree, and two Meeting Houses emerged, one at Sidmouth and another at Sidbury. Murch, *op. cit.*, p. 344–5.

Order'd that Mr Brinley be ordain'd some time before September next, by Mr Halsey, Flammank, Tingcomb, Hallet, Sandercock, Daniel and Thomas Kellow. His Question: An libri, vulgo Apocryphae vocati, sint canonici? That Mr John Stoddon be ordain'd at Crediton, on Thursday the 11th of July, by Mr Tross, Hooper, Hallett, and Hall. That he preach at Exon, Tuesday the 11th of June on Romans [10, v.13;[1]] How shall they hear without a Preacher? His Question: An ministerium Evangelicum sit necessarium? Mr Hugh Brown, and Mr Bishop, examin'd by Mr Ball, Hallet, Gilling, approv'd, and permitted by the Assembly to preach.

Whereas Mr John Prew hath been charg'd with several immoral and scandalous practices, of which there is too great reason [fo. 145r.] to believe him guilty; and having been sent for, to come, and justify himself before the Assembly, if he could, which he refus'd to do: we therefore disown him, and judge him unfit to preach under his present circumstances, untill he shall give sufficient satisfaction as to his repentance and reformation.

A petition of some of Barnstaple desiring another minister with Mr Peard during the indisposition of their Pastor Mr Hanmer. After a long and full hearing of Mr Peard and his friends objections, the Assembly came to this resolution. Tis the opinion and advice of this Assembly, that 'twill be most for the glory of God, the peace & good of the Church, that another minister go to Barnstaple, to settle & join there with Mr Peard; and tis their earnest request and advice that the people choose such a minister, against whom there may be no just cause of objection either by Mr Hanmer or Mr Peard.

[fo. 146r.]
EXETER, 1706, Sept. 3, 4. At the Meeting of the United Brethren of Devon & Cornwall.

[Present:] Mr George Tross, moderator, Isaac Gilling, scribe; Mr Samuel Tapper, John Balster, Benjamin Hooper, Joseph Hallett, William Horsham, Jacob Sandercock, Samuel Wood, John Moor, Deliverance Larkham, John Withers, John Ball, Samuel Hall, Richard Evans, Jelinger Symonds, Peter Kellow, Thomas Kellow, John Enty, John Walrond, Samuel Mullins, William Giles, Thomas Edgely, George Bowcher, Samuel Short, Henry Atkins, John Cox, Josiah Eveleigh, John Slowly, John Hughes, John Norman, Charles Gillingham, Ebenezer Taylor, William Bartlett, Peter Baron, Matthew Hody, Samuel Grigg, William Palk, Benjamin Wills, John Stoddon, Majendie.
From Somerset: James, Cornish, Humphry Berry.
From Dorset: Joseph Manston.
Candidates: Mr Edward Bearn, Samuel Stoddon, Hugh Brown, Samuel Carkeet, Bishop, Copplestone, Thomas Jones, Brampton,[2] Alexander Walker, N. Molton,[2] Cornelius Bond.
Candidates from Somerset: Short, Furse.

Mr Evans preach'd, Mr Henry Atkins pray'd.

[1] Left blank in the text.
[2] i.e. Thomas Jones of Braunton, and Alexander Walker of North Molton. Copplestone is the name of a person, however.

Brought in to the Fund.

	£	s	d
By Mr Eveleigh	8	0	0
Mr Ball	2	5	0
Paid Mr Eveleigh for Halberton	3	0	0
Mr Ball for Stephen Edwards, Midsummer Quarter	2	10	0
Mr Bond, Midsummer Quarter	2	5	0

[fo. 147r.] Order'd that Mr Bond's £9 per annum be continu'd untill next Assembly. That Mr Grigg have but £4 per annum from Michaelmas next. That Lawrence Hext of Staverton have £5 per annum at present.

Mr Samuel Stoddon of Sidbury proposes himself to Ordination. Agreed. That he be ordain'd at Ottery St. Mary the 26th of December by Mr Tross, Mr Ball, Mr Evans and Mr Walrond. That he preach at Exon the last Tuesday in November on this Text: [1 Tim. 4, v.15.[1]] Meditate on these things, give thy self wholly to them, that thy profiting may appear. His Question: An Paedobaptismus sit institutio Christi?

Hatherly people desire Mr Bishop for their Pastor and Minister. He refuses to settle, but promises to take a turn there once a month.

Ashburton people desire Mr Woods positive answer whether he will settle among them. He at length refuses. Upon which some ministers promis'd to supply them for a month: and Mr Cranch propos'd to get a Minister from London.

[fo. 148r.] Some of Barnstaple appear, and inform that Mr Peard and his friends refus'd to comply with the advice of the last Assembly, and that they had rejected all offers of peace and union: that hereupon about two hundred had withdrawn from Mr Peard's ministry, and had set up another meeting, which had hitherto been supply'd by several ministers of the County. They desir'd this Assemblies advice and assistance in order to their being further supply'd. The Assembly recommended Mr Bearne to them, who promis'd to settle among them this winter. Resolv'd, nemine contradicente, that those ministers who have been at Barnstaple, and have preach'd to those who are come off from Mr Peard upon his refusing to comply with the advice of the last Assembly, answer'd the design of that Assembly, and did very well in so doing. A copy of this resolution subscrib'd in the name, and by the order of the Assembly, by the Moderator, was given to Mr Richard Parmynter, junior.

South Molton people's call to Mr Thomas Kellow read. He desir'd the advice of the [fo. 149r.] Assembly whether he should continue in Cornwall or remove from thence. They left it to him whether to stay or remove: but advis'd him that if he did remove, he would accept of the call given him by South Molton people. He promis'd to give a positive answer in a months time to South Molton people, whether he would accept of their call.

Some of Sidmouth again appear'd, insisting on their right to the Meeting House erected there. The Assembly being inform'd of the inconveniences of that place, as lying remote from several of the most substantial persons of Sidbury Meeting, & that Mr Samuel Stoddon

[1]This was left blank in the MS.

deceas'd had order'd that house to be sold, and the money to be laid out in building a Meeting Place in Sidford, again earnestly persuaded Sidmouth people to join with those of Sidbury who are ready to build a convenient place to meet in at Sidford; and declar'd that they should take it ill if any of their members should [fo. 150r.] preach at Sidmouth while the people of that place separate from those of Sidbury.

Mr James of Taunton gives an account of the method which he, Mr Darch, & Mr Grove take with their Pupils.[1] The following approbation drawn up by Mr Ball, read, approved, subscribd and given to Mr James. Exon, Sept. 5, 1706: Whereas Mr James of Taunton came to this Assembly, and propos'd to the Assembly the method that he, Mr Darch and Mr Grove intended to take in the educating of young men for the Ministry: this Assembly did approve of that design, not doubting but they will continue in their good resolutions, we have subscribed our names, wishing all good success to them. Subscribd in the name & by the order of the Assembly by George Tross, Moderator, Isaac Gilling, scribe.

Resolv'd that tis fit that we should pray for the House of Hanover on which the Succession to the Crown is settled by Act of Parliament.

Mr Walrond to preach next Assembly, or if he fail, Mr Enty. Mr Cox to pray. [fo. 151r.] Propos'd, whether it be convenient that those who are absent from Prayers during the Assembly, or go out of the Assembly without leave, should be liable to some forfeitures? Negative. Question: What is to be done to prevent confusion & disorder in our debates? It appeared that seats were wanting, & the room not convenient to receive the number of Ministers & Candidates that meet.

[fo. 151r.]
EXETER, 1707, May 6th & 7th. At the Meeting of the United Brethren of Devon and Cornwall.

[Present:] Mr Nathaniel Harding, moderator, Isaac Gilling, scribe; George Trosse, John Balster, Benjamin Hooper, Stephen Towgood, Joseph Hallet, William Horsham, Jacob Sandercock, Samuel Wood, Thomas Walsh, John Rosewel, John Moor, Deliverance Larkham, Jacob Bailies, Samuel Hall, Richard Evans, Michael Martyn, John Ball, Jelinger Symonds, John Enty, John Walrond, Samuel Mullins, William Giles, Thomas Edgeley, George Bowcher, Samuel Short, Henry Atkins, John Cox, Josiah Eveleigh, John Slowly, William Bartlett, John Hughes, John Norman, Charles Gillingham,[2] Ebenezer Taylor, Jaspar How, Samuel Grigg, Richard Glanvil, Robert Wood, William Palk, Benjamin Wills, John Stoddon.
From Somerset, Ministers: Stephen James, Humphrey Berry.
From Dorset: Joseph Manston, Matthew Clode.
Candidates, Devon: Edward Bearne, Henry Brett, Samuel Carkeet, Thomas Bishop, Hugh Brown, Henry Rutter, John Bushrod, Eliezer Hancock. Candidates, Somerset: John Short, John Talbot, Samuel Baker, Furse, Roger Beadon, James Strong.

[1]Matthew Warren, founder of the Nonconformist Academy at Taunton had died on 14th June, 1706. These were his assistants seeking approval for the continuance of this institution. Calamy, *op. cit.*,
[2]Added to his name is: " ob. Jan 13, 1707/8 ".

[fo. 152r.] Mr Walrond preach'd, Mr Cox pray'd.

Brought in to the Fund.

	£	s	d
By Mr Ball	2	3	0
By Mr Walrond	8	0	0
Given by some of the Ministers to Mr Balster	2	11	3

Ordered that Mr William Youat of Tiverton who is now a pupil to Mr Hallett have £5 per annum out of the Fund. That Mr Bond's £9 per annum be continu'd. That Mr Carkeet have the £4 per annum given to Mr Thomas Kellow.[1] The Ministers were earnestly desir'd to bring in something to the Fund.

Mr Daniel & Thomas Kellow propos'd as fit persons to be desir'd to preach to this Assembly. Mr Enty to preach next Assembly in September, or if he fail Mr Bailies. Mr Eveleigh to pray or if he fail Mr Slowly.

Resolv'd that to prevent inconveniences at Ordinations the Candidates Confession of Faith be perus'd some time before the Ordination by two at least of the Ordainers. That tis expedient that Candidates should preach sometimes privately before some ministers, where it may be done conveniently, before they enter upon publick preaching.

That the Scribe bring in to the next Assembly a copy of the Rules agreed upon to be subscrib'd by those that have not yet done it.

[fo. 153r.] Resolv'd that tis convenient for us ordinarily to administer the Lords Supper at least once in two months in our respective congregations. Upon inquiry it appear'd that the Lords Supper was administered once a month in Exon, Plymouth, and Bytheford.

Resolv'd that catechizing be kept up in our congregations, and reading the Scriptures.

Mr Henry Brett, Assistant to Mr Harding of Plymouth, propos'd himself to Ordination. Order'd that he be ordain'd at Plymouth August 20th next: by Mr Hooper, Gilling, Sandercock, Harding. His Question: An Satisfactio Christi fuit necessaria? Mr James Strong of Taunton propos'd himself to be examin'd in order to be licens'd to preach. Mr Ball, Hallet, Enty,[2] appointed to examine him reported that they found his qualifications such that they thought fit he should have the approbation of the Assembly to preach as a Candidate. This following certificate drawn up. At the Meeting of the United Brethren at Exon, May 6th, 1707: Mr James Strong of Taunton having been [fo. 154r.] this day examin'd by some of this Assembly who declar'd that they were satisfy'd with his parts learning and qualifications, the Assembly do approve of his preaching as a Candidate for the Ministry for some time until a fit opportunity present itself for his Ordination. Subscrib'd in the name and by the order of the Assembly by Nathaniel Harding, moderator, Isaac Gilling, scribe.

Edward Wordell and Abraham Follet of Sidmouth appear with a letter from Mr Coles, and desiring to have a Minister settled among them, or to be repaid the money they have spent in building the Meeting

---

[1] He had moved, in the autumn of 1706, to South Molton, an unaided church.
[2] A space was left here for another name, to complete the customary number of four ordainers.

House in that place. The following Minute drawn up and approv'd. At the Meeting of the United Brethren at Exon, May the 6th, 1707. Whereas the case of Sidmouth hath been now a 3d time laid before this Assembly, and some more papers of Sidmouth people been consider'd: tis the earnest advice of this Assembly nemine contradicente that Sidbury and Sidmouth do both join heartily together in a Meeting House [fo. 155r.] to be erected at Sidford: and that Mr Tross and Mr Hallett when they shall keep a Fast at Sidmouth, do communicate this advice to Sidmouth people, and persuade them to acquiesce therein, as what we judge is the only expedient to prevent the ruin of one if not both Meetings. Subscrib'd in the name & by the order of the Assembly. One copy given to Edward Wordel & Abraham Follett, and another to Mr Tross.

Bovey people desir'd a supply for 8 or 10 weeks until they can get another minister, Mr Bowcher being about to remove to Barnstaple. Mr Bishop & Mr Brown promis'd to supply them upon Mr James's undertaking that Plymtree Meeting should be supply'd by some of Taunton.

Order'd that Mr Carkeet go to Bodmin for one year.

Hatherly people acquaint the Assembly that they have given a Call to Mr John Bushrod of Taunton. Mr Bushrod show'd an inclination to accept of it, if he and the people can agree, and promised however to supply the place until the next Assembly.

[fo. 156r.]
EXETER, 1707, Sept. 9th & 10th. At the Meeting of the United Brethren.

[Present:] Mr John Walrond, moderator, Isaac Gilling, scribe; Mr Samuel Tapper, George Trosse, Benjamin Hooper, Joseph Hallet, William Horsham, Samuel Wood, Deliverance Larkham, John Withers, John Hughes, Ebenezer Taylor, Majendie, Henry Brett, John Ball, John Moor, Samuel Hall, Richard Evans, Jelinger Symonds, Thomas Kellow, William Giles, John Enty, John Norman, Samuel Grigg, Benjamin Wills, John Balster, Samuel Mullins, Thomas Edgeley, George Bowcher, Samuel Short, Henry Atkins, Josiah Eveleigh, John Cox, John Slowly, Nicholas Brinley, Samuel Stoddon.
Candidates: Rutter, Bond, Hugh Brown, Bishop, Walker, Samuel Carkeet, George Brett. From Somerset: Darch, Humphry Berry. Candidates: Short, Beadon.

Mr Eveleigh pray'd, Mr Enty preach'd, and was desir'd to print his sermon.

Brought in to the Fund.

						£	s	d
By Mr Eveleigh	...	...	...	...	...	9	10	0
Mr Horsham	...	...	...	...	...	3	17	0
Mr Gilling	...	...	...	...	...	2	14	0
Mr Ball	...	...	...	...	...	2	6	0
						18	7	0

Paid to Mr Balster...	...	...	...	...	3	0	0
to Mr Symonds	...	...	...	...	3	0	0
to Mr Ball for Mr Stephen Edwards			...		2	10	0
to Mr Gilling for Mr Lawrence Hext			...		5	0	0

The Assembly being inform'd of the low circumstances of Oakhampton and Bow Meetings order'd £3 out of the money brought in to the Fund for Oakhampton and £3 for Bow.

[fo. 157r.] A letter from Holsworthy to Mr Tross informing him that Mr Bond had a mind to leave them, declaring their desire that he would continue with them. Mr Bond declares that his wife is sickly and that he hath met with such things there as make him uneasy. He promis'd to stay there untill Midsummer next, if his wife's health will permit. Mr Tross & the other Exon ministers have writ to the people to exhort them punctually to pay Mr Bond his contribution.

Mr Thomas Hoore of Beaminster's letter desiring some contribution out of our Fund for Mr John Syms read.

The contributions to the Fund failing very much. The following paper to recommend it to our Hearers drawn up by Order, read & approv'd: At the Meeting of the United Ministers of Devon & Cornwall at Exon, Sept, 9th, 1707. Whereas the education of such as are to be imploy'd in the Ministry is highly necessary to the maintaining the Gospel, & propagating it unto posterity, and several young men of promising parts & good inclinations are willing to devote themselves to the service of Christ in his church whose parents are not capable of bearing the whole charge of a learned education: and whereas it appears there are some congregations who are unable to afford a competent [fo. 158r.] subsistence to their Ministers: it is the unanimous advice and desire of the Ministers now assembled, that such persons as have a due regard to the honour of Christ, and the promoting the salvation of souls would cheerfully contribute to these useful and pious designs.

A letter from Mr Bushrod of Hatherly declaring that he is willing to continue with that people one year more.

A petition from Bovey people to Mr Hugh Brown, desiring him to settle among them as their Minister, read. He promis'd to supply them for one year. The Assembly advis'd him to be Ordain'd, and desir'd him to change no oftener than need during this year. Order'd that Mr Brown be ordain'd at Moreton by Mr Tross, Hallet, Gilling, Spark, the Thursday in the Easter week, April 8th, 1708. His Question: An Paedobaptismus sit licitus?

Shoobrook people desire the Assembly to recommend a Minister to them. Mr George Brett, Mr Coppleston, & Mr Short of Taunton were propos'd.

A petition from Carolina for a Minister to be sent thither, read. Mr Darch propos'd Mr Billingsly.[1]

Mr Hallett acquainted the Assembly that he had read the order of the last Assembly at a Fast [in [2]] Sidmouth, at which Mr Coles was not

[1] He did not go, but became minister at Ashwick, Somerset 1710–40. Ebenezer Taylor left Cofton (Dawlish) in 1709 for S. Carolina, however. See Murch, *op. cit.*, p. 161, and below p. 147.
[2] The bottom of fo. 158r. is slightly damaged at this point.

present. [fo. 159r.] Mr Stoddon says that Sidmouth people threaten to bring their affair before Justices of the Peace, at the Sessions, to get their wages for building the Meeting-House. Wordell demands £7, Follett £9, Coles £40.

Upon advice that the County of Gloucester hath not held Meetings of Ministers for several years, that examinations of Candidates, & Ordinations are carried on by private hands, and that tis all things are in disorder: and that tis the desire of some of the Ministers of that county, that this Assembly would write a letter to Mr Forbes of Gloucester to encourage them to assemble. The following letter was drawn up by order of the Assembly, read, approv'd, and order'd to be sent.

At the meeting of the United Brethren of Devon & Cornwall at Exon, this 10th of September, 1707. Reverend Sir. Whereas we are credibly inform'd that for some years past there have been no stated Assemblies of Ministers in your county, which by above 16 years experience we have found to be highly advantagious for the preventing & healing of breaches, the promoting order & unity in the Churches of Christ committed to our care, and the confirming love and concord among ourselves: as also for the strict examination of candidates, and impartial proceedings in admission to the Ministry by general approbation; as well as the more regular ordination of those who have been approv'd (which experience has shewn us to have added the greater respect to their persons, & weight to their labours among their people][1]: and likewise to have contributed not a little to the allaying animosities [fo. 158v.] between Ministers & People, and between the people themselves, by hearing the complaints brought before us, and reconciling many differences. We your Brethren, Servants of the same Lord, and fellow labourers in the same work, do earnestly desire you to call upon your brethren in the Ministry of your neighbourhood and county to hold Assemblies at such times and places as shall be judged most convenient, that you may the better answer those important ends. Not doubting but you will put a favourable iterpretation upon this our request, we wish you such success as we hope, thro' the blessing of God we can say has attended us, in this work: and desiring your prayers for his presence with us in our Assemblies & ministrations, we commend you, and our Brethren with you, to his blessing. Subscrib'd in the name & by the order of the Assembly by John Walrond, moderator, Isaac Gilling, scribe. To the Reverend Mr Forbes, Minister of the Gospel in Glocester.[2]

Inquiry made how the advice of the last Assembly has been follow'd as to Catechizing, & administring the Lords Supper once in 2 months. Resolv'd that those Ministers who take turns at any Meetings inform the people that tis the advice of the Assembly that some of those who preach among them, or some neighbouring Minister administer the Lords Supper among them: & that catechizing be kept up among them. This advice to be communicated to Plymtree people by Mr Evans, to Beer People by Mr Bishop.

[1]This second bracket was omitted by Gilling.
[2]James Forbes (1629?–1712) was ejected from Gloucester Cathedral in 1660. He continued his work both under persecution, 1662-87, and afterwards, at Barton St. chapel, Gloucester. He was the most eminent minister of his neighbourhood. *Calamy Revised*, ed. A. G. Matthews.

Orderd nemine contradicente that none of the Brethren withdraw from the Assembly before the conclusion of each session without leave first obtain'd from the Assembly.

Resolvd. That in cases of discipline which are difficult tis convenient for young ministers especially to desire the advice & assistance of their Brethren.

Next Assembly the 1st Tuesday & Wednesday in May, Mr Bailies to preach, if he fail Mr Thomas Kellow. Mr Slowly to pray, if he fail Mr Bartlett.

[fo. 157v., reversed.]
EXETER, 1708, May 4th. At the Meeting of the United Brethren.

[Present:] Mr Deliverance Larkham, moderator, Mr Josiah Eveleigh, scribe; Mr George Tross, John Balster, Benjamin Hooper, Joseph Hallet, Isaac Gilling, Jacob Sandercock, John Moor, John Withers, John Walrond, Jacob Bailies, John Ball, William Horsham, Powel, Richard Evans, Jellinger Symonds, Humphry Berry (Somerset), Samuel Short, George Bowcher, Henry Atkins, John Sloly, William Giles, Samuel Grigg, John Norman, William Palk, Benjamin Wills, Majendie, William Bartlett, Joseph Manston, Ebenezer Taylor, Peter Baron, Matthew Hody, John Stoddon, Samuel Stoddon, Jaspar How, Henry Brett, Hugh Brown. Candidates: Hugh Goffe, Lobb, John Bushrod, Thomas Bishop, Eleazar Hancock, Samuel Carkeet, Cornelius Bond.
From Somerset: Candidates: John Short, John Coppleston.

Brought in to the Fund.

	£	s	d
By Mr Walrond	8	0	0
Mr Gilling	4	15	0
Mr Horsham	3	0	0
Mr Ball	2	0	0
Paid Mr Gilling for Mr Lawrence Hext	2	10	0
Mr Walrond for Philip Moor	1	1	6
Mr Ball for Stephen Edwards	2	10	0

Mr Baron reports that Mr Enty's Congregation contribute £6 per annum to John Geby[1] for his education. Order that Mr Cornelius Bond who had £9 per annum whilst be continu'd at Holdsworthy, having left that people be struck out of the Fund. That the following sums be continu'd.

	£	s	d
To Mr Balster, per annum	2	10	0
To Plimtree Meeting	3	0	0
To Holdsworthy Meeting	4	0	0
To Mr Symonds	2	10	0

[fo. 156v., reversed] A petition of Dr Henry Lewis Nagel, complaining of deep poverty.

[1]Sic. This probably should be " Greby ".

A petition from the people of Holdsworthy desiring a Minister in the room of Mr Bond, and for assistance out of the Fund. Resolved that another Minister be got for them if possible, and that they have £4 per annum out of the Fund.

A petition from Okehampton for some help for Mr Balster. Resolv'd that he have £2 10s out of the Fund continu'd. That Mr Symonds £2 10s out of the Fund be continu'd, and his and Mr Balsters contribution be augmented next Assembly, if possible.

Resolv'd that a particular request be deliver'd to every Minister and his congregation to raise something yearly for the Fund.

Mr Walrond informs the Assembly that he had received a thankful answer from Mr Forbes of Gloucester to the letter sent to him & the Gloucestershire Ministers by the last Assembly.

A petition from several of the parish of Budleigh remonstrating the condition of their parish, and desiring the Assembly to recommend a Minister to them. Mr Roger Beadon was recommended to them.

Mr Goff and Mr Lob desire ordination. Order'd that they be ordain'd at St. Ives in Cornwal by Mr Sandercock, Enty, Daniel Kellow, July, 1708. Mr Goff's question: An S. Scriptura sit perspicua et perfecta fidei et morum regula? Mr Lob's question: An Christus sit $\Theta\epsilon\alpha\nu\Theta\rho\omega\pi\circ\varsigma$?[1]

A petition from Buckril[2] for help from the Fund, refer'd to next Assembly, because of the poverty of the Fund.

William Henery, being able to speak Welsh, recommended to be educated for the Ministry, in order to be sent back to Wales. Mr Hallett, Gilling, Sandercock, Baron order'd to examine him: report that he appeard tolerably well skill'd in the Latine tongue, and that he understood somewhat of the Greek. [fo. 155v., reversed] The Assembly thought him fit to be encourag'd, to be educated for the Ministry: and the Fund being low, some Ministers, and others promis'd to contribute something yearly towards his education.

The Moderator, by order of the Assembly, return'd thanks to Mr Baylys for preaching, & Mr Sloly for praying, before the Assembly. Order'd that Mr Thomas Kellow of S. Moulton preach before the next Assembly, and if he fail Mr Daniel Kellow of Foy. [Mr Thomas Kellow dy'd the latter end of May, 1708.][3] That Mr Joseph Manston pray, and if he fail, Mr William Bartlett.
[Out of Mr Eveleigh's Minutes.][3]

[fo. 155v., reversed]
EXETER, 1708, Sept. 7th & 8th. At the Meeting of the United Brethren of Devon and Cornwall.

[Present:] Mr George Tross, moderator, Isaac Gilling, scribe; Joseph Hallett, Deliverance Larkham, William Horsham, Jacob Sandercock, Samuel Wood, John Moor, John Withers, Samuel Hall, Richard Evans, John Ball, Jelinger Symonds, Daniel Kellow, John Walrond, Thomas Edgeley, George Bowcher, Samuel Short, Henry Atkins, John Cox,

[1]Theanthropos is literally "God-Man". Christ was so described often in 18th century theology. See this word in *New English Dictionary*.
[2]Buckerell.
[3]These words were underlined in the MS.

Josiah Eveleigh, John Slowly, William Bartlett, Ebenezer Taylor, Joseph Manston, John Stoddon, Samuel Stoddon, Hugh Brown, Majendie. Candidates: Thomas Bishop, Cornelius Bond, Bushrod, Roger Beadon, Samuel Carkeet, Rutter. From Somerset, Ministers: Stephen James, Humphrey Berry. Candidates: Eleazar Hancock, Strong, Standard, Cornish.

Brought in to the Fund.

						£	s	d
Mr Eveleigh	...	...	...	...	...	9	2	6
Mr Samuel Stoddon		...	...	...	...	4	7	6
Mr Horsham	...	...	...	...	...	2	4	0
Mr John Stoddon ...		...	...	...	...	2	0	0
Mr Ball ...	...	...	...	...	...	1	14	0
						19	8	0

	£	s	d
Paid Mr Ball for Stephen Edwards Michaelmas Quarter	2	10	0
Mr Eveleigh for William Henery	1	1	6
Given by the Ministers present to Monsieur Brial, a Minister at Bideford	3	0	0

[fo. 154v., reversed] Order'd that if the Fund will bear it Mr Coulton's son have £5 per annum and William Henry £2. But if the Fund will permit of but £5 in all then Mr Coulton £4 and Mr Henry £1.

Mr Bennet Stephenson[1] offers himself to be examin'd in order to have the approbation of the Assembly to preach. Mr Ball, Hall, and Withers who were order'd to examine him, report that they find him a very good scholar. The following certificate drawn up and given him. Exon, Sept. 8th, 1708. Mr Bennet Stephenson being examin'd by persons deputed for that purpose: it is order'd by the Assembly that he have leave to preach upon the report of the examiners that he is well qualify'd. Subscrib'd in the name & by the order of the Assembly of the United Brethren of Devon & Cornwall by George Tross, moderator, Isaac Gilling, scribe.

Mr John Stoddon of Ashburton declares that Mr Tozer will no longer entertain him, and that none else in this town can but Mr John Goswell.

Thanks given to Mr Joseph Manston for praying, and Mr Daniel Kellow for preaching, and he desir'd to print his sermon.

Mr William Day and Edward Knight of South Molton inform the Assembly that Mr Rutter who hath preach'd some time there since Mr Thomas Kellows death, doth not give satisfaction: that they cannot profit by him; that he is not popular, nor lively, that he doth not rouse them. [fo. 153v., reversed] Mr Rutter informs the Assembly that on Monday last he had sent for some of the people, advising them to apply themselves to the Assembly for another minister: but that they would not be satisfy'd without him, he having a vast majority, there being about 50 for him, 15 against him. Mr Rutters friends desire the advice of the Assembly what to do. Whether tis fit for them on such a majority to give

[1]Here inserted in shorthand above the line is " tutor to Sir W. Judson ".

him a Call. Mr Thorn & 4 others declar'd that there are 10 or more families against Mr Rutter; that their subscriptions amount to near £8 per annum. That tho' they are very desirous of Mr Rutter, yet are loth to have a breach made in the congregation. The objections against Mr Rutter appear'd to be very weak, and trivial. Resolv'd, nemine contradicente, that whilst Mr Rutter is of so clear a character, and the objections against him are so trivial, it is the opinion of this Assembly, that the minor part of the congregation of South Molton ought to have comply'd with the major in an unanimous call to Mr Rutter. Resolv'd, that it be left to Mr Rutter whether he will go to South Molton or not. Whereas Mr Rutter hath voluntarily quitted his interest in the people of S. Molton, (foreseeing some difficulties that may probably ensue on his going thither],[1] the Assembly recommend to them Mr Hancock, Mr Coppleston, and Mr Walker, as fit persons to settle among them; earnestly desiring them to be unanimous in their [fo. 152v., reversed] choice of one of these, or some other fit person. Both parties heartily and thankfully acquiesc'd in the advice of the Assembly.

Mr Coles and Edward Worden of Sidmouth desire a Minister. They say they can raise £20 per annum. Mr Serle and Mr Stoddon of Sidbury produce Mr Samuel Stoddon's Deeds by which he settled the new Meeting House at Sidmouth on them, and his account of receipts for it, and disbursements about it. Viz:

	£	s	d
Received	102	1	1½
Laid out	198	11	8
Paid Mr Coles	16	0	0
Laid out in all	214	11	8
More than received	112	10	7½

Mr Coles' account of receipts.

	£	s	d
By memory	141	18	6
Mr Stoddon promised to give	50	0	0

Propos'd to Mr Coles whether they will give £50 for the Meeting House & Dwelling House, provided they use it for a Meeting House: if not that it return to the Trustees.

Mr Peter Kellow to preach next Assembly in May, or if he fail, Mr Samuel Mullins. Mr William Bartlett to pray, if he fail, Mr John Hughes.

[fo. 151v., reversed.]
EXETER, 1709, May 3rd & 4th. At the Meeting of the United Brethren of Devon and Cornwall.

[Present:] Isaac Gilling, moderator, Thomas Edgly, scribe; John Balster, Benjamin Hooper, Joseph Hallet, William Horsham, Jacob Sandercock,

---

[1]This second bracket was omitted by Gilling.

Samuel Wood, John Moor, Deliverance Larkham, John Withers, Samuel
Hall, Richard Evans, Michael Martyn, John Ball, Jelinger Symonds,
Peter Kellow, William Giles, Samuel Short, Henry Atkins, John Cox,
Josiah Eveleigh, John Slowly, John Norman, Ebenezer Taylor, Jaspar
How, Samuel Grigg, William Palk, Benjamin Wills, John Stoddon,
Hugh Brown, Lobb, Majendie, Joseph Manston, Wheeler.
Candidates: Coppleston, Roger Beadon, Walker, Samuel Bishop, Samuel
Carkeet, Darricot, Eliezer Hancock, Benjamin Flavel, Furse.
Ministers of Somerset & Dorset: Stephen James, Cornish, Bernard Banjer,
Humphry Berry, Theophilus Lobb of Shaftesbury.
Candidates: James Strong, Groves, Standard, Batesby.

[fo. 150v., reversed.] Brought in to the Fund.

	£	s	d
Mr Ball	2	0	0
Mr Walrond sent	5	7	6
Given by Mr Weeks	12	10	0
James' Meeting	8	5	0
Mr Horsham	3	9	8
Bow Meeting	2	9	0
Mr Hallet of the money brought in September 1708	19	8	0
	53	9	2
[Paid out now]	32	6	6
	21	2	8

	£	s	d
Paid, to Mr Ball for Mr Edwards to Lady Day ...	2	10	0
Mr Hallet paid Mr Edwards for Michaelmas & Christmas	5	0	0
Mr Eveleigh for Mr Henry	1	1	6
Mr Savage, Christmas & Lady Day	2	10	0
Mr Coulton, Christmas & Lady Day	2	10	0
Mr Youat	8	15	0
Mr Gilling for Mr Hext, 1 year	5	0	0
Mr Symonds, Lady Day	2	10	0
Mr Wood paid Mr Balster, Lady Day	2	10	0
	32	6	6

The present charge of the Fund

	£	s	d
Mr Stephen Edwards	10	0	0
Mr Youat	5	0	0
Mr Coulton	5	0	0
Mr Hext	5	0	0
Mr Angel Shapland	10	0	0
Mr Savage's son	5	0	0
Scholars, per annum	40	0	0

Mr Grigg, Kingskerswel ...	...	...	...	4	0	0
Mr Carkeet, Bodmin	...	...	...	4	0	0
Holdsworthy Meeting	...	...	...	4	0	0
Mr Balster, Oakhampton ...	...	...	...	2	10	0
Mr Symonds, Bow ...	...	...	...	2	10	0
Plymtree Meeting ...	...	...	...	3	0	0
Ministers and Meetings per annum	...	...		20	0	0

A letter from Buckril, another from Ufculm desiring help from the Fund. Buckril can raise but £21 7s 0d, Ufculm but £26, Kings Kerswell but £17. Ufculm people desire that tho' the Fund will not at present afford anything for their Meeting they may be consider'd as soon as it will.

[fo. 149v., reversed] Angel Shapland of Crediton was examin'd by Mr Hallet, Hall, Larkham, Eveleigh, as to his parts & progress in grammar learning: upon their report that he deserv'd to be encourag'd, order'd that Angel Shapland have £10 per annum out of the Fund, if Crediton contributions amount to that sum.

Order'd that Mr. Hallet, Hall, Larkham, Eveleigh, examine Mr George Hallet & Mr Webber, two of Mr Hallet's pupils. The examiners declaring themselves well satify'd in their learning & qualifications, and they having promis'd the Assembly to be ordain'd in a short time after they are constant preachers, and have a call to the Pastoral Office, the following Certificates given them. At the Meeting of the United Brethren of Devon & Cornwal at Exon, May the 4th, 1709. Mr George Hallet having been this day examin'd by some of this Assembly deputed for that purpose, upon the report of his examiners that he is well qualify'd: order'd that he have leave to preach as a Candidate for the Ministry for some time until a fit opportunity present for his ordination. Subscrib'd in the name and by the order of the Assembly, etc. etc.,

Order'd that Mr Roger Beadon be ordaind by Mr Hooper, Ball, Walrond, Withers, Manston. The time to be fix'd by himself. His Question: An Christus sit Deus ab aeterno, against the Arrians. His text: Acts 20;28. Feed the Church of God which he hath purchased with his own blood.

[fo. 148v., reversed] Edward Worden of Sidmouth presents a petition to the Assembly. Order'd that Mr Walrond be desir'd to consider his petition and to do him justice.

The following letter drawn up, read, approv'd & order'd to be sent. Exon, the 3rd of May, 1709. Sir: The Ministers now assembled earnestly desire that if it stand with your convenience you would be pleas'd to take upon you the trouble of keeping an account of what is brought into & paid out of our Fund, in the room of Mr Thomas Wood who hath for many years done it with much fidelity, but is now incapacitated by reason of age. Subscrib'd, etc. To Mr John Pym, merchant.

A letter from South Molton desiring Mr Hancock might be settled there to prevent a new breach in that Congregation, he being unanimously chosen. Mr John Atkins of Exon & Mr Pardew of Penzance appear in the behalf of the Congregation at Penzance who also earnestly desire Mr Hancock for their Minister, in the room of Mr Lobb who has left them. They inform the Assembly that he was invited to Penzance 3 years

ago. That they thought he [fo. 147v., reversed] had given them encouragement to hope that he would settle among them. That no other person
could be thought on so proper as he. On the other hand Mr Hancock
being recommended to South Molton by the last Assembly, and that
people having given him an unanimous call, and he referring himself to
the Assembly, the following Minute was drawn up and approv'd.
Exon, May 4th, 1709: The Ministers now assembled having consider'd
Mr Hancock's call to South Molton, and heard some in behalf of Penzance
who also earnestly desir'd him for their Minister; after mature deliberation gave him their advice to accept of the call to South Molton. This
is a true account of the opinion and advice of the Assembly.

Mr Strong at the desire of the Assembly promis'd to go to Gunrownson[1] in Cornwall, and continue there upon trial for some time.

Exon, May 4th, 1709. These are to certify whom it may concern
that Mr John Copplestone at the earnest desire of the Assembly promis'd
to go to Penzance for some time, but declar'd that he had no inclination
to settle among that people, but only to preach to them for some months,
that they may endeavour to get another to fix with them.

[fo. 146v., reversed] Upon complaint that some candidates who are
settled and constant preachers to particular congregations, and are called
to the Pastoral Office, defer their Ordination, whence several inconveniences proceed, viz: some children die unbaptiz'd, Dissenters are
forc'd to carry their children to the Publick Churches to have them
baptiz'd, etc. Resolv'd that for the future no Licence be given to any to
preach before they have promis'd before the Assembly to offer themselves
to be ordained in a short time after they are constant preachers and have
a call to take the Pastoral Charge of some particular congregation. Mr
Furse, Hancock, Carkeet, and Bishop were advis'd to be ordain'd, and to
apply themselves to the next Assembly for that end. Propos'd that
ordinarily no person be Licens'd to preach till he be 22 years of age.

Mr Bartlett and Mr Hughes who were appointed to pray, both
fail'd. Mr Norman was prevaild upon to pray. Thanks to Mr Peter
Kellow for preaching and Mr Norman for praying. Order'd that Mr
Mullins or if he fail Mr Edgly preach, Mr Hughes or if he fail Mr Bartlet
pray next Assembly.

[fo. 145v., reversed] The following paper drawn up by Mr Eveleigh.
Whereas in order to the compleat settlement of the peace of South Molton
happily united in the choice of Mr Hancock, it is desir'd that something
be said by this Assembly relating to the conduct of the Messengers of
that Church to the last Assembly. We declare it our opinion that they
behaved themselves like impartial faithful men. This paper was a long
time debated, and at length the signing it rejected by a great majority,
who thought it neither needful nor proper for the Assembly to make
such a declaration.

Mr Evans, Hallet, etc., desir'd leave to depart before the conclusion
of the Assembly, which was granted.

[1]Gunrownson or Goon Rounson is in the parish of St. Enoder, Cornwall. Henry Flamank
ejected Rector of Lanivet, seems to have begun a society there, licensed 1672. He
moved to Tavistock c.1697, and his place was taken by his elder brother Roger
Flamank, ejected Vicar of Sithney, Cornwall, who died in December, 1708, a few
months before this Assembly. It was a very small cause. *Calamy Revised*, ed. Matthews.

Question whether Licenses should be granted to any to preach who are not in Communion with some Church.

[fo. 144 v., reversed]

EXETER, 1709, Sept. 6th & 7th. At the Meeting of the United Brethren of Devon and Cornwall.

[Present:] Mr John Enty, moderator, Isaac Gilling, scribe; Mr Tross, Balster, Hooper, Hallet, Horsham, Sandercock, Samuel Wood, Harding, Moore, Larkham, Ball, Evans, Giles, Mullins, Walrond, Eveleigh, Cox, Sloly, Short, Atkins, Hughes, Norman, Hody, Grigg, Glanvil, Robert Wood, Wills, John Stoddon, Brinly, Manston, Wheeler, Samuel Stoddon, Brown, Beadon, Majendie. 36.[1] Candidates: Bishop, Furze, Isaac Clark, Hancock, Flavel, Coppleston, Hornabrook. From Somerset: Mr Humphry Berry. Candidates: James Cornish, Henry Webber. Mr Chorley of Norwich.

Thanks given to Mr Mullins for preaching and Mr Hughes for praying, & keeping time. Mr Edgley to preach next Assembly, or if he fail, Mr Giles. Mr Bartlet to pray, if he fail Mr How.

[fo. 143v., reversed] Brought in to the Fund.

						£	s	d
Mr Eveleigh	...	...	...	...	...	8	0	2
Mr Gilling ...	...	...	...	...	...	2	12	4
Mr Horsham	...	...	...	...	...	2	10	0
Paid: To Mr Eveleigh for Mr Shapland				...		2	0	0
Mr Gilling for Mr Hext, ½ a year ending at Michaelmas	...	...	...	...	...	2	10	0

Orderd that Stephen Edwards be paid 20s and Mr Savages son 50s now, & then both be struck out of the Fund. That Mr Bond who is settled in Dorsetshire have £3 out of the Fund to pay for removing his Goods. That Ufculm, Hatherly, & Buckrel Meetings have each 40s for one year, and Kings Kerswel an addition of 40s for one year.

Ordinations. Mr Walter Furse of Chulmleigh, Mr Thomas Bishop of Shoobrook, Mr[2]Hancock of South Molton, and Mr Benjamin Flavel of Holdsworthy desire to be Ordain'd. Order'd that Mr Furse, Hancock & Flavel be ordain'd at South Molton or Chulmleigh by Mr Hooper, Hallet, Hall, Sandercock & Eveleigh. And at Mr Furse's desire 'twas permitted that Mr Moor of Bridgwater might also be one of his Ordainers, tho' none of our Counties. The Ordainers and Ordained to agree upon time & place.

[fo. 141v., reversed] Hatherly people want a minister. Mr Brown with them at present, designs to leave them. They say they have about about 150 Hearers, near 50 communicants. They raise about £15 per annum themselves, and have about £9 per annum more. Order'd that Mr Manston write to Taunton to endeavour to get Mr Hamlyn to go to Hatherly, the answer to be given to Mr Tross.

[1]There were actually 37 ordained ministers. Majendie's name was added at the end of the list.
[2]A space was left here for his Christian name, Eliezer.

Mr Hony Church of Penzance desires the Assembly to recommend a Minister to the Meeting in that place, Mr Coppleston who went thither at the request of the last Assembly having left them. They raise about £30 per annum, & hope to get something from London. About 150 or 200 Hearers, 30 communicants. Mr Cornish & Mr Webber desir'd to go thither declin'd it. Mr George Brett of Lupton promis'd to go thither.

A letter from Cofton Meeting desiring Mr Brown to supply them, upon Mr Ebenezer Taylor's leaving them (who is said to be going for Carolina). Mr Brown promis'd to supply that Meeting for a while.

[fo. 140v., reversed] Mr Bishop to be ordain'd at Topsham by Mr Ball, Gilling, Horsham, Withers, Walrond, at Christmas. Their Questions[1]:

Mr Furse's: An Ordinatio per Presbyteros sit valida?
Mr Bishop's: An officium Apostolicum sit perpetuum?
Mr Hancock's: An detur Peccatum Originale?
Mr Flavel's: An Dies Dominicus sit moralis?

Resolved N.C. that no person be licens'd to preach who is not in full communion. That for the future particular inquiry be made into the prudence and conduct as well as the learning & piety of persons to be ordain'd.

That no poor scholars have any contributions out of the Fund but such as appear to the Assembly, or some deputed by the Assembly to examine them, to have pregnant parts, and to be serious, and well inclin'd.

Order'd that Mr Gilling transcribe the Rules for regulating our Meetings, and all other Rules relating to general practice, and bring in a Copy to the next Assembly, to be perus'd, in order to subscription.

Agreed that tis expedient that only Davids Psalms, & Scriptural Hymns, be ordinarily us'd in our publick assemblies for religious worship.

[fo. 139v., reversed] Edward Worden & [2] of Sidmouth desire the Assembly to use their indeavours to persuade Mr Stoddon's trustees to let them have the new Meeting House there. The following paper drawn up, read, approv'd, subscribd & deliver'd to Mr Walrond. Exon, Sept. 7, 1709. The Ministers now assembled desire Mr Ball, Mr Walrond, and Mr Manston to discourse Mr Serle & Mr Stoddon, Trustees to Mr Samuel Stoddon deceas'd, and to dispose them to settle the Meeting House at Sidmouth on Trustees, to be us'd as a place of Religious Assemblies by the Dissenting Protestants of Sidmouth, since it appears to us that Sidbury people resolve to fix their place of Meeting in Sidbury Town. Subscrib'd in the name & by the order of the Assembly.

Order'd that Mr Hooper, Hallet, Withers, & Norman inspect Mr Thomas Wood's Book & Papers relating to the Fund, adjust his accounts, & pay in the money in Mr Wood's hand to Mr Pym the present Receiver.

Question: Whether the consent of 2 persons to take each other as Man & Wife, without a declaration of this consent before competent wittnesses, be lawful marriage according to the 7th Commandment. Negatived.

Sept. 6, 1709. Mr Pym has of the Fund money, £28 17s 8½d.

[1] i.e. all those to be ordained.
[2] Blank in MS.

[fo. 138v., reversed]
EXETER, 1710, May 9th & 10th. At the Meeting of the United Brethren
of Devon and Cornwall.

[Present:] Mr Joseph Manston, moderator, Isaac Gilling, scribe; Mr Tross,
Hallet, Horsham, Sandercock, Samuel Wood, Harding, Walsh, Moor,
Larkham, Withers, Ball, Evans, Martyn, Symonds, Peter Kellow, Giles,
Enty, Mullins, Edgeley, Walrond, Bowcher, Short, Atkins, Cox, Eveleigh,
Slowly, Norman, Baron, Hody, Grigg, Glanvil, Palk, Wills, How,
Stoddon, Wheeler, Brown, Beadon, Bishop. 41. Candidates: Furse,
Bond, Carkeet, Strong, Copplestone, Flavel, Walker, Hancock, Edmonds,
Coulton. 10. From Somerset: James, Berry, Rabjent. Candidates:
Bernard Banjer, Lissant, Darracot.   57.

Thanks given to Mr Edgley for preaching & to Mr Baron for praying,
Mr How being much tir'd with his journey, on his desire was excus'd
from praying.

Brought in to the Fund.

						£	s	d
Mr Walrond	...	...	...	...	...	5	7	6
Mr Horsham	...	...	...	...	...	2	9	0
Mr Ball	...	...	...	...	...	1	13	0

Resolv'd that Zachary Mudg[1] whom Mr Tross recommends as an
excellent grammar scholar, and very serious, have £10 per annum out of
the Fund. He is now with Mr Hallet.

[fo. 137v., reversed] A petition of Edward Worden of Sidmouth
desiring the Assembly to consider his poor and mean circumstances.

Some of the Meeting of Bovey-Tracy appear, declaring that they
were under a necessity to purchase the land of their Meeting house,
which cost them £90, and that they must make an addition to it, their
Meeting increasing, which would cost them about £30 more. That they
would themselves contribute about £40. The following ministers ingag'd
for the following sums. Mr Harding 30s., Mr Enty 20s., Mr Walrond 20s.,
Mr Manston, Horsham, Edgley, Mullins, Bishop, Larkham, Atkins,
Norman, Wheeler, 10s. apiece. Mr Ball 20s. Mr Moor, Sandercock,
Evans, Wills no certain sum.

Budleigh people desir'd the Assembly to recommend their case and
petition to the London Fund. Exon, May 10, 1710. Reverend Sirs,
The United Brethren of Devon & Cornwall now assembled having perus'd
this petition do judg that the petitioners have truly represented their case;
and therefore desire you to take it into consideration. Subscribd, [etc.,]
by Joseph Manston, moderator, I. G., scribe.

[fo. 136v., reversed] A letter from Mr Ebenezer Taylor[2] in South
Carolina, giving an account of the coming away of Mr Joseph Boon, Mr
George Smith, Mr Fenwick, & Mr Nairn, and mentioning some names of
Parliament men: 'twas thought not proper to be read out in our Assembly.

[1]He later became Headmaster of Bideford Grammar School, and, after conforming,
    Vicar of St. Andrew's, Plymouth. In Sept., 1746, he paid to the Assembly £52 10s
    " as a grateful return for what he had formerly received ". *Trans. Devon. Assoc.*,
    1897, xxix, pp. 86–94.
[2]Formerly at Ashburton and Cofton.

Mr Edward Coulton who has been with Mr Hallet about 4 years, and is 22 years of age, propos'd himself to be examin'd, & was examin'd by Mr Harding, Walrond, Gilling; who reported their being satisfy'd with his qualifications, on which the Assembly gave him their permission to preach in order to Ordination.

Mr Hody having left Plymton, and being unwilling to return thither again, tho' at present without any invitation to fix elsewhere; the Assembly advis'd Mr Edmonds to go thither for some time.

Mr How desir'd the advice of the Assembly whether 'twere proper to bring the Meeting of Penryn to Falmouth, it being there wholly heretofore. About half the communicants are inhabitants in or about Penryn, who are very unwilling to have the meeting house kept wholly at Falmouth. [fo. 135v., reversed] The Assembly upon the representation made them, advis'd Mr How to continue for a while to preach as formerly.

One whose parents were Baptists, and whose Baptism ('tis well known) was upon that account omitted for a considerable time; yet cannot tell whether she was baptiz'd afterwards or not. Question, whether this person should be admitted to the Sacrament of the Lords Supper before she is baptiz'd? If not, what method is to be taken in Baptizing her? Exon, May 10, 1710. The Ministers now assembled think it not adviseable to admit this person to the Lords Supper without being baptiz'd; and advise the Minister to use words to this effect before baptism. I take it for granted that thou art not Baptiz'd, and therefore N. I baptise thee, etc.

Unordain'd preachers were earnestly press'd to be ordain'd. Mr Strong & Mr Carkeet consented to be ordain'd between this and the next Assembly. The Ordainers, Mr Halsey, Harding, Enty, Baron, Sandercock, Martyn, Daniel Kellow, & Horsham. They & the Ordainers to appoint time and place. [fo. 134v., reversed] Mr Walker to be ordain'd with Mr Hancock Furse, and Flavel. They & the ordainers to fix time & place. The Ordination to be between this & the next Assembly. Mr Isaac Clark agrees that the Assembly shall fix the time for his ordination at their next Meeting. Mr Copplestone to be ordain'd. Mr Carkeet's Question: An Ordinatio per Presbyteros sit valida? Mr Strong's: An Secessio nostra ab Ecclesia Anglicana sit schismatica? Mr Clark's: An Dies Dominicus sit moralis? Mr Copplestone's: An mors Christi sit sacrificium stricte propitiatorium? Mr Walker's: An Christus sit verus et supremus Deus?

One of the Brethren, Mr Ball, spake with much warmth against Ministers wearing long light powder'd wigs, as that which gives great offence to serious people, and is a great hindrance to the success of our Ministry. [The persons who gave this offence were Parr and Huxham.][1]

Thanks given to Mr Withers for the pains he hath taken to vindicate the Dissenting Cause.[2]

[fo. 133v., reversed] Mr Gilling according to the Order of the last Assembly brought in an Abstract of all the Rules relating to General Practice which have come to his knowledge at the several meetings of the

---

[1] This is a note in thicker ink, possibly not in Gilling's hand, at the bottom of the page.
[2] He had been in controversy with the Rector of St. Mary Arches, Exeter, a Mr Agate. His chief pamphlet was *Truth Try'd, or Mr Agate's pretended truth proved an untruth.* (1708).

United Brethren of Devon & Cornwall from March 17th & 18th 1690/1 to this time, which were read & approv'd. Resolv'd that the following words be added to the Rule about fixing ministers:
—first offering his reasons for so doing to the next Assembly, if there be any within two months: or, if not, to some of the neighbouring ministers; and that he have the approbation of four, at least, of them, under their hands, who are to give an account of it to the next Assembly.

Tis the advice of the Assembly that Ministers should acquaint their people, that they judg it generally expedient that children be baptiz'd in publick; and that they endeavour to persuade their people to bring their children into the publick congregation to be there baptiz'd.

Resolv'd that the Moderator declare to all candidates to be licens'd to preach that they be responsible to the Assembly that licenses them for the orthodoxy of their doctrine, and the regular conduct of their lives.

[fo. 132v., reversed] Mr Giles to preach next Assembly, if he fail Mr Martyn, Mr Bartlet to pray, if he fail Mr How, Mr Evans to be Moderator.

Can: LXXII, Ecclesiae Africanae.[1] Item placuit de Infantibus, quoties non inveniuntur certissimi Testes, qui eos baptizatos esse sine dubitatione testentur, neque ipsi sunt per aetatem de traditis sibi sacramentis idonei respondere, absque ullo scrupulo eos esse baptizandos.[2]

Synodica luce Patriarchae Constantinop. Cap: XII, ibidem statuit Tales ὀφείλειν Baptizari quod nesciant, an in Infantia fuerint Baptizati, nec ulli inveniantur, qui Baptismum affirment.[3]

Mr Edward Coulton having proposd himself to the Assembly of the United Brethren of Devon & Cornwall at Exon, May 9th & 10th, 1710 to be examind; and his examiners reporting that they were satisfy'd as to his qualifications; the Assembly gave him their permission to preach in order to his Ordination. This is attested by Joseph Manston, moderator, Isaac Gilling, scribe.

[fo. 131 v., reversed]
EXETER, 1710, Sept. 5th & 6th. At the Meeting of the United Brethren of Devon & Cornwall.

[Present:] Mr Richard Evans, moderator, Isaac Gilling, scribe; Mr Tross, Balster, Hooper, Hallet, Horsham, Moor, Samuel Wood, Withers, Ball, Larkham, Symonds, Martyn, Walrond, Edgley, Short, Atkins, Cox, Eveleigh, Enty, Slowly, Majendie, John Stoddon, Samuel Stoddon, Hughes, Giles, Hody, Bartlet, Norman, Manston, Robert Wood, Wills, Brett,[4] Bowcher, Hancock, Wheeler, Brown, Bret,[4] Bishop, Lissant. Mr Thomas Rowe of London.

[1]These are rulings of the Early Church relevant to the problem discussed above at this meeting whether a person whose original baptism is not proved should be baptized afresh.
[2]Translation. It is satisfactory concerning infants, when sure witnesses are not to be found who can unhesitatingly testify that they have been baptized, and when they themselves are not of an age to answer concerning sacraments administered to them, that they ought, without any scruple, to be baptized.
[3]Translation. Legislates that such ought to be baptized when they do not know whether they have been baptized in infancy and when none can be found who can affirm that they have been baptized. The exact source of Gilling's quotation has not been identified.
[4]This name definitely occurs twice, with different spelling.

Candidates: Isaac Clark, John Greby, Stevenson, Edmonds, Webber, Darracot, Coulton, Bond.

Thanks given to Mr Giles who preach'd and Mr Bartlet who pray'd.

Brought in to the Fund.

						£	s	d
Mr Eveleigh	...	...	...	...	...	8	1	0
Mr Manston	...	...	...	...	...	3	16	0
Mr Horsham	...	...	...	...	...	2	2	6
Mr Ball	...	...	...	...	...	1	16	6
Paid Mr Gilling for Mr Hext	...	...	...			5	0	0
To Budleigh Meeting out of Mr Manston's money							15	0

Order'd that Mr Grigg have £5 given him at present besides the £4 per annum formerly granted him. That the 40s per annum to Buckrel Ufculm and Hatherly Meetings be continu'd. That Mr Balster who had formerly £26 per annum at Oakhampton & now has not above £14 or £15 have £5 for one year out of the Fund. [fo. 130v., reversed] Tis the general sense of the Assembly that we cannot afford any contribution out of the Fund to the Meeting at Sidmouth.

Brought in for Bovey Meeting House.

						£	s	d
Mr Harding	...	...	...	...	...	1	10	0
Mr Enty	...	...	...	...	...	1	10	0
Mr Ball	...	...	...	...	...	1	0	0
Mr Hughes (not paid)	...	...	...	...	1	3	6
Mr Atkins ...	...	...	...	...	...		16	0
Mr Larkham	...	...	...	...	...		10	0
Mr Bishop ...	...	...	...	...	...		10	0
Mr Manston	...	...	...	...	...		10	0
						7	9	6

Mr Bartlet promised to propose Bovey Meeting House to his people. Mr Eveleigh can do nothing.

Mr Alexander Stephenson a North Brittain who hath liv'd about Bristol & Manchester, & was ordain at Manchester, had 20s given him by the Ministers, but having no certificate from the Bristol Ministers was not admitted to be present at our debates.

Mr Carkeet & Mr Strong ordaind at Bodmyn July 19th, 1710. Mr Hancock, Furse & Benjamin Flavel ordain'd at South Molton, Aug. 23, 1710. Mr Isaac Clark to be ordain'd at Christmas, by Mr Ball, Walrond, Manston and Horsham. His Question: An secessio nostra ab Ecclesia Anglicana sit schismatica?

Mr Slowly proposes Richard Milford's son of Thorverton to the Fund desiring £4 per annum. The following question put whether [1] Milford provided when he is examin'd he be approv'd shall have four pounds per annum out of the Fund? Negative. [fo. 129v., reversed] Resolv'd that it is not proper, under our present circumstances, to take in any more young

[1] A space was left for his Christian name, Richard.

men upon the Fund, whose parents can contribute little or nothing towards their education, while we have so considerable a number already educated, and under Tutors; and no vacant places for several who are already ingag'd in the work of the Ministry.

Inquiry made into the reasons of Mr Bond's leaving Sandwich[1] in the Isle of Purbeck. The Moderator told him, that he had by his carriage given great scandal, etc. And advis'd him, to be more careful of his conduct for the future.

Mr Martyn to preach next Assembly; if he fail Mr Symonds. Mr How to pray, if he fail, Mr Palk.

[fo. 174r., reversed.[2]] *Tottness, September, 1710. To Mr Webber. We whose names are hereunto subscribed members and delegates of a congregation of dissenting Protestants in Tottness being, by the wise and just providence of Almighty God, to our great sorrow deprived of our worthy and dearly beloved Pastor Reverend Mr Samuel Mullins, though through the divine goodness we have not been left altogether destitute since his decease, but have had weekly supplies, yet knowing that it is our duty to make choice of a fixed minister to instruct us and watch for our souls, and God having brought you among us whose labours we have enjoyed with good satisfaction, we therefore apply ourselves to you earnestly desiring you to come and settle among us as our Pastor, to administer all the ordinances of Christ to us. And if it shall please God to incline your heart to comply with this our desire, we trust our subjection to the Gospel and cheerful contribution to your maintenance will be to your satisfaction.*

[fo. 128v., reversed.]
EXETER, 1711, May 8th & 9th. At the Meeting of the United Brethren of Devon and Cornwall.

[Present:] Mr Thomas Edgley, moderator, Isaac Gilling, scribe; Mr Tross, Balster, Hooper, Hallet, Horsham, Moor, Wood, Sandercock, Larkham, Withers, Evans, Martyn, Jelinger Symonds, Peter Kellow, Enty, Giles, Bowcher, Short, Atkins, Manston, Majendie, Eveleigh, Sloly, Bartlett, Hody, Grigg, Glanvil, Palk, Wills, Wheeler, Stoddon, Brett, Brown, Beadon, Bishop, Hancock, Flavel, Furse, Carkeet, Strong, Clark. From Somerset: Mr Stephen James, Taunton; Mr Berry, Wellington; Candidates: Munckley, Lavington, Bond, Hornibrook, Colton, Walker, Youatt, Greby, Cudmore, Symonds. Lennet of London.

Thanks given to Mr Palk for praying and to Mr Martyn for preaching.

Brought in to the Fund.

						£	s	d
Mr Walrond	...	...	...	...	...	5	0	0
Mr Horsham	...	...	...	...	...	1	15	6
Paid to Mr Gilling for Mr Lawrence Hext				...		2	10	0

Ordered that 24s gather'd by Mr Ball of Honiton be according to his desire given to Up-Ottery meeting. That Mr Coulton, Mr Youatt, and Plymtree Meeting receive no more out of the Fund. That Mr Hext now

---

[1]Sic. The identification is difficult. It is possibly Swanage.
[2]This shorthand passage is an example of the invitations sent to young ministers by churches in search of a pastor.

a pupil to Mr Hallet have for the future £9 per year. That Foy[1] Meeting have £5 for one year, North Molton 40s and Mr Edgley [fo. 127v., reversed] (the Moderator) promis'd to give 10s per year more. That Halberton and Sidmouth Meetings have 40s each per year provided the Fund will bear it. That Mr Hooper, Mr Hallett and Mr Gilling inspect the Fund to see whether it will bear it. That Hatherly Meeting can have no more than 40s per year. That £4 per annum be continu'd to Kings Carswell Meeting. That Mr Grigg's case be consider'd next Assembly. The Ministers present gave Mr[2] Symonds who is at present at Oldscomb two & forty shillings.

Mr Hallett, Withers, Short, appointed to examine Mr[2] Cudmore: and the Exon ministers who examind Mr William Youatt, declaring that they found them well qualify'd for preaching, the Assembly approv'd of their preaching in order to Ordination, and order'd a Certificate to be given them under the hands of the Moderator and Scribe, of this their approbation.

Inquiry made why Mr Walker whose ordination was appointed by the Assembly in May 1710 was not ordain'd at the time appointed: Mr Walker said he was hinder'd by a journey into Wales, which he could not put off. [fo. 126v., reversed] Agreed that Mr Cornelius Bond, Mr Edward Coulton and Mr[2] Walker be ordain'd at Chudleigh the third Tuesday in July. Mr Tross to pray over Mr Coulton, Mr Hooper over Mr Bond, Mr Hallet over Mr Walker. Mr Edgley to preach, Mr Spark to give the exhortation, or if he fail, Mr Withers. Mr Bond's question: An Sancta Scriptura sit divinitus inspirata ? Mr Coulton's: An Christus sit supremus Deus ?

The following Minute drawn up, read & approv'd. At the Assembly of the United Brethren of Devon & Cornwall at Exon, May the 9th, 1711. The Assembly being inform'd that Mr Jones of Branton[3] hath preached for several years without ordination, desir'd Mr Bowcher, Mr Palk, Mr Bartlet, and Mr Wills to acquaint him that they are concern'd at his practice, and desire him to propose himself to be ordain'd or give his reasons to the next Assembly why he refuses. This is a true Copy. I. G. Scribe.

A representation of the difference between Mr Roswel of Colyton, Minister, and some of his hearers with their appeal to the Assembly, and desire to have liberty granted them to choose an Assistant, and that the Assembly would persuade Mr Roswel to accept of one. Subscrib'd by Mr William Lymbrey, Richard Thompson, John Bussel, and Benjamin Slade, who appeard, and gave some account of their case. [fo. 125v., reversed] Resolv'd that Mr Hallett & Mr Eveleigh draw up a letter to Mr Roswel in the name of the Assembly to exhort him to refer the difference between him, & his Hearers, to the hearing and determination of Mr Ball, Mr Walrond, Mr Horsham, Mr Withers, & Mr Manston; who are desir'd to meet for this end, at Colyton within a month from this time: and if, upon hearing the matter, they think it proper, that they advise Mr Roswell to accept of an Assistant, in order to the healing of

[1] Fowey, Cornwall.
[2] A space was left for his Christian name.
[3] Braunton, N. Devon.

this breach, and preventing the sinking of the Meeting. The following letter read, approv'd, and order'd to be sent:

Revd. Sir. Some persons of your congregation have given an account to the associated Ministers of Devon & Cornwall met at Exon, this 9th of May, 1711, of some differences risen among you, from a desire some of them have that an Assistant may be joined with you. They have given us reason to fear that if their request as to this matter be not granted them, a very considerable part of the supporters of the meeting will leave you, and some probably quit the Dissenting interest. But, not intirely relying on the representation they have given us of this affair, we have thought it most advisable to request some of your Brethren, viz: Mr Ball, Mr Horsham, Mr Walrond, Mr Withers and Mr Manston, to make a visit to you at Culliton, within a month from this time, to gain a more full information of [fo. 124v., reversed] the state of things. As it is our desire to have a due regard to your peace and usefulness, so are we oblig'd to consult the peace and edification of the Church. We are fully persuaded that our brethren will make this their rule in the whole of their conduct. We also hope and presume that for the Glory of God, the peace and edification of the Church, you will have an impartial regard to the advice of your brethren, which upon a full hearing of the case they will better be able to give than we at present can. Begging God to direct you to those things that make for peace, we conclude ourselves, Sir, your affectionate friends and brethren in the Lord. Subscrib'd in the name & by the order of the Assembly by Thomas Edgley, moderator, Isaac Gilling, scribe. To the Revered Mr Roswell, Minister in Culliton.[1]

Mr Enty acquaints the Assembly that Mrs Vinson of Plymouth desires their advice about distributing a hundred pounds left by her husband Dr Vinson to the poor Ministers of Devon and Cornwall. The words of his will are these: " I give unto such poor Presbyterian Ministers (Non-Conformists) as at the time of my death shall dwell only in the Counties of Devon [fo. 123v., reversed] and Cornwall the sum of a hundred pounds sterling to be distributed among them within two years after my death. And for the more equal and proportionable doing thereof, it is my desire that my executrix for the most part, do crave and follow the directions and advice of the Assembly of the Presbyterian Ministers that usually meet twice a year at Exon." Mr Tross, Hooper, Hallett, Gilling, Withers, Martyn, Edgley, Brett, appointed to advise with Mr Enty about distributing the money. They advis'd that Mr Sandercock, Grigg, Tingcomb, Walker, Balster, Merrion, Halsey, Brinley, Hody, Bond, Cudmore, Knight, Short, Giles, Cox, Sloly, Strong & the French Minister at Plymouth, should have it distributed among them, 10, 9, 8, 6, 6, 6, 6, 6, 5, 5, 5, 4, 4, 4, 4, 4, 4, 4.

Mr Isaac Clark was ordained at Sidbury the Wednesday in Easter week, April 4, 1711.

Mr Jelinger Symonds to preach next Assembly, if he fail Mr Bowcher. Mr How to pray, if he fail Mr Wills.

[1]Colyton Nonconformity had begun in 1662 with the ejection of the Vicar, John Wilkins. Rosewell had become minister about 1705. As will be seen below (pp. 88–9) the differences proved irreconcilable, and he had left the society by the beginning of 1712, preaching to a small group in a private house in the town. After his death some of them turned Baptists, which may indicate the reasons behind the disagreement. Evans, G. E., *Colytonia*, 1898.

Mr John Atkins of Exon. desir'd the Assembly to recommend a minister to Bodmyn upon Mr Carkeet's removing from thence to Tottness. Mr[1] Lennet propos'd. He having been but a little while in the country (coming down with Mrs Jillard, Mr Eveleigh's sister) twas not thought proper for the Assembly to recommend him, without a Testimonial from London, of his good conversation. [fo. 122v., reversed] Resolv'd. That Mr Eveleigh with the Exon. ministers indeavour to provide for Bodmyn, while they inquire about Mr Lennet: and if they receive a good testimonial of him, that then they recommend him to Bodmyn.

Cases propos'd. Whether a Man that hath by Bond obliged himself in marriage to make his eldest son worth a Thousand Pounds, can in conscience (thinking it best afterwards to make all his children equal) destroy the said Bond, by and with the consent of his wife and her father, who are the persons to whom the Bond is made, and all that are concern'd, except the eldest son himself, who is very young and not capable of giving his consent? Or, whether 'tis consistent with justice to make void the said Bond, without the consent of the eldest son, supposing that otherwise by the frowns of Providence there will be nothing for the younger children, be they four or five, or more or less of them? Tis the general opinion of the Assembly that 'tis consistent with Justice to make void the Bond, by the consent of the wife and her father, without the consent of the son, in order to make provision for the younger children.

[fo. 166v., reversed. Shorthand] *To the Reverend Assembly of Divines who are to meet together on the 8th day of this instant May 1711 at Exon. Reverend Sirs. Your judgment and opinion is desired on the case which is here underwritten viz: A. of D. taking a voyage to H., about 20 years since, he had bought of B.I.S. and W. several parcels of goods and had also goods sent by him as a factor which he was to carry and dispose of for the account of C. and P. The said A. proceeded in the voyage and sold a considerable part of the aforesaid goods and the rest he left with a factor beyond the sea; at his return from the sea he absconded, and sent word to his creditors that he was pirated upon the sea, and had many of the goods taken from him, by reason of which he said he could pay the half but promised if ever it pleased God to bless him in the world he would pay the other half, yea promised it as he trusted to see the face of God. The creditors feared the said A. would go on board a man of war, and so lest they should lose all they consented to take half and release him of his promise. With the other half of his creditors' money (for he was not pirated as he falsely said) he purchased a commission on board a man of war, and died beyond the sea in Her Majestie's service, and left behind him an estate (according to report) of more than £2000. For he gave £500 legacy to a daughter who is since married to a young Professor of Religion. Now, Reverend Sirs, your opinion is desired in this case by your answer to these 2 questions. 1. Whether the widdow of the said A. that was his executrix be not obliged in conscience to pay these debts aforesaid? 2. If she refuse to pay them whether the [fo. 167r., reversed] Professor who married the daughter and had the legacy of £500 or more be not obliged in [2] and conscience to pay these just debts which he knew of before marriage and promised [2] should be done, and gave as his judgment when his wife (who had the legacy of £500) was like to marry another man, that they ought in conscience*

[1] A space was left for his Christian name.
[2] Not clear, but the characters probably signify "faith" and "faithfully".

to pay these just debts or else could expect no prosperity to attend them. Mr Ch—t of Dartmouth, Mr Hughes.

Young Colton brought and Edgley opened the case. [fo. 166v., Margin] *'Tis the opinion of the greater number of the ministers assembled that, as the case is here stated, the debts of A. here specify'd ought to be paid out of his effects. That the widow of A. who was his Executrix is obliged in conscience to pay them.*

[fo. 173r., reversed.[1]] *Dear Sir, You were pleased to intimate to me last Wednesday by Mr Pulling that you were desired to preach a Funeral Sermon here at Chudleigh next Lord's day, and therefore did desire me to exchange in the afternoon. I should readily comply with your desires on another occasion, but I shall not in this, for though I would gratify Mr Rendall in any thing that is reasonable, yet I care not to trot about the country to please his silly humour. I thought I should have seen you here yesterday, and then I would have discoursed with you about it; but seeing I did not, I have sent you this that you might not be at any uncertainty. In haste I remain your affectionate and humble servant, Edward Colton. Chudleigh, July 17, 1711. For the Reverend Mr Samuel Stoddon in Bovey Tracey.*

[fo. 121v., reversed]
EXETER, 1711, Sept. 4th & 5th. At the Meeting of the United Brethren of Devon and Cornwall.

[Present:] Mr William Giles, moderator, Isaac Gilling, scribe. Mr Tross, Hooper, Hallett, Withers, Harding, Edgly, Manston, Symonds, Norman, Martyn, Larkham, Sandercock, Atkins, Short, Eveleigh, Sloly, Grigg, Palk, Brett, Hancock, Wills, Furse, Brown, Bishop, Beadon, Carkeet, Bond, Walker, Coulton, Candidates: Mr George Brett, Greby, Hornibrook, Jones of Branston, Youatt, John Lavington. Mr Thomas Powel of Swanzey in Glamorganshire, Mr James Cornish of Dulverton, Mr George Lissant. Mr Edwards of Taunton, candidate.
    Brought in to the Fund.

						£	s	d
Mr Eveleigh	...	...	...	...	...	8	2	6
Mr Manston	...	...	...	...	...	4	9	0
Mr Ball	...	...	...	...	...	1	13	0
						14	4	6

[fo. 120v., reversed] The Fund being low and many Meetings having never contributed anything, the ministers present were desir'd to do something. Resolv'd that Budleigh Meeting have twenty shillings per annum for four years at Mr Manston's request. The first payment to be made at this time twelve months. A petition of Mr Hugh Henry a North Brittain to have something out of the Fund, and to be settled in some Meeting in this County. Resolv'd that we cannot give him anything out of our Fund. That the consideration of his petition be referr'd to the Exon Ministers, when he applies himself to them. A letter from Buckrel desiring help from our Fund. Mr Penuel Symonds who was there doth not give satisfaction. Order'd that five pounds be paid at present out of

[1]This shorthand passage is included to show the tendency of the younger of the Presbyterian ministers to stand on their dignity even in connection with funeral arrangements. Edward Colton was at this time only 23 years old.

the Fund, to Mr Symonds, who is in low circumstances. Mr Edmond's case propos'd. That he hath but £27 per year at Plymton. Order'd that Plymton Meeting have forty shillings for one year if the Fund will bear it.

[fo. 119v., reversed] A petition in behalf of Mr Thomas Powel of Swanzey in Glamorganshire read. The following state of his case drawn up by Mr Martyn & Mr Eveleigh, read, and after an amendment, approv'd and subscribd, to be sent to absent ministers.

Exon, September 5th, 1711. Whereas tis represented to us, that Mr Thomas Powel, now Pastor at Swanzey, is, by Gods hand, reduc'd to great distress, having had a large family, a wife and five children, and an aged mother to maintain, and preaching five years in Brecconshire gratis, and afterwards at Cardiff, where he had only £15 per annum to support them for several years together: where he sustain'd a great loss by a violent inundation, and also by some methods he was advis'd to for the better support of his family; in which it pleas'd God not to succeed him, and thereby contracted a considerable debt which he must unavoidably sink under without charitable assistance: and, whereas the said Mr Powel is recommended as a person of great learning, [fo. 117v., reversed][1] eminent piety, and conduct, an excellent preacher, a very laborious, successful & unblameable minister, on whom the eyes of the favourers of the Dissenting Interest are mostly fix'd as the main credit and support thereof in that region, and, who has in time past deny'd himself great offers to serve his native country, (and at some times in the Welsh tongue) and being now call'd to one of the chief towns in South Wales, where, 'tis hop'd, he would be very useful, were it not that his debt lies heavy upon his spirits, daily threatening the ruine of his family, or friends, who, to inable him to support his great charge, as they hop'd, became ingag'd for him: the deep distress, and excellent character of the said Mr Powel are to us very evident from a letter attested by several ministers, whose testimony is confirm'd by several other persons present. We therefore, the Associated Ministers of Devon and Cornwall, do hereby unanimously advise and agree to represent the case of the said Mr Powel to our congregations, or friends, as uncommon, and him as a proper object of charity. [fo. 116v., reversed] Resolv'd that the collections made for him be transmitted to Mr Anthony Vicary,[2] grocer in Exon: and that an account be given to the next Assembly, how much each minister hath sent.

Mr Walker proposes the case of the people of North-Moulton. That Mr How of London got them something out of the Fund there. That fourty shillings was sent to one of that Meeting when they had no settled minister, but only lecturers, viz. Mr Samuel Wood and others. That the people thought the money ought to be equally divided among the ministers who by turns preach'd there. That Mr Wood claim'd all for his. That the people understand that four pounds per annum issued out of the Fund at London for [3] years past for the benefit of that meeting hath never since been paid to the people, but taken up by Mr Wood. That Mr Walker hath preach'd there for five years past: and Mr Wood hath preach'd there upon exchange but four times in those five years.

[1]118v. is taken up by part of Gilling's list of Ministers and Candidates in 1701.
[2]One of the Presbyterian Committee of Thirteen in Exeter, from 1714 to 1723.
[3]Left blank.

[fo. 115v., reversed] Mr Wood's letter to Mr Hallet alledging that the four pounds per annum were given to him upon the account of his aged Mother. Mr Weeks hath an express order from London to pay the four pounds per annum to Mr Walker.

Order'd that Mr Grigg have eight pounds for one year, the first payment to begin at Michaelmas next.

The Ministers appointed by the last Assembly met at Honiton, and the difference between Mr Rosewell and his Hearers was there accommodated, and he complying with the advice of the Assembly, he and his people went away seemingly good friends.

Mr Jones of Branton appears, and says the reason why he doth not seek for ordination is, because the people to whom he preaches never gave him a Call; nor doth he apprehend that they desire to have him for their settled Pastor. That several of his Hearers [fo. 114v., reversed] are communicants at Barnstaple (with Mr Peard) which is five miles distant. That tis the general opinion of his Hearers that his being ordain'd and administring the Lords Supper would break the Meeting: some substantial people would thrust themselves upon Communion, whom others would not care to sit down with. That he hath been settled among that people about five years. That he was invited to preach among them.

Question: Ought not a man to be ordain'd in order to his preaching with authority, when the Apostle tells us, he was sent, not to Baptize but to preach the Gospel. And, How shall they preach except they be sent?

Question: What shall be done as to the Heathen World? May not a man be a minister before he is a settled Pastor? Must he not preach in order to convert souls? If so, may he do it without Ordination? Then every man may preach.

Twas the general advice of the Assembly, to Mr Jones, that he be ordain'd. And on his desiring not to be urg'd to it at present, he was desir'd to consider of it between this and next Assembly.

Mr Bowcher to preach next Assembly, or if he fail Mr Short, Mr How to pray, if he fail Mr Hody.

[fo. 113v., reversed] Mr Hallett proposes Mr Milner of Bridgwater, educated by him to be examin'd, in order to be licens'd to preach. Upon inquiry as to his age, the regular conduct of his life, and his being in full communion: it appear'd that he behav'd himself well; was in communion with Mr Moor of Bridgwater; but was but little past one and twenty.

Question: Shall this Assembly order Mr Milner to be examin'd, tho' he is not of the age ordinarily requir'd? Resolv'd that seeing he is very much desir'd to supply a congregation at Wrington, in Somersetshire, he be examin'd by Mr Sandercock, Harding, Withers, Hooper, in presence of Mr Hallett. Mr Milner was examin'd, approv'd, and had a license.

[fo. 112v., reversed] An account of some proceedings in Wales against Mr Matthias Maurice for harsh expressions, viz: Of our being justified from eternity; of God's willing Sin; and his ill conduct in thrusting himself into Mr Jeremy Owen's pulpit, read. Order'd that Mr Withers draw up a paper to be sign'd by the Assembly to condemn his harsh expressions and ill conduct.[1]

[1]The last two-thirds of 112v. are blank.

[fo. 111v., reversed] Mr Powels letter to the Assembly. September, 1711.

Reverend Fathers and Brethren. It was with the utmost satisfaction I observ'd the order, unity, and moderation of all your well weighed proceedings. The gravity of the seniors with the becoming seriousness and promising usefulness of the juniors exceedingly rejoiced my soul. As to your great readiness to commiserate my distressed condition and to extend your charity towards me, all that I shall at the present take liberty to say, is, that I hope one day will make it appear, your charity hath not been misplac'd, neither shall it be unrewarded. All the returns I am capable of making are acknowledgments and thankfulness, which I do in the most solemn and hearty manner, with earnest request you would still extend your greater charity in constant prayers, that this your charity may quicken to more diligence and faithfulness, Reverend Sirs, your highly oblig'd and unworthy fellow-labourer, Thomas Powell.

[fo. 110v., reversed]
EXETER, 1712, May 6th, 7th. At the meeting of the United Brethren of Devon and Cornwall.

[Present:] Mr John Ball, moderator, Isaac Gilling, scribe; Mr Tross, Balster, Hooper, Hallet, Horsham, Sandercock, Moor, Larkham, Withers, Evans, Martyn, Jelinger Symonds, Enty, Walrond, Edgley, Giles, Bowcher, Short, Atkins, Cox, Eveleigh, Sloly,[1] Norman, Manston, Baron, Hody, Grigg, Glanvil, Palk, Brett, Brown, Bishop, Beadon, Lissant, Hancock, Flavel, Carkeet, Bond, Walker, Coulton, Clark, Strong, Majendie, Short, Penuel Symonds. Candidates: Lavington, Edmonds, Batten, Hornabrook, Greeby, Youat.
From Dorset: Mr John England. From Taunton: Candidates Langdon, Liddon, Simon, Hamlyn, Webber. From Wales: Mr Thomas Powel. From London: Mr Archer, Baker, Hall.

Mr Bowcher preach'd, Mr Hody pray'd.

Brought in to the Fund.

					£	s	d
Mr Adams' Legacy	...	...	...	...	5	9	0
Mr Walrond	...	...	...	...	5	7	6
Mr Horsham	...	...	...	...	2	3	6
Mr Ball	...	...	...	...	1	11	0
					14	11	0

[Mr Edgley, N. Molton... ... ... 10s.][2]

[fo. 109v., reversed] Order'd that Hatherly Meeting have 40s per annum added. That Bow Meeting have 50s per annum added. That Mr Hody have 40s per annum added to Kerswel Meeting for one year. That Mr Penuel Symonds have £3 given him at present. That Mr Mudg have 40s per annum added. He has already £8 per annum. The Assembly was inform'd that Mr Mudg took a journey to London. Some thought

[1]The name of Bartlett was inserted here but crossed out.
[2]Apparently added later.

that he had a mind to conform. Mr Hallett his tutor says that he is now very steady. Some dislike his fine Wig, etc., and think he ought to go as one maintain'd by charity.[1]

Mr Slade, Bussel, and Thompson of Culliton acquaint the Assembly that Mr Rosewell hath left them & preaches at present in his own house. That about 25 of the old communicants adhere to him, and about the same number continue to hear in the old Meeting House. That Mr Batten of Somerset a candidate preaches there. That several have left the Meeting and are gone to Church. They desire to have a Minister to administer the Lords Supper to them. [fo. 108v., reversed] Resolv'd that Mr Withers draw up a letter to Mr Rosewell in the name of this Assembly to advise him to keep to his former agreement at Honiton, provided the people pay him £4 12s which he told Mr Withers he would be contented with, and also to request him to consent that such other ministers as the dissatisfy'd people shall desire may sometimes administer the Lords Supper in the Congregation. The following letter by him drawn up, read, approv'd, subscrib'd, and order'd to be sent:

At the Meeting of the United Brethren of Devon & Cornwal at Exon, May the 7th, 1712. Reverend Brother, Tis to our great grief we understand that the differences betwixt you and some of your people are grown to such an height as to divide the congregation. We were in hopes that the Honiton Agreement might have prevented such a fatal conclusion, and are sorry to find our selves disappointed. The design of these lines is to let you know that some of the old Meeting House have apply'd themselves to this Assembly desiring that one or other may be appointed to administer the sacraments to them as a distinct society: and being sensible what a wound and scandal these quarrels have given to religion we have resolvd to make one essay more in order to reunite you. We do therefore most earnestly intreat you so far to consult your own quiet, the honour of the Dissenting Interest, and [fo. 107v., reversed] above all the glory of our common Lord and Master, as to admit of a union with your former flock, upon the terms agreed on at Honiton, by both parties. The ends which we have propos'd are certainly so very valuable, that some even of your just pretensions may well be sacrific'd in order to obtain them. We have also written a letter to such as are at present divided from you, intreating them to perform their part of this Agreement: particularly to pay you the money promis'd, excepting 20s per annum, which you told Mr Withers you were willing to deduct, upon Mr Clode's death. We have desir'd two of our body, Mr Ball and Mr Walrond, to discourse these gentlemen on this head, and they are furnished with such arguments as (we flatter ourselves) may prevail with them to comply. But if upon their performing their part you shall refuse a coalescence upon the terms formerly consented to, we know not how to discourage any member of our Assembly from administering the Sacrament to them in their present circumstances. Begging God to inspire you all with the sentiments of concord peace and love, we remain, yours, subscrib'd by the order of the Assembly, J. Ball, moderator, I. G., scribe.

[1]The whole of the passage about Zachary Mudge is marked by a thick marginal bracket for emphasis. For an explanation of his journey to London, see *Trans. Devon. Assoc.* 1897, xxix, p. 87.

[fo. 106v., reversed] Resolv'd that Mr Manston draw up a letter in the name of the Assembly to those of Culliton people who are dissatisfy'd with Mr Rosewell as their sole minister, to advise them to make up the £4 12s per annum to Mr Rosewill which was formerly promis'd him, provided he will consent to his former agreement at Honiton. Which advice, if Mr Rosewill refuses, that he acquaint the people that the Assembly consent that they apply themselves to a Minister to administer the Lords Supper among them. The following letter by him drawn up, read, approv'd subscrib'd and sent:

To that part of the congregation at Culliton which desires another Minister. Your case being this day represented to the Assembly by Mr Slade, Mr Thompson, etc., the Assembly is willing to do all that possibly lies in their power to heal the breach that is unhappily begun in your Congregation. And as the state of the case appears to us upon the most serious consideration we advise you to use all Christian prudent endeavours to obtain union & peace with Mr Rosewell, and that part of the Congregation that adheres to him. And in order to this we do particularly advise you to make up the £4 10s per annum to Mr Rosewell which was formerly promis'd him, provided he will stand to the Agreement, that you all mutually consented to: which sum we hope you will not find very difficult to raise, £2 of it being promis'd by [fo. 105v., reversed] two of yourselves. If Mr Rosewell absolutely refuse your offer, the Assembly unanimously consents that you apply yourselves to another Minister to come and administer the Lord's Supper unto you: but we desire you not to run too hastily into this untill you have try'd all just ways to restore peace to the whole Congregation. Earnestly beg God, in your several places to direct you into the ways of peace & truth that all may be built up in faith & holiness. The Lord guide you in the whole affair for his glory the good of your souls and the promoting the interest of Christ in these parts. We subscribe ourselves in the name and with the consent of the Assembly, J.B., moderator, I.G., scribe, Exon, May 7, 1712.[1]

The Assembly advis'd those of the congregation of Culliton who desir'd another Minister to make up the £4 10s per annum to Mr Rosewell which they formerly promised him provided he will make good his former Agreement at Honiton, which if [fo. 104v., reversed] he refuses to do they consented that they might apply themselves to a Minister to administer the Lord's Supper among them. This is a true copy signd by Moderator [&] Scribe.

Agreed. That Monsieur Majendie be desir'd to preach to the French Church at Dartmouth once in six weeks; and that Mr Enty be desir'd to request the French ministers in Plymouth to preach at the aforesaid place twice in six weeks likewise; and that Monsieur Majendie be desir'd to write to the Plymouth ministers to that purpose.

A paper sign'd by several of North Moulton setting forth that their Meeting House was purchas'd about 9 years since by Mr Wood and William Burgess: that the right by purchase is still theirs: that they have requested them to give an account of what money there was collected

---

[1] At this point on 105v. is interposed a note already given relating to 1699. The next passage continues after the renewed heading " At the Meeting of the United Ministers of Devon and Cornwall at Exon May the 7th, 1712 ".

towards the purchase and rebuilding the said house, and, if any be due to Mr Wood, they would pay him and have the House transferred over to them, or to some in Trust for them. That they have been with Mr Wood since last Assembly, and he refuseth to do it, etc.
Exon, May 7, 1712. Mr Wood, we had before us a letter from North Moulton people, complaining that you will come to no account with them about the money collected for their Meeting-House, neither will transfer it to them. We should have been glad to have seen [fo. 103v., reversed] you here, and have heard your reasons, for every good man would act so as to approve himself to all good men: and it is reasonable that the Meeting should be settled according to Law, and not left to uncertainties, especially when publick monies have been collected to help them. We hear they are for continuing Mr Burgess for one of the Trustees, and we hope you will not be wanting to give the people all reasonable satisfaction, that the Ministry be not blam'd. Subscrib'd in the name and by the order of the Assembly by Moderator and Scribe.

Mr Short to preach next Assembly, if he fail Mr Henry Atkins. Mr Wheeler, Glanvil, Stoddon, to pray.

Moneys collected for Mr Thomas Powel.

	£	s	d
In Exon	60	0	0
Mr Harding, Plymouth	6	8	9
Mr Enty, Plymouth	6	5	0
Mr Peard, Barnstaple	5	4	3
Mr Eveleigh, Crediton	5	8	3
Mr Bere & Partners, Tiverton	5	0	0
Mr Gilling, Newton	2	12	3
Mr Giles, Modbury	2	0	0
Mr Hancock, South Molton	2	17	6
Mr Glanvil, Liskeard	2	0	0
Mr Beadon, Budleigh	2	0	0
Mr Sloly, Silferton	2	8	6½
Mr Henry Atkins, Puddington	1	17	0
Mr Cox, Kingsbridge	1	16	0
Mr Short, Ufculm	1	12	0
Mr Norman, Biddeford	1	10	0
Mr Walsh, Stoke in Ham	1	10	0
Mr Ball, Honiton	1	7	0
Mr Evans, Cullompton	1	5	6
Mr Wills, Appledore	1	0	0
Mr Coulton, Chudleigh	1	0	6
Mr Jones, Braunton	1	0	0
Mr Clark, Sidbury	1	0	0
Mr Bond, Ashburton		14	0
Mr Samuel Sketchley		10	0
Mr Manston, Lymptsone		10	9
Mr Jonathan Heyer		10	0
Mr Brinley, Townsend, Hatchfield.[1]	119	7	3½

[1]These would be the names of the auditors, or collectors, or both. The first was one of the Exeter Presbyterians' Committee of 13.

[fo. 101v., reversed]

EXETER, 1712, Sept. 9th and 10th. At the Meeting of the United Brethren of Devon and Cornwal.

[Present:] Mr John Withers, moderator, Isaac Gilling, scribe; Mr Tross, Hallet, Horsham, Ball, [1] Hall, Larkham, Evans, Daniel Kellow, Edgley, Hughes, Samuel Wood, Moor, Eveleigh, Atkins, Short, Wheeler, Giles, Glanvil, Hancock, Stoddon, Brown, Majendie, Manston, Eveleigh, Lissant, Flavel, Carkeet, Coulton, Walker, Bond, Wheeler, Short. From Somerset: Mr Cornish,

Candidates: John Lavington, John Munkley, Hornabrook, Stephenson, Youat, Adams of Biddeford. [2]

Mr Short preach'd, Mr Wheeler pray'd.

Brought in to the Fund.

						£	s	d
Mr Horsham	...	...	...	...	...	1	16	3
Mr Ball	...	...	...	...	...	1	12	0
Mr Eveleigh	...	...	...	...	...	7	6	6
						10	14	9

Order'd that Mr Penuel Symonds have £1 8s. Mr Wheeler and Mr Moor promis'd to get something for Mr Penuel Symonds. Order'd that the contributions to Mr Grigg, Mr Shapland and Plympton Meeting be continued. That the Meeting at Liskeard in Cornwall. [fo 100v., reversed] have five pounds for one year: the first quarterly paiment to be made at Michaelmas next.

A minister was desir'd for Bodmyn in Cornwall. Mr Coulton promis'd to go thither and to preach there the Lords Day after Michaelmas, October 5th.

The affair of Chudleigh Meeting propos'd. Resolv'd that seeing the people belonging to that Meeting do not apply themselves to us, tis not proper for us at present to intermeddle in their affairs.

Mr Samuel Wood promis'd the Assembly to transfer the Trust of North Molton Meeting, to such persons as Mr Walker, and the majority of the contributors of that Meeting shall approve, on their reimbursing him what he hath laid out, and settling it for the use of the United Brethren.

Question: Whether the children of profane and scandalous parents may be admitted to Baptism, upon the parents confessing their faults and promise of future Reformation? Affirmative.

Mr Glanvil or Mr Stoddon to pray, Mr Atkins or Mr Cox to preach next Assembly.

---

[1]Here the name of Sandercock was first included, then deleted.
[2]Wheeler, Short and Eveleigh are mentioned twice in error in the MS.

[fo. 99v., reversed.]

EXETER, 1713, May 5th and 6th. At the Meeting of the United Brethren of Devon and Cornwall.

[Present:] Mr Balster, Hooper, Hallet, Gilling, Sandercock, Wood, Horsham, Ball, Harding, Moor, Larkham, Withers, Hall, Evans, Martyn, Jelinger Symonds, Peter Kellow, Giles, Enty, Walrond, Bowcher, Short, Atkins, Cox, Eveleigh, Sloly, Bartlet, Hughes, Norman, Manston, How, Baron, Gough, Hody, Peard, Grigg, Wheeler, Glanvil, Palk, Wills, Brinley, Stoddon, Henry Brett, Brown, Bishop, Strong, Hancock, Furse, Flavel, Beadon, Clark, Bond, Walker, Coulton, Majendie, Lissant, Penuel Symonds.

Candidates: John Edmonds, Samuel Adams, Greby, Cudmore, Hornabrook, Facy, Joseph Hallett, Youat, Stevenson, Par, Tooels of Somerset, Pierse of Dorset, Towgood ' unlicensed '. Dr Edmond Calamy of London. Mr Humphrey Berry, Rabjent, Blake, of Somerset.[1]

[fo. 98v., reversed] Mr Bowcher was chosen Moderator, Mr Gilling, scribe.

[Shorthand] *Mr Hallet proposed Mr Hooper, put to the vote and carried for Mr Bowcher.* Resolv'd [that henceforward we proceed to choose a Moderator at the beginning of the Assembly, when twelve ministers are present.][2] Mr How, who was formerly appointed to pray, but fail'd by reason of the length of the journey, was desir'd to pray.

There being some demur as to Dr Calamy's preaching before the Assembly, the following questions were propos'd, viz: Whether this Assembly shall desire Dr Calamy with Mr Atkins's consent, to preach tomorrow? Affirmative. Whether this Assembly shall desire Mr Atkins to give his consent that we make this request to Dr Calamy? Mr Atkins said he had writ to him to desire it, and the Dr refus'd. Resolv'd that Mr Atkins, with the Moderator and Scribe do in the name of this Assembly desire Dr Calamy to preach to us tomorrow. Accordingly they waited on the Dr Tuesday night and he granted their request.

Brought in to the Fund.

					£	s	d
Mr Weeks, Mr Adams' legacy	...	...	....		5	0	0
Mr Harding	...	...	...	...	7	0	0
Mr Walrond	...	...	...	...	6	9	0
Mr Ball	...	...	...	...	...	2	0	6
Mr Horsham	...	...	...	...	2	18	0
					23	7	6

[fo. 97v., reversed] Order'd that Mr Harding have 2 guineas out of the money he brought for an aged Minister, [*Mr Tingcombe of*][3] St. Germans. That Goon Rounson Meeting have 40s per annum out of such money as Mr Enty shall bring in from Plymouth. That Mr Tross having given Mr Mudg many of his books the 40s per annum given him to buy books be

[1] The names of the United Brethren were arranged by number. Except for the last three, these seem to coincide with the order in which they were ordained.
[2] Underlined in the MS.
[3] Shorthand.

taken off so that for the future he receive but £10 per annum. The present contributions to be paid out of the Fund:

Devon	Per annum £	Cornwall	Per annum £
Kings Kerswell Meeting	6	Fowey Meeting	5
Bow Meeting	5	Liskard	5
Hatherly	4	Bodmin	4
Holdsworthy	4		
North Molton	2	*Devon*	
Sidmouth	2	Zachariah Mudge ...	10
Buckerel	2	Mr John Balster	5
Halberton	2	Mr Samuel Grigg ...	8
Ufculm	2	Angel Shapland ...	8
Budleigh	1		—
Plymton	2		45
	—		32
	32		—
			77

Added now Goon Rounson ...   2
79

Resolv'd, the Fund being in debt, that the Treasurer be orderd to forbear paying one quarter's contributions to the Meetings & Ministers. Mr Manston promis'd Mr Strong 20s and Mr Harding 40s for one year.

[fo. 96v., reversed] A petition in behalf of Mr Majendie desiring help out of the Fund, read. Resolv'd that it be left to the Exon ministers, who promis'd to endeavour to get somthing for him by private subscriptions.

Mr John Bushel & Robert Hitchcock of Culliton present a petition desiring help from our Fund to uphold their Meeting, some being dead, some remov'd, others unable to pay what they subscrib'd. Mr Youat and Mr Batten supply the Meeting. They have rais'd £26 but now can't raise above £18 or £20. Resolv'd that the Fund being in debt we can't at present contribute anything to Culliton Meeting, but that some of the Ministers will write to London Fund in their behalf, and their case shall be further consider'd next Assembly.

Mr Bishop informs the Assembly from Sir John Davy, that a new College being erected in Connecticut Colony in New England, their agent Mr Dummer desires encouragement from this Assembly for a Library. Sir John Davy will give £10. The following Ministers promis'd to give [fo. 95v., reversed] some books: Mr Walrond, Gilling, Enty, Peard, Harding, Horsham, Bartlet, Hooper, Eveleigh, Hallett, Bowcher, Ball, Evans, Balster, Bishop, Hughes, Brett, Manston, Sandercock, Larkham, Baron, Palk, Hancock, Atkins, Stoddon, Brown, Wills, Gough, Sloly, Clark.[1]

A petition of some poor people of South Molton, desiring relief, read. Resolv'd that this Assembly can take no cognizance of such petitions.

[1] This was the beginning of Yale University, first granted a Charter in 1701, but which did not really establish itself until about 1718. Sir John Davy lived at Creedy House in the parish of Sandford, near Crediton. His name occurs elsewhere in the MS. For the Davy (Davie) Family see Lysons, S. & D., *Topographical and historical account of Devonshire*, 1822, Vol. 1, pp. cxii–cxiii.

Upon complaint of Mr Atkins that some present had reported some things debated in the Assembly last night about Dr Calamy's preaching, which drew on him severe censures. Resolv'd that if any Brother divulge any matters discours'd of, or debated in, the Assembly to the prejudice of any of the Brethren, such Brother be liable to the censures of the Assembly.

Mr Samuel Wood gave an account of what he had done in pursuance of the order of the last Assembly as to North Molton Meeting. [fo. 94v., reversed] Resolv'd that upon hearing Mr Wood's defence and seeing the accounts with respect to North Molton Meeting House, as far as it appears to this Assembly he hath done nothing unfair in that matter, but hath been unjustly and undeservedly reflected upon. This is a true Copy of the Resolution of the Assembly. Isaac Gilling, Scribe. Exon, May 6, 1713.

Thanks given to Mr How for praying, to Dr Calamy for preaching, and he was desir'd to print his sermon.

Mr Joseph Hallett & Mr John Par of Exon, & Mr John Pierce of Sherborn in Dorset propose themselves to be examin'd in order to be licens'd to preach. The 2 first near 22, the latter 21½ years of age. All three in communion and of good conversations. Mr Pierce produc'd the following certificate:

Bridgwater, Feb. 26, 1712/13. This is to certify whom it may concern that Mr John Pierce hath gone thro' a course of philosophy with us, and the preparatory studies usual, to our satisfaction: he hath also read a body of Theology. He hath been partaker of the Lord's Supper in the congregation at Bridgwater. We have observed the unblamableness of his conversation, and believe him [fo. 93v., reversed] serious and sincere in his Christian profession. We recommend him to the approbation of our Reverend Brethren judging it would be for the promoting of the interest of our Lord that he preach occasionally where God's Providence shall call him. John Moore, John Moore, junior. There was a debate whether any of these candidates should be examin'd, seeing they were not full 22 years old, the age required by our rule; and whether we should examine Mr Pierce, who liv'd at Sherborn in Dorset, and might be examin'd by order of the Assembly in that County. But the question being put, twas agreed by the majority, that they should all be examin'd. Mr Gilling, Harding, Enty, Withers, Larkham, appointed to examine them, reported that they were satisfy'd in their qualifications. On their promise before the Assembly to offer themselves to be ordain'd in a short time after they are constant preachers, and have a call to the pastoral office by some particular congregation, they were permitted to preach as Candidates.

Mr Samuel Adams of Chudleigh desir'd to be ordain'd at Chudleigh where he is settled. Order'd that who ever offers himself to Ordination, not having been examin'd and licens'd to preach by some Assembly, be examind and approvd before any Order be made for his being ordaind. [fo. 92v., reversed] Orderd that Mr Adams not having been examin'd, be now examin'd by Mr Hallet, Ball, Gilling. They being well satisfy'd in his qualifications, order'd that he be ordain'd, and Mr John Edmonds of Plymton, at Chudleigh, June the 18th. Mr Adams' Question: An detur Peccatum Originale inherens?   Mr Edmond's: An Christus officio sacerdotali fungatur in coelis? Memorandum: They were ordain'd at the time & place appointed. Mr Hooper began with prayer, Mr Hallett preach'd, Mr Hooper prayd over Mr Edmonds, Mr Hallet over Mr Adams, Mr Gilling gave the Exhortation, Mr Withers concluded with Prayer.

Mr John Atkins, Thomas Jeffery, John Vowler, and Aaron Tozer, inform the Assembly that they hop'd Mr Pierce of Newbury would come hither, if he had a letter from this Assembly. That he shew'd an inclination to it, but had left it to be determind by the 6 Lecturers at Salter's Hall, London. Dr Calamy inform'd the Assembly that he heard what was urg'd in the behalf of Newbury, & Exon, at Salter's Hall: that the Lecturers gave it as their judgment that if Mr Pierce apprehended his health was at stake by his continuance at Newbury, he ought to come to Exon; being desirous to preserve [fo. 91v., reversed] a useful life. Mr Robinson mov'd that Physicians might again be consulted. Accordingly he went with Mr Pearse [sic] to Dr Mead, who said, if Mr Pearse did study less and divert himself more, and had more help, he might have his health tolerably well. Mr Pearse own'd that he was willing to come & settle at Exon, but hath been so useful at Newbury, and God hath so own'd him there that he doth not know how to leave that people, or to give them a denial to stay there: and having sent such a letter to Exon, he said, he hop'd that matter was over.

Twas pleaded on behalf of Newbury, that it was a very particular providence brought him thither. The people were much at a loss, that they did set apart a time for Prayer, with great solemnity, to look up to God to direct them in the choice of a man who might carry on the interest of the Gospel among them: and soon after, by a concurrence of particular providences they were pointed to Mr Pearse, as one who was uneasy in the post where he was. He came thither, was received with great unanimity, entertain'd with great respect, hath been very useful, hath a number of young people just growing up, who are under his conduct [fo. 90v., reversed] ready to receive instruction from him, who own him for their spiritual father, among whom 'tis hop'd he may be singularly useful. They also pleaded, that whereas there are two congregations in Newbury, and a division among them, 'tis fear'd his removal will heighten this division, and they will difficultly be again provided for. That Mr Henry had been drawn from Chester to London, and his place not yet supply'd. Twas fear'd twould be the same at Newbury. That Mr Pearse went with great regret to Cambridge, promis'd to stay there but 3 years, whereas he stay'd there twice three. That God had much more own'd him at Newbury than at Cambridge. Mr Collings of Newbury was very zealous to keep Mr Pearse there. Mr Robinson pleaded strenuously for his stay at Newbury, and mov'd that at the importunity of Newbury people an assistant might be got for him: to which Mr Pierse consented. Mr Clark thought that if he stay'd there, he ought to remove out of the Town, and to live somewhere upon the hills. Dr Clark could not be very forward to persuade him to remove from a people that lov'd him so well.

[fo. 89v., reversed] The arguments urg'd at Salter's Hall in favour of Exon were, the unanimity of Ministers and people there, which, it was affirm'd, was not likely to be great in the choice of any other person, if Mr Pearse should refuse to go thither. It was also urg'd that Exon was a healthful air, approv'd as such by physicians; whereas Newbury is looked upon otherwise. That the ways and methods of Exon, where 3 congregations are united, were agreeable to him. Mr John Munckley[1] pleaded zealously in the behalf of Exon: which Dr Williams favour'd.

Letters from Exon people and Mr Pearse's last answer read, in which he shews a great inclination for Exon. He is afraid, tho' now Newbury people subscribe for an Assistant, they would grow weary if the danger of Exon were over. If any way could be found by which Newbury people might be satisfy'd, or there were any on whom he might cast the blame of his removal, he would come to Exon.

Upon hearing Dr Calamy's narrative of what passed at Salter's Hall, and reading Mr Pearse's letters; there being very weighty considerations [fo. 87v., reversed] in behalf of Newbury people: some of the Assembly gave it as their opinion, that since London ministers had declin'd to decide this case, who were better acquainted with the circumstances of Newbury, it would be more difficult for us at such a distance to do it; when there were none of Newbury here to plead for themselves. At length 'twas resolv'd that a letter be drawn up by Mr Sanderock, Enty, Walrond, Eveleigh, to encourage Mr Pearse further to consider Exon people's call. Accordingly, a letter was drawn up and read in the Assembly before Exon men, who not being satisfy'd with it, but insisting that the advice of this Assembly should be given Mr Pearse to remove from Newbury upon the account of the air, and his health, as that which only was like to be effectual to determine him for Exon. Exon men being desir'd again to withdraw, twas proposed whether we should alter this letter at their request and give Mr Pearse our advice to remove from Newbury. [fo. 86v., reversed] Twas offer'd on one hand, that none of Newbury were present, that Mr Pearse had not ask'd our advice, that the Lecturers at Salters' Hall had declin'd to advise[2] his removal from Newbury, that when we were told that he wanted some upon whom to lay the blame of his removal it would not be proper for us to take it upon our selves, by giving him such advice, when we had not heard both sides. On the other hand twas urged that we should go far to gratify the citizens of Exon to whom we were so much oblig'd for their generosity towards us, etc. After long debates, the greater number of the Assembly being gone, the following [fo. 85v., reversed] clause was propos'd to be added to the letter, viz: (In consideration of the ill state of your health at Newbury, we think it advisable that you remove to a better air). And after candles were brought in, this clause was agreed to be added (Which makes us think your removal from that Air adviseable). The letter was as followeth:

Exon, May 6th, 1713. Reverend Sir, Whereas we, the United Ministers of Devon & Cornwal being now assembled in the City of Exon, have understood by the principal citizens thereof that you have receiv'd from them (together with their surviving ministers) an unanimous call to

[1]He was not one of the six Salters' Hall Lecturers in 1713, and must have attended as the representative of the Exeter Presbyterians, amongst whom his family occupied a prominent position according to the Minutes of the Committee of Thirteen.
[2]The words " determine for " were deleted and " advise " written above.

supply the vacancy occasion'd by the death of the late Reverend Mr Tross, whom we esteem'd our common Father, we shall heartily rejoice in your compliance with it: and cannot but express our great satisfaction to see your own inclinations towards it, in the letters you have lately sent them: understanding from your physicians, from your [fo. 84v., reversed] brother Allein, and yourself, that your health is in no small danger at Newbury (whose life and welfare we are all concern'd for) which makes us think your removal from that air adviseable: and being likewise of opinion that the well supplying of this post is of the utmost consequence to religion in these two counties, therefore we hereby signifie our hearty desire of your presence and assistance in these parts. Subscrib'd in the name and by the order of the Assembly by George Bowcher, moderator, Isaac Gilling, scribe.

[fo. 83v., rev.[1]] *Mr Sandercock said at Mr John Vowler's before Mr and Mrs Walrond and myself to Mr Vowler. You would not have gained your point had not I gone out of the Assembly and carried away 5 or 6 with me.*

[fo. 84v., reversed (continued)] 38 ministers dined with Henry Walrond, Esquire, and 38 with Mr Tristram.

Memorandum: Mr Nathaniel Cock is said to have preach'd without being examin'd or licens'd, and when but 20 years of age. Propos'd whether it be not expedient that candidates state & defend a theological question, preach a sermon before some of the United Brethren, & perform other exercises before they be licens'd? And whether such ministers being deputed by the Assembly having examind them and heard them dispute and preach, may not have power to license them, if satisfy'd in their qualifications.

[fo. 83v., reversed] Poor widdows of Ministers, Mrs Par of Ottery St. Mary, Mrs Taylor of Holdsworthy, Mrs Palk of East Ogwell, Mrs Sprague of Tiverton, Mrs Mortimer, Mrs Hallet[2] of Exon, Mrs Berry of Barnstaple, Mrs Cudmore of Chulmleigh.

[fo. 82v., reversed.]
EXETER, 1713, Sept. 8th & 9th. At the Meeting of the United Brethren of Devon and Cornwall.

[Present:] Mr John Walrond, moderator, Isaac Gilling, scribe; Mr Balster, Hooper, Hallett, Sandercock, S. Wood, Ball, Horsham, Hall, Evans, Moor, Hancock, Lissant, Symonds, Edgley, Giles, Short, Atkins, Cox, Eveleigh, Sloly, Majendie, Grigg, Walker, Coulton, Manston, Hody, Henry Brett, Wills, Glanvil, Palk, Samuel Stoddon, Brown, Beadon, Bishop, Adams.
From Somerset: Batson, James, Cornish, Groves. Candidates: J. Lavington, Joseph Hallett, Par, Cudmore, Stevenson.

Mr Short who was chosen Moderator desir'd to be excus'd, having of late been indisposd of an ague. Order'd that Mr Short be Moderator next Assembly, that Mr Stoddon pray, or if he fail Mr Henry Brett. Mr Cox being appointed to preach, and desiring that Mr Pierce, (who hath accepted Exon people's call) might preach in his turn, resolv'd that

[1]This shorthand passage comes at the very end of the minutes for this Assembly.
[2]The wife of Joseph Hallet I, who had died in 1689.

Mr James Pierce preach next Assembly at Mr Cox's request, and Mr Cox the Assembly following.

[fo. 81v., reversed] Brought into the Fund

	£	s	d
By Mr Eveleigh	7	19	0
Mr Ball	1	14	6
Mr Manston for Goon Rounston ...	1	0	0
More	5	5	6
	15	19	0

Paid

	£	s	d
To Mr Penuel Symonds	1	8	0
More[1]		5	6
To Mr Manston for Beer Meeting-house	5	0	0
To Mr Coulton for Goon Rounston	1	0	0

The Ministers present gave Mr Symonds 22s more to buy him a coat. Resolv'd that such as took up Midsummer Quarter last Assembly have 1 quarters contribution abated now by the Receiver of the Fund, according to the order of the last Assembly, except Budleigh Meeting, which is to have no abatement. A petition from Hatherleigh Meeting desiring help from the Fund. Mr Lissant is their minister. The Meeting consists of about 150 Hearers above 50 of whom are communicants.

Mr Manston informs the Assembly that Mr Broadmead who says he has laid out about £70 about Beer Meeting House is willing to sell it for £15 or £20, and give up his title to it. He desires some of the ministers to make collections in order to buy it, that it may not be sold away. Mr Walrond and Mr Beadon promis'd to endeavour to collect some money to that end.

Exon., Sept. 9, 1713. Whereas the Ministers now assembled are inform'd by some of the Congregation in Beer that their Meeting House is speedily to be sold, which would [fo. 80v., reversed] be a great prejudice to the Meeting should it be bought by any other than the people concern'd, we have already allotted £5 towards the purchase in case they can obtain a good title and procure the money that shall be further needful for that purpose. Accordingly we recommend their case to all well disposed Christians. Subscrib'd in the name of the Assembly by John Walrond, moderator, Is. Gilling, scribe.

A petition from Looe in Cornwall representing that by Mr Merryon's removal to London they are destitute of a settled Minister, desiring the Assembly to recommend one to them. Mr Cudmore who has preach'd among them with approbation by the advice of the Assembly consented to supply the Meeting till next Assembly.

Exon, Sept. 9th, 1713. The case of Mr Samuel Wood with relation to some of the people and the Meeting House in North Moulton being again heard & debated in the Assembly of the United Ministers after the said Mr Wood had been heard and what was offer'd on the behalf of the people of North Moulton, the Assembly unanimously came to the following resolution, scilicet: that there is no manner of ground or reason

[1]This presumably means that Penuel Symonds had 5s 6d extra.

for the accusations brought against Mr Wood, but in that whole affair he hath carry'd himself with justice and integrity as becomes a Christian and a Minister. John Walrond, Isaac Gilling.

[fo. 79v., reversed] Mr Bishop in behalf of Sir John Davy desires the advice of this Assembly about an annuity given by his Uncle Sir John Davy to the Vicar of [¹] on condition that he preach & expound the catechism Lord's Days in the afternoon: whether he is oblig'd to pay this annuity to the present incumbent who doth not perform the condition on which it was granted? Resolv'd, that 'tis not proper for this Assembly to intermeddle in this affair.

Mr Thomas Lavington who was one and twenty years old the [¹] day of August last propos'd himself to examination in order to be licens'd to preach. He was inform'd that it was contrary to a resolution of the Assembly to license one of his age. When he persisted earnestly to desire it, alledging that otherwise some might reflect upon him as if he was rejected for want of due qualifications; the matter was further debated. But there being no present necessity for his entering upon preaching, the Assembly did not think fit to act contrary to their own Rule by granting his request. And advis'd him to follow his studies for one year longer.

[fo. 78v., reversed] Resolv'd that to prevent young men from entring upon preaching without due qualifications, for the future all candidates who propose themselves to be licens'd, be examin'd during the Assembly by some deputed therby, and if so far approv'd be oblig'd to state and defend a Theological Question in Latine, and to preach a Sermon upon a Text given them before four or more of the United Brethren in some private licens'd house, where they are also to pass under such further trials and examinations as to their skill in languages philosophy divinity etc., as those brethren shall think fit, before whom these exercises are performed. Resolv'd, that notwithstanding such approbation and license to preach, whenever any candidates offer themselves to Ordination the Ordainers have liberty further to examine them and put them upon such further exercises as they think fit.

[fo. 79r., reversed] To Mr Nathaniel Cock of Chulmleigh. Exon,. Sept. 9th, 1713. Sir, It being agreed upon by the Assembly that no candidate should preach before he be in full communion and hath been examin'd by some of the Ministers, the Assembly having heard that you have preach'd twice upon the desire of neighbour ministers, and as they tell us in a case of some necessity, yet desire you would forbear for the future, that some order may be kept up among us, and the Ministry be not reflected upon. So we wish you well in your studies and increase in knowledg and piety. Subscrib'd, in the name & by the order of the Assembly, by John Walrond, moderator.

[fo. 78v., reversed, continued] Mr Evans inform'd the Assembly that Mr Walsh frequently leaves his congregation for one or 2 Lord's Days and takes no care to get it supply'd. Mr Cox desir'd to discourse with him about it.

[fo. 77v., reversed] The following letter read. For the Reverend the President of the Assembly of Dissenting Ministers in Exon. To be com-

¹Blank in MS.

municated to his brethren. Sandford, Sept. 7, 1713. Reverend Sirs, In a sermon which I preach'd in Exon April 16th last past (the true and whole design of which was in that critical juncture to promote peace and love and national unity[1]) I took notice that two of your body (like men of candour and judgment) had publicly owned the Church of England to be a noble part of the Reformation (as doubtless it is). But this sermon of mine being printed, another of your body hath since persecuted me with his angry letters about it; and (among other reflecting passages, reflecting, I say, not only on my self, but on the whole Church of England) hath sent me the following words: viz:

"The Church of England is so noble a part of the Reformation that no other is fit to be nam'd on the same day with her, and noble indeed she is if you regard her edifices, her dignities, and revenues: but the truest nobility of any Church lies in a conformity to the pattern received in the Mount; without which the former is but vain pageantry. And could I see that she had any apostolical discipline, apostolical terms of communion, or so much as one apostolical officer, I should more readily join with you (he should have [fo. 76v., reversed] said with my Brethren) than as yet I can in giving her that character."

This expression I look upon as a plain denial of our having in the Church of England any of the aforesaid things; without which I see not how she (or any other) can be so much as a Christian church. If you can show me how it may be so, I shall be thankful for the light which you are pleased to afford me. But for preventing of an increase of our discord and animosities and of our unhappy divisions (which eat out the very heart of all true religion and indanger our best interests) and because I would not charge a whole body of men with what one or some few only are to be charg'd: I make it my humble request that you will be pleas'd to inform me (in such friendly manner as you think best) which of your aforesaid Brethren's sentiments you do adhere to, and in particular, whether you do approve of Mr Samuel Hall's words. Your more judicious answer is expected and will be acknowledged as a favour by a sincere well wisher to peace, love and charity, and who is, sirs, your affectionate friend and humble servant, Robert Ham.

For the Reverend Mr Robert Ham, Rector of Stockly English. Exon, Sept. 9, 1713. Reverend Sir, We have received your friendly letter, which [fo. 75v., reversed] we have carefully perus'd with that which inclos'd it. We are not a little pleas'd that you so fully declare your resolutions to pursue peace; and we can as sincerely assure you that it is our settled purpose to do what in us lies towards the restoring and preserving peace unity & love; and for the healing of our breaches. We are satisfy'd, that the Particular Churches of England, according to the National Establishment, are true Christian Churches, and that their Presbyters are Ministers of Christ; which our brother, Mr Hall, readily owns in concurrence with us. However, we judg there is so much weight in the objections which have been offer'd by our fathers and brethren against some things with reference to the terms of communion, discipline & officers of those churches, as obliges us to dissent from them. And we

[1]This was the time of a High Church reaction culminating in the abortive Schism Act of 1714.

still desire to increase in that light & love which may teach us to manage our dissent with as much Christian temper and peace as possible (all possible peace & Christian temper). And we should heartily rejoice to find you, and your brethren entertaining the same charitable sentiments with relation to us and our congregations; which, in a great measure, would prevent those ill consequences of our unhappy differences, which may otherwise eat out the heart of true religion, and indanger all our best interests. We conclude with assurances of our great respect for you, and our prayers for your health and success in your labour. Subscrib'd in the name and by the order of the Assembly, by John Walrond, moderator.

[fo. 74v., reversed]
EXETER, 1714, May 4th.

[Present:] Mr Benjamin Hooper, moderator, Thomas Edgley, scribe; Mr Hallet, Gilling, Horsham, Harding, Sandercock, Walsh, Rosewell, Moor, Larkham, Withers, Evans, Martyn, Ball, Symonds, Kellow, Enty, Walrond, Peirce, Giles, Majendie, Bowcher, Short, Atkins, Cox, Eveleigh, Slowly, Baron, Huddy, Grigg, Palk, Wills, Stoddon, Beadon, Bishop, Carkeet, Strong, Hancock, Furse, Clark, Bond, Colton, Adams. Candidates: Lavington, Greby, Youat, Hornabrook, Hallett, Parr, Facy, Stogdon, How. Foreign ministers: Powel, Batson, James, Lobb, Blake, Warren. Candidates: Hallett, Pearse, Batten, Bale.

Brought in to the Fund.

	£	s	d
Mr Enty	5	6	0
Mr Harding	9	11	6
Mr Walrond	6	0	0
Mr Ball	1	10	0
Mr Adams' legacy	5	0	0
	27	7	6

[fo. 73v., reversed] Thanks given to Mr Stoddon for his good prayer, and to Mr Pierce for his excellent sermon, and he was desir'd to print it.

Order'd that the Moderator, Scribe, and persons to examine candidates for the future be chosen by ballotting. That no Moderator be chosen unless fifteen ministers are present: and any Minister who appears to be in town and is chosen, tho not present, is to serve the Assembly in that capacity, when he comes into it. That candidates propose themselves on Tuesday in the afternoon. That every candidate who is examined & licensed be recommended to the grace of God in his work, by the Moderator, in his concluding prayer.

Mr Cox to preach next Assembly, if he fail Mr Eveleigh. Mr Bret to pray, if he fail Mr Brinley.

Mr Stogdon[1] examin'd in order to publick preaching, by Mr Ball, Walrond, Withers, Enty, Evans, who gave a good account of his abilities.

[1] A student at Hallet's Academy in Exeter. He was orthodox at this time but later caused scandal by adopting Arian beliefs. *Dictionary of National Biography*: Hubert Stogdon.

Orderd that he make and defend a thesis on this Question: An Christus sit Mediator secundum utramque naturam? That he preach on Fight the Good Fight of Faith. That if the 5 City ministers approve his performances they give him a license and recommend him to the Grace of God by solemn prayer.

[fo. 72v., reversed] Mr Par agreed to settle at Oakhampton for one year, if the people can give him a tolerable maintenance. Mr Youat promis'd to comply with the request of the Assembly to be ordain'd next September.

[fo. 71v., reversed] The State of the Fund, Sept. 8th, 1714. Places and persons in stated pay:

Devon							Per annum, £
Kings Carswel	...	...	...	...	...		6
Bow ...	...	...	...	...	...	...	5
Hatherly	...	...	...	...	...	...	4
Holdsworthy	...	...	...	...	...	...	4
Ufculm	...	...	...	...	...	...	2
Halberton ...	...	...	...	...	...	...	2
North Molton	...	...	...	...	...	...	2
Sidmouth	...	...	...	...	...	...	2
Buckerel	...	...	...	...	...	...	2
Plympton	...	...	...	...	...	...	2
Budleigh	...	...	...	...	...	...	1
Mr Mudge ...	...	...	...	...	...	...	10
Mr Grigg	...	...	...	...	...	...	8
Mr Balster, dec.	...	...	...	...	...	...	5
							—
							55
Cornwall							
Liskard	...	...	...	...	...	...	5
Bodmin	...	...	...	...	...	...	4
Fowey	...	...	...	...	...	...	5
Goon Rounston	...	...	...	...	...	...	1
							—
							15
							—
					[Grand total]		70

[fo. 70v., reversed]
EXETER, 1714, Sept. 7th, 8th.

[Present:] Mr James Peirce, moderator, Thomas Edgley, scribe; Mr Hooper, Hallett, Gilling, Horsham, Sandercock, Walsh, Larkham, Withers, Evans, Martyn, Ball, Symonds, Walrond, Giles, Majendie, Short, Atkins, Cox, Eveleigh, Sloly, Hughes, Bartlet, Norman, Manston, Glanvil, Wills, Brett, Brown, Gough, Beadon, Bishop, Carkeet, Hancock, Furse, Lissant, Bond, Walker, Colton, Edmonds. Candidates: Lavington, Stevenson, Hallett, Hornabrook, Force, Shapland, Cock. Ministers Foreign: James, Aycrigg, Cornish, Force, Billingsley.

Brought in to the Fund.

					£	s	d
Exon ministers	...	...	...	...	62	17	0
Mr Eveleigh	...	...	...	...	9	0	0
Mr Horsham	...	...	...	...	2	12	0
Mr Ball ...	...	...	...	...	1	12	6
					66	1	6[1]

Order'd that the arrears of the Fund be paid in full to the 24th of June last. That Ufculm, Hatherly, and North Molton have 40 shillings yearly added to each of them, the 1st quarter payable at Christmas. That 3 pounds be paid to Mr Symonds, & 40s to Mr Tingcombe.

[fo. 69v., reversed] Mr Larkham, Evans, Carkeet, and Manston, appointed to examine Mr Shapland in order to his publick preaching, report that he was competently qualify'd. Order'd that he make and defend a thesis on this Question: An Foedus gratiae sit conditionatum? That he preach on Matthew 1:21, and that if the neighbouring ministers approve his performances they give him a license.

Resolv'd that balloting be laid aside on the account of some inconveniences that attend it. That no person less than forty years of age be chosen Moderator for the future.

Orderd that Mr Eveleigh preach next Assembly, and if he fail Mr Manston. That Mr Brinly pray, and if he fail Mr Gough.

[fo. 68v., reversed]
EXETER, 1715, May 3rd.

[Present:] Mr John Enty, moderator, Thomas Edgley, scribe; Mr Isaac Gilling, William Horsham, Jacob Sandercock, Thomas Walsh, John Rosewell, John Moor, Deliverance Larkham, Richard Evans, John Ball, Jelinger Symonds, John Walrond, James Peirce, William Giles, Andre Majendie, Samuel Short, Henry Atkins, Josiah Eveleigh, George Bowcher, John Sloly, William Bartlett, Joseph Manston, Peter Baron, Matthew Huddy, Samuel Grigg, Richard Glanvil, William Palk, Benjamin Wills, Jonathan Wheeler, Henry Brett, Hugh Brown, George Lissant, Roger Beadon, Thomas Bishop, James Strong, Cornelius Bond, Alexander Walker, Samuel Adams, Edward Colton.
Candidates: Cudmore, John Parr, George Brett, John Lavington, Facey, John Force, William Youatt, Hornabrook, Greby, Shapland.
Ministers of other counties: James, Edward Bearne, Darracot.
Candidate: Whitty.

Brought to the Fund.

					£	s	d
Exon ministers	...	...	...	...	56	19	6
Mr Harding ...	...	...	...	...	8	10	0
Mr Enty ...	...	...	...	...	6	0	0
Mr Walrond ...	...	...	...	...	6	0	0
Mr Horsham ...	...	...	...	...	1	18	9

[1]Note error in addition. The total should be £76 1s 6d.

Mr Ball	...	...	...	...	...	1	0	0
Mr Peirce received for the Fund	...	...	6	18	9

86	17	0[1]

[fo. 67v., rev.] Order'd that

Mr Grigg have	...	...	...	...	10	0	0
Mr Majendie this year	...	...	...	8	0	0
Cofton meeting this year	...	...	...	4	0	0
Added to Hatherly this year	...	...	2	0	0
Given now to Mr Walrond for Upottery	...	2	0	0
That there be added yearly to Ufculm	...	2	0	0
That Penzance have yearly	...	...	2	0	0
That Mr Strong have	...	...	...	2	0	0
Mr Cox	...	...	...	...	...	1	0	0
Mr Edmunds...	...	...	...	...	1	0	0
Buckeril Meeting	...	...	...	...	1	9	0

Mr Cox, Mr Edmunds, Buckeril Meeting — quarter year

Agreed that the following persons have the following sums out of Mr Harding's money (at his desire):

	£	s
Mr Strong...	...	...	2	0
Mr Palk	...	...	1	0
Mr Edmunds	...	...	1	0
Mr Symonds	...	...	1	0
Mr Grigg ...	...	...		10

Mr Beadon desir'd to pray, the persons appointed failing. Resolv'd that Mr Hughes preach next Assembly, and if he fail Mr Manston; that Mr Gough pray, & if he fail Mr Brown.

That Mr Youatt be ordaind at Culliton June 28 by Mr Ball, Walrond, Manston, Withers, Horsham, and Evans. His Question: An ordinatio per Presbyteros sit licita? That Mr Parr be ordaind at Okehampton July 20 by Mr Hallett, Peirce, Sandercock, Enty, Edgley, Eveleigh. His Question: An Secessio nostra a Communione Episcopali sit schismatica?

[fo. 66v., rev.] Some of Silferton lodgd a petition against Mr Sloly on Tuesday. Orderd that his case be heard tomorrow morning at 7 a Clock, by the whole Assembly, not by a Select Committee. That none but ordain'd ministers be present. A letter sent to desire him to be present at that time with such friends as might contribute anything to his vindication. Mr Sloly propos'd that Mr Adams might withdraw while his case was under debate. Resolvd, nemine contradicente, that Mr Adams do not withdraw. That the crime acknowledg'd by Mr Sloly was a sufficient reason for his being desired to desist from preaching. Tis the determination of this Assembly that Mr Sloly desist from preaching for 3 Lord's Days: and that a solemn day of fasting and prayer be afterwards appointed in his congregation for his own and people's humiliation before God, at which some neighbouring ministers are desired to assist.

Out of Mr Edgley's minutes.

Mr [2] Preach'd. Mr [2] pray'd.

[1]Note error in addition. The total should be £87 7s 0d.
[2]These spaces were left blank.

[fo. 65v., reversed]
EXETER, 1715, September 5.

[Present:] Mr Jacob Sandercock, moderator, Thomas Edgley, scribe; Mr Joseph Hallett, Isaac Gilling, Edward Bishop, Thomas Walsh, John Rosewell, John Moor, Deliverance Larkham, John Withers, Richard Evans, Michael Martyn, John Ball, Jelinger Symonds, John Walrond, James Peirce, William Giles, André Majendie, Samuel Short, Henry Atkins, John Cox, Josiah Eveleigh, John Sloly, John Hughes, Joseph Manston, Peter Baron, Samuel Grigg, Richard Glanvil, Benjamin Wills, Samuel Stoddon, Henry Brett, Hugh Brown, George Lissant, Roger Beadon, Thomas Bishop, Samuel Carkeet, Isaac Clark, Cornelius Bond, Alexander Walker, Edward Colton, Samuel Adams. 41. Ministers of other Counties: John Moor, John Moor [jun.], Thomas Moor, Edward Bearne, Towgood. Candidates: George Brett, Stephenson, John Lavington, Joseph Hallett, Hornabrook, James How, Nathaniel Cock, Hubert Stogdon, John Force. Candidates of Somerset, London, etc.: Rowe, John Munkley, Milner, Milner,[1] Facey.

Brought in to the Fund

	£	s	d
Mr Ball	1	12	9
Mr Adams	1	19	0
[fo. 64v., reversed] Given to Mr Symonds at Mr Adams request	1	19	0
to Alesbeer Meeting now	2	0	0
to Mr Lissant now (besides his yearly contribution)	2	0	0
Orderd that Mr Palk of Ilfercomb have yearly ...	3	0	0
Mr Bond of Ashburton yearly	3	0	0
Cofton (or Cockwood) Meeting an yearly addition of	3	0	0

The first payment of these 3 to begin at Michaelmas. That the contribution to Holdsworthy be stopt.

Orderd that Mr Hallett preach if Mr Hughes fail. Thanks given to Mr Hughes for preaching, to Mr Brown for Praying. Order'd that Mr Manston preach next Assembly or if he fail, Mr Bartlett. That Mr Gough pray, and if he fail, Mr Bishop or Mr Lissant.

That Mr John Lavington, Mr Joseph Hallett, and Mr James How be ordain'd at Exon, Sept. 28, by the 4 Exon ministers, Mr Ball & Mr Walrond. Mr Lavington's question: An Foedus gratiae sit conditionatum? Mr Hallett's: An S. Scriptura sit divinitus inspirata? Mr. How's: An Signam Crucis in Baptismo sit licitum?

The following ministers desir'd to make a collection for Hatherleigh Meeting in 2 months. Messrs Ball, Harding, Enty, Atkins, Carkeet, Beadon, Evans, Edgley, Giles, Peard, Wills, Bishop.

Out of Mr Edgley's *short and compressed*[2] minutes.

[1]This name is written twice without qualification.
[2]These three words were in shorthand.

[fo. 63v., rev.]
EXETER, 1716, May 8, 9. At the Meeting of the United Ministers of
Devon & Cornwall.

[Present:] Mr Isaac Gilling, moderator, Samuel Carkeet, scribe; Mr
Joseph Hallett, Senr., William Horsham, Jacob Sandercock, John
Rosewell, Samuel Hall, John Moor, Deliverance Larkham, John Withers,
John Evans, Michael Martyn, Daniel Kellow, John Ball, Jelinger
Symonds, James Peirce, Thomas Edgley, William Giles, André Majendie,
George Bowcher, Samuel Short, Henry Atkins, Josiah Eveleigh, John
Sloly, William Bartlett, John Norman, Peter Baron, Samuel Grigg,
Robert Wood, William Palk, Benjamin Wills, Hugh Brown, George
Lissant, Roger Beadon, Thomas Bishop, James Strong, Eliezer Hancock,
Isaac Clark, Cornelius Bond, Alexander Walker, Edward Colton, John
Edmunds, Samuel Adams, William Youatt, John Parr, John Lavington,
Joseph Hallett junior, James How. Candidates: Nathaniel Cock, Stephen
Towgood, Jones, Pyke, Nicodemus Harding, Stogdon, Force, Greby,
Baker, Hornabrook, Facy, Hanmer, Walrond.

Thanks given to Mr Bishop for praying & to Mr Bartlett for
preaching. Tis the unanimous desire and request of this Assembly that
Mr Bartlett [fo. 62v., rev.] would print his sermon, making such correc-
tions as he shall think fit. Mr Manston to preach next Assembly, if he
fails Mr How, if he fails Mr Baron. Mr Lissant to pray, if he fails Mr
Carkeet.

Brought to the Fund.

						£	s	d
By Mr Harding	...	...	...	...	...	9	0	0
Mr Hall	...	...	...	...	...	8	6	0
Mr Walrond	...	...	...	...	...	5	7	6
Mr Baron	...	...	...	...	...	5	2	6
Mr Ball	...	...	...	...	...	1	16	0
Mr Bond, Ashburton	...	...	...	...		1	16	0
						31	8	0

Mr Larkham was desir'd to make a collection for the Fund, the
same day they make it at other meetings in Exon.[1] Moreton, Bideford,
Barnstable, Puddington, to be desir'd to collect for the Fund.

					£	s	d
Paid to Mr Thomas Elms at Mr Hallett's Mr Hall's money, viz	...	...	...	...	8	6	0
to Mr Theophilus Tingcomb	...	...	...	4	0	0
to Mr Edward Bishop	...	...	...	...	2	0	0
to Chulmleigh Meeting at the desire of Exeter at present	...	...	...	...	5	0	0
to Mr Strong out of Mr Harding's and Mr Enty's money	...	...	...	...	4	0	0

[1]A few words of undecipherable shorthand occur here.

		£	s	d
to Hatherleigh Meeting out of Plymouth money at the same ministers desire towards building their Meeting House		3	0	0
to Mr Palk out of Mr Harding's	⎫	1	0	0
& to Mr Penuel Symonds	⎭		10	0
to Plympton Meeting out of Mr Baron's ...		1	0	0
to Buckrel Meeting out of Mr Ball's		1	10	0
Paid		30	6	0

[fo. 61v., reversed] A petition from Ashburton desiring more assistance from the Fund. They have £3 per annum already. Orderd that Ashburton have more £2. That Bovey have per annum £4. That Chulmleigh have per annum £5. The 1st half year to be paid next Assembly. The 1st quarterly payment for Ashburton and Bovey to be made at Midsummer.

A letter from Hatherleigh[1] representing the state of the Congregation, and desiring assistance from the Fund. Orderd that Mr Lissant have at present £6 out of the Fund for himself, and that his case be further consider'd in order to a yearly allowance. Mr Arnold promis'd the Moderator and Mr Lavington to lend £10 in order to pay off the Notes for building the Meeting House, Collected towards the Meeting at Hatherleigh:

	£	s	d		£	s	d
Plymouth ...	3	0	0	In Mr Arnold's hands	3	0	0
Barnstable ...	3	0	0	Mr Withers's...	1	1	6
Totness	3	0	0	Mr Atkins's ...	1	0	0
Mr Sandercock ...	2	0	0	Mr Lissant's ...	1	0	0
Mr Gilling ...	2	5	6	Mr Lavington's		5	0
Budleigh	1	0	0				
Mr Bishop ...		13	6				
Mr Evans ...		5	0				

	£	s	d
[fo. 60v., rev.] Promised more by Mr Hallet	1	10	0
Mr Lavington ...	1	10	0
Mr Eveleigh ...	1	0	0

if it can prevent breaking the Meeting.

Towards paying off Mr Combe of Hatherleigh.

Mr Benjamin Flavel of Holdsworthy having sent no answer to the letter from the Assembly, the following letter was drawn up, read, and subscrib'd. Exon, May 9th, 1716. Sir, By the order of the Assembly I acquaint you, that since you have taken no notice of the admonition they gave you by a letter, and have neither come, nor sent to them, as they desired you, they are resolved not to own you any longer as a Brother, unless you take some fair course to give them satisfaction.[2] Isaac Gilling, moderator, p[ro] t[empore.]

[1]See also Appendix A 15–16.
[2]The nature of the offence was not recorded by Gilling.

A petition of John Marley of S. Molton undone by Suretiship desiring the Assembly to raise money for him, read. Mr Edgley gave an account of his poverty.

[fo. 59v., rev.] Some objections were made against the Additional Minute about fixed Ministers removing (made May 9, 1710) viz; that greater power is given to four Ministers than to the whole Assembly; and that it takes away from the Minister the judgment of discretion. After some debate the Minute was thus alter'd: Resolved, N.C., that no Minister settled in any congregation shall remove from it and settle in another, without offering his reasons for so doing to the to next Assembly if there be any within two months: but if there be not, that he give them in writing to four neighbouring ministers; and if they do not approve of his removal, that then he give them to the next Assembly.

Mr Stephen Towgood[1] proposed himself to be examined in order to Ordination. Mr Nicodemus Harding and Mr George Hanmer propos'd themselves to be examined in order to preaching. Mr Evans, Peirce, Baron, Eveleigh, appointed to examine them reported that they [fo. 58v., rev.] were well satisfied in their ministerial abilities. Order'd that Mr Ball, Peirce, Walrond, and Evans ordain Mr Towgood, and appoint exercises, time, and place. Memorandum: Mr Stephen Towgood was ordain'd at Axminster, [July 4][2] 1716. Mr [Evans][2] preach'd, Mr [Ball][2] pray'd, at the imposition of hands, Mr [Peirce][2] gave the Exhortation. Order'd that Mr Harding and Mr Hanmer have licence to preach as candidates till an opportunity present for their ordination.

Mr Jones his case was debated. The Assembly expect that he propose himself to ordination at their next Meeting or give sufficient reasons for his refusal.

Mr Larkham and Mr How complain'd against Mr Stoddon and Mr Force for exchanging congregations, Mr Stoddon leaving Bovey to Mr Force, & taking the charge of Ailsbeer from whence Mr Force remov'd. Resolv'd that Mr Stoddon be desir'd to appear, without fail, at the next Assembly.

[fo. 57v., rev.] The French Minister of Plymouth, Monsieur [3] desires the opinion of this Assembly whether a French Refugee who is married to his sister in law by a Church of England minister, may be admitted to the peace of the Church. The Assembly can't see how the Consistory can restore him to the peace of the Church, while he continues in this incestuous state. This was the case of King Henry 8th. The foreign universities judg'd his taking his brother's wife to be an unlawful incestuous marriage. Vid=Quick Synodic. vol. [4] pag. [4].

Twas propos'd that no particular minister should give a certificate

---

[1]The younger son of Stephen Towgood of Axminster, the Independent, who has already appeared in these Minutes.

[2]These spaces were left blank on this page, but the details have been provided from MS. f39v.

[3]The minister of the Conformist Huguenot Church at Plymouth from 1685–1723 was James Dejoux. The names of those directing the Nonconformist Huguenots in Plymouth at this date are not known. *Trans. Devon. Assoc.*, 1934, LXVI, p. 178.

[4]These spaces were left blank. The reference may be to John Quick's *Synodicon in Gallia Reformata*, 1692, i, pp. 18, 40, but it is more likely that Gilling intended John Quick's *A serious inquiry . . . 1703*, p. 3.

to any of his people (I think in order to ask relief or make collections) without the advice and consent of an Assembly.

The following letter read: To the Reverend Ministers of Christ of the County of Devon, etc., assembled at Exon: Portsmouth, May 5th, 1716. Reverend Sirs, The Congregation of Dissenting Protestants in this place, lately under the pastoral [fo. 56v., rev.] care of the Reverend Mr Simon Brown, by whose removal to London we are become destitute of a minister having had a recommendation from him of the Reverend Mr John Norman now of Bideford and seen a very large & honourable testimonial concerning him from several Reverend members of your Assembly, do generally conclude him a proper person to supply their present vacancy, but are willing to have the way clear'd for his removal: and understanding it to be a custom for your Assembly to be advised with in all such cases relating to any of your members have thought it proper to communicate their purpose to him by your hands. We therefore whose names are subscribed having been deputed by the body for this purpose do by this letter give him an invitation to take the pastoral care of us, if it may be done consistently with the relation wherein he stands to his people at present, to whom we have signified our purpose by another letter, as we do to you by this. And we doubt not but you will advise him and them on this occasion as shall be most for the honor of God, and the good of the Church in general, as well as for our particular advantage and satisfaction. We subscribe ourselves, Reverend Sirs, your very humble servants, Thomas Barton, William Palmer, Henry Seager, Thomas Hammond, Philemon Powel, Caleb Wroth, James White junior, William Chapman.

[fo. 55v., rev., Shorthand] *To the Congregation of Dissenting Protestants in Bideford, now under the pastoral care of the Reverend Mr John Norman. Portsmouth, May 5, 1716. Christian Brethren, We, Protestant Dissenters in the town of Portsmouth, upon the recommendation of our late minister now removing from us to London, and other Testimonials concerning him have come to a resolution to invite the Reverend Mr John Norman your worthy minister to fill up the vacancy. But as we would in such a proceeding do nothing unfair or unchristian, and wishing to do it with your approbation and consent, and we cannot doubt that your regard to the common interest of Christians which you should prefer to your own private advantage, and which he may be much more serving here than with you, and your regard to the welfare of himself and family, which, we are informed, has not among you an income sufficient to subsist him, will prevail with you to yield him up to us. We have at the same time referred ourselves in this matter to the Assembly at Exeter to whose judgment and advice we doubt not you will conform yourselves. We subscribe in the name of the congregation being thereunto deputed, your affectionate Brethren, Thomas Barton, etc., ut supra.*

[fo. 55v., rev.] The following answer drawn up by Mr Hallett senior and Mr Ball was agreed unto and orderd to be subscribed by the Moderator, and sent:

At the Assembly of the United Brethren of Devon & Cornwal at Exon, May 9th, 1716. To the Congregation of Dissenting Protestants in Portsmouth. Christian Friends. It has always been our opinion that the removal of a minister from his congregation is a matter of no little importance and difficulty. We have therefore made it a Minute in our Assembly that none of us should remove to another people without first acquainting a considerable [fo. 54v., rev.] number of our Brethren with it. We take it kindly that you have been pleased to communicate to us your invitation of Mr Norman to be your Pastor; and have discours'd our brother in relation to the offer you have made him. The continuance of such a person as Mr Norman among us (to whose undissembled piety ministerial abilities & soundness in the Faith we readily give our Testimony) would be very agreeable. You have offerd us several reasons to induce us to consent to his removal: but it being not possible (because of the little time we are to continue in this city, and the considerable distance of Bideford from hence) to hear what his people may offer against it; we judge it proper to leave the matter to Mr Norman himself, who after he has debated it with his people, and seriously made his address to God for direction will best determine what may be his duty in the present case. We have nothing to add but our hearty prayer that his determination may be for God's glory and the Churches good. Subscrib'd in the name and by the order of the Assembly, by Isaac Gilling, moderator, p[ro]t[empore.]

[fo. 54v., rev. Shorthand.] *Mr Ball gives his service to Mr Barton.*[1]
To Mr Brown. Reverend Sir, having perused what Mr Norman has written, I think he has given a true account of the sentiments of the ministers in our Assembly, there has been no objection made against his accepting Portsmouth people's invitation, though they did not judge it impart any more to them than you will find in the enclosed. I am, Reverend Sir, Your affectionate Brother and humble servant. Isaac Gilling.

The Ministers dined at Capt. Lydston's, Mr Arnold's, Mr John Starr's, & Mr Hales's.

[fo. 53v., rev.]
EXETER, 1716, Sept. 4, 5. At the Meeting of the United Brethren of Devon & Cornwall.

[Present:] Mr John Ball, moderator, Isaac Gilling, scribe; 1. Joseph Hallett. 2. Isaac Gilling. 3. William Horsham. 4. Thomas Walsh. 5. John Moor. 6. Deliverance Larkham. 7. John Withers. 8. Richard Evans. 9. John Ball. 10. Jelinger Symonds. 11. James Peirce. 12. Thomas Edgley. 13. William Giles. 14. Andre Majendie. 15. Samuel Short. 16. Henry Atkins. 17. John Cox. 18. Josiah Eveleigh. 19. John Sloly. 20. William Bartlett. 21. Joseph Manston. 22. Samuel Grigg. 23. Benjamin Wills. 24. Jonathan Wheeler. 25. Samuel Stoddon. 26. Hugh Brown. 27. George Lissant. 28. Roger Beadon. 29. Thomas Bishop. 30. Samuel Carkeet. 31. James Strong. 32. Eliezer Hancock. 33. Walter Furze. 34. Benjamin Flavel. 35. Isaac Clark. 36. Cornelius Bond. 37. Alexander Walker. 38. William Youatt. 39. John Parr. 40. John Lavington. 41. Joseph Hallett junior. 42. James How. Ministers from Somerset: Stephen James, Darracot, James Cornish, Candidates: Nathaniel Cock, Facey, John Force, Hubert Stogdon, Hornabrook, Jacomb, Angel Shapland, Walrond of Wellington.

---

[1]This might be placed as a postscript to the note from Gilling to the Rev. Simon Brown, but is probably more correctly added to the official letter to Portsmouth immediately preceding.

Brought to the Fund.

						£	s	d
By Mr Eveleigh	...	...	...	...	...	7	2	0
Mr Horsham	...	...	...	...	...	4	10	0
Mr Manston	...	...	...	...	...	4	0	6
Mr Gilling ...	...	...	...	...	...	2	8	0
Mr Ball	...	...	...	...	...	1	11	0
Mr Walsh ...	...	...	...	...	...	1	10	6
						21	2	0

				£	s	d
Paid: To Mr Eveleigh for Shapland	...	...	7	2	0
To Mr Ball for Ed. Bishop	...	...	...	1	0	0
To Mr Stogdon ⎱ out of Mr	...	...	...	1	1	6
To Mr Bishop ⎰ Manston's	...	...	...	1	1	6
To Mr Ball for Buckrel	...	...	...	...	1	11	0
				11	16	0

In Mr Withers' hand: £9 16s 0d

[fo. 52v., rev.] Yearly contributions, 1716, out of the Funds.

MEETINGS	MINISTERS	EXON			LONDON		
		£	s	d	£	s	d
Cofton	Hugh Brown	9	0	0			
	Samuel Grigg	10	0	0			
	Andre Majendie	8	0	0			
Kings Carswell	Edward Colton	6	0	0	6	0	0
Ufculm	Samuel Short	6	0	0	5	0	0
Hatherleigh	George Lissant	6	0	0	5	0	0
Bow	Jelinger Symonds	5	0	0			
N. Molton	Alexander Walker	4	0	0	8	0	0
Ashburton	Cornelius Bond	5	0	0			
Ilford-Combe	William Palk	5	0	0	5	0	0
Bovey Tracey	John Force	4	0	0			
Sidmouth	Youatt, Stevenson	2	0	0	8	0	0
Sidbury	Isaac Clark	2	0	0			
Plympton	John Edmonds	2	0	0	8	0	0
Halberton	Samuel Wood	2	0	0			
¹Buckerel		2	0	0			
Chulmleigh	Walter Furse	5	0	0			
Budleigh	Roger Beadon	1	0	0	4	0	0
Torrington	Peter Kellow				8	0	0
Stoke in Ham	Thomas Walsh				6	0	0
Culliton					5	0	0
Kingsbridge	John Cox				4	0	0
Oakhampton	John Parr				5	0	0
Beer					3	0	0
Stockland					3	0	0

¹The name " Ball " is written in the margin in minute characters beside the word
' Buckerel ".

[fo. 51v., rev.]

CORNWALL. Yearly contributions.

MEETINGS	MINISTERS	EXON			LONDON		
		£	s	d	£	s	d
Liscard	Richard Glanvil	5	0	0			
Fowey	Daniel Kellow	5	0	0			
Bodmin	John Greby	4	0	0			
Pensance	Matthew Huddy	2	0	0			
Silferton	——		——			——	
Loo					10	0	0
Holdsworthy	——		——			——	

[fo. 49v., rev.][1] At Mr Walrond's desire 40s per annum was granted to Sidbury Meeting, which raises but £19 per annum.

A petition from 2 of South Molton, (*prosecuted for words spoken against Mr Courtenay, a non-juror*),[2] desiring help, was read. Resolv'd that we will not be concern'd.

That Mr Majendie's £8 per annum be continued. That Ilford-Combe and Cofton Meetings have each an addition of 40s per annum. The first quarterly payments to be made at Michaelmas.

The following letter from the London managers of the Fund read. We have consider'd your case, as it is at present represented to us; and accordingly have allocated to you [£93[3]] for this present year, towards the support of the Gospel amongst you. But yet we think it necessary to acquaint you, that we find there is too much cause to apprehend that there are many who address to us in this kind who fall exceedingly short of their duty by being too narrow hearted and straithanded towards their Ministers, either from too great a love of the world, and too low a value that they put upon spirituals, or from a partial judgment of their own abilities, or from the discouraging examples of some leading men among them, which they [fo. 48v., rev.] mistakingly think themselves to be regulated by; or lastly, by a groundless opinion taken up by them, that the obligation to the maintenance of a Gospel Ministry is by a rule of charity and not of justice: whereas the Spirit of God placeth it wholly upon the latter, and makes it a standing duty in the days of the Gospel, upon that very account. See and consider well, I Cor: 9:11,13,14. More-over, the Trust committed to us is to incourage the preaching of the Gospel in places truly indigent, where (upon the best inquiry) we find the people willing and forward to the utmost of their abilities, but not sufficiently able. It is far from the design of this undertaking to give to the rich, or indulge others of meaner capacity in the neglect of their duty: and therefore they who think themselves unconcerned to do their duty, must not expect the continuance of this supply from us, who are press'd upon by persons and places really indigent to do beyond what is in the power of our hands to do. Thus hoping you will consider what we say, and accept what we do, we subscribe, [etc.]

[1]fo. 50v. was not used in this sequence.
[2]In Shorthand.
[3]i.e. The total of the amounts allocated above. Space left blank in MS.

[fo. 47v., rev.] Mr Lissant was excus'd from praying on account of the perplexity of his affairs: and Mr Carkeet was desired to pray in his room.

Mr Benjamin Flavel brought a Testimonial of his regular carriage for a year past; with which the Assembly was satisfied.

Ordinations appointed. Mr Nathaniel Cock, who succeeds Mr Norman at Bytheford, Mr Bennet Stevenson, and Mr John Force of Bovey, offer'd themselves to be examined, in order to Ordination. Agreed, that Mr Ball, Horsham, Evans, Walrond, Peirce, Manston, ordain Mr Stevenson and Mr Force, and fix time and place. Mr Stevenson's question: An Lumen internum sit regula fidei et morum? Mr Force's: An S. Scriptura sit divinitus inspirata? That Mr Edgley, Bowcher, Kellow, Palk, Hancock, Wills, and Furse, ordain Mr Cock, and that they fix time and place. His question: An Satisfactio Christi sit necessaria? Memorandum: Mr Cock was ordain'd at Bytheford, October 24, 1716. Mr [1] preached, Mr [1] prayed over him, Mr [1] gave the Exhortation. [fo. 46v., rev.] Mr Stevenson was ordain'd at Topsham April 25, 1717. Mr Ball preach'd, Mr [1] pray'd over him, Mr Walrond gave the exhortation.

Mr Stoddon. Some of Bovey came with a complaint that Mr Stoddon had kept £6 14s collected in Exon, and that he had received for his salary money which he had collected to pay for the Meeting-House. And that he had deliver'd up 3 notes of £4 6s each, to some of Chudleigh, etc. Twas propos'd that the arbitration of this matter should be referr'd to Ministers. Mr Stoddon was not willing to refer it to any other Umpirage but that of the whole Assembly. The people would have left it either to particular ministers, or the whole Assembly. Mr Edward Wotton spake something in vindication of Mr Stoddon. Mr How complain'd that Mr Stoddon had taken from him his turn at Mr Stokes's (at Alesbeer). Mr Force, who began that Meeting declar'd [fo. 45v., rev.] that Mr Stoddon took upon him wholly to supply it with Mr How's consent. The further consideration of Mr How's complaint was put off till Mr Stokes should be present, which was expected on Wednesday in the afternoon. But no more was said about it for want of time.

Thanks given to Mr Manston for preaching, and to Mr Carkeet for praying. Mr Jaspar How to preach next Assembly, or if he fail, Mr Baron. Mr Lissant to pray, or if he fail Mr Strong.

Mr Thomas Bishop. Resolv'd N.C., that 'tis not lawful for a person to marry a child without the parent's consent. That Mr Bishop in marrying (Mary) the daughter of Sir John Davie (Bart) without his consent when he knew Sir John's aversion to it, is guilty of a sin. That his marrying her contrary [fo. 44v., rev.] to his promise that he would not marry her without her father's consent, is an aggravation of his sin. And that by both of these he hath brought a reflection upon the Ministry. Mr Bishop declar'd his sorrow for his sin in marrying Sir John Davie's daughter without his consent; his greater sorrow for the aggravation of it in doing it contrary to his own promise; and profess'd, that it more nearly touch'd his heart that hereby he had brought a reflection upon the Ministry. He also begg'd pardon of God, Sir John Davie, and the

[1]Blank in MS.

Ministers: and said he was ready to declare this his sorrow and repentance to the chief of his people, and to any others. Resolv'd that Mr Bishop in this Declaration of his Repentance hath given satisfaction to this Assembly. Dissentient only Mr Eveleigh and Mr Lavington. The question was propos'd a second time, and all the Ministers [fo. 43v., rev.] declared their satisfaction again, but 3 or 4: there being above 30 present. Resolv'd that the Moderator, in the name of the Assembly, give Mr Bishop an Admonition to prove the sincerity of his repentance by his future conduct.[1] Order'd that the Scribe give a Minute of what past in this matter to Mr Eveleigh or Mr Jacomb. Which he did; and thereupon Mr Bishop readily promis'd to endeavour to do it.[1]

[fo. 43v., reversed. Shorthand.] *The Moderator admonished him so to behave himself that his action might give nobody occasion to think he stood upon his vindication, but that he should declare that he had done amiss* [2] *and added, We trust you will take care to carry yourself humbly and admonish others when there is occasion not to take example by you; and that your diligence in your ministry and care of your conversation will show that you* . . . . .[3]

After the 1st Resolution the moderator persuaded Mr Bishop to make an ingenious confession of his fault in acting contrary to his duty. He said he promised and resolved not to marry Sir John Davie's daughter; that he was sorry for breaking those promises, begs pardon of God, of his Brethren in the ministry, and of Sir John Davie, and desired the prayers of the Assembly, resolving for the future so to behave himself in his ministry and whole conversation as to endeavour to get the blessing of God upon him and his. When he was asked whether he thought it was a fault to break his promise, [fo. 42v., rev.] he said he was sorry for anything that appeared to be sinful in what he had done, that he was sorry he had broken his promise, but would not say he was sorry that he had marry'd his wife. After the 2 last Resolutions had been past and reported to him, then he made the former full and ingenuous confession.

The Ministers dined with Capt. Lydston, Mr Trobridge, Mr Bastard, Mr Fryar.

[fo. 42v., rev.]
EXETER, 1717, May 7, 8. At the Meeting of the United Brethren of Devon and Cornwall.

[Present:] Mr Harding, moderator, Gilling, scribe; Mr Hallet, Horsham, Sandercock, Walsh, Hall, Moor, Larkham, Withers, Evans, Ball, Symonds, Enty, Walrond, Edgley, Giles, Majendie, Short, Atkins, Cox, Eveleigh, Sloly, Baron, Grigg, Palk, Wheeler, Brinley, Stoddon, Brown, Lissant, Beadon, Carkeet, Hancock, Furse, Flavel, Clark, Bond, Walker, Colton, Adams, Youatt, Lavington, Hallett junior, James How, Stephen Towgood, Cock, Stephenson. Candidates: Penuel Symonds, John Force, Hornabrook, Shapland, Stogdon, Greby, Jones of Tewkesbury. Of Somerset & Dorset: Berry, Wellington, Webber, Peirce, James of Yeovil.

[1] Although the whole passage is written in this order, the sentence ending *do it* is a comment on that ending *future conduct* and both are marked with an asterisk in the MS. for connection.
[2] This was left blank in the MS.
[3] This sentence was not finished in the MS.

[fo. 41v., rev.]

Brought to the Fund.

	£	s	d
Mr Hall	12	0	0
Mr Harding	7	0	0
Mr Enty	6	0	0
Mr Walrond	5	7	6
Mr Horsham	3	2	3
Mr Ball	1	10	0
	34	19	9

Twas orderd last Assembly that Mr Flavels contribution should be continued.

Paid: Out of Mr Hall's money to him:

	£	s	d
For Mr Elms	6	0	0
For Halberton	2	0	0
For Silferton	2	0	0
For Mr Palk	2	0	0

Out of Mr Harding's:

	£	s	d
For Gunrownson	2	0	0
For Plimpton	2	0	0
To Mr Penuel Symonds	1	1	6

Out of Mr Enty's:

	£	s	d
To him (viz. P. Symonds)...	2	0	0
To Mr Cox	1	0	0
To Gunrownson	2	0	0

	£	s	d
Mr Ball's to Buckril	1	10	0
To Mr Sloly. ½ year	3	0	0
To Mr Arnold	5	0	0

A petition from Silferton in behalf of Mr Sloly. Order'd that Silferton Meeting have £6 per annum, that £3 be paid Mr Sloly now for ½ a year ending at Ladyday last. Order'd that £5 be paid Mr Arnold now out of the money brought in, and the remaining £5 borrow'd of him for Hatherleigh Meeting another Assembly. A petition from Loo for help. They have £10 per annum from London, yet cannot make up £30. Order'd that an addition of 20s per annum be made to Cofton Meeting, 20s formerly given by 2 of Exon being withdrawn, so tis to have £10 per annum.

[fo. 40v., rev.] A petition from the Meeting at Ford or Stoke in Ham desiring help for their Meeting House which cost £80 the rebuilding. About £35 remains to be paid. The Assembly recommended it to such ministers as could to make collections and bring in the money next Assembly. Mr Bowcher & Hancock exhorted to get contributions for the Fund. A letter drawn up by Mr Eveleigh & Mr Edgley to be sent to the ministers of Biddeford, Barnstaple, Axminster, Puddington, Appledore, South Molton, to press them earnestly to make a collection for the

Fund in their congregations. The letter read. [Mr Edgley & Evans orderd to withdraw and soften some passages in it.]¹

[Shorthand] *At the meeting of the United Brethren of Devon and Cornwall at Exon, May 8, 1717. Reverend Brethren, The miserable circumstance of 30 poor congregations, and some of our distressed Brethren who have none* [sic], *together with the incapacity of the Fund to give them such relief as is equal to their necessities, oblige us to request you to use your best endeavours to procure some assistance from your Churches. We are firmly persuaded from the Word of God, that God will bless your people the more and make up trebly to what shall be laid out in so great a good work and shall bless you the more in your good labours if you shall encourage it by your renewed opportunity. The urgency of circumstances will be our apology for laying this matter afresh before you. We commend you, dear Brethren and your flocks to the divine blessing. Subscribed in the name and by order of the Assembly.*

[fo. 39v., rev.] Gunrownson desir'd the Assembly to recommend a Minister to them in the room of Mr Strong, who is remov'd to Pitminster in Somerset. Mr Facey who hath preach'd to them declines to settle among them. Mr Hanmer was recommended to them, to preach to them.

Ordinations. Order'd that Mr John Force (whose ordination was differ'd) be ordain'd at Bovey the last Thursday in June, viz: June [²] 1717. Mr Hallett to pray over him, Mr Gilling to preach, Mr Spark to give the Exhortation which was done accordingly. Mr Edgley began Mr Cox concluded with prayer.³

Examinations of Candidates. Dr May, Mr John Forse, Mr John Star, and Mr Thomas Lavington propos'd themselves to be examined in order to be licensed to preach. Dr May hath taken his degree of Doctor of Physick & been examined in Natural Philosophy, & hath Testimonials of his good conversation from his tutors in Scotland. [fo. 38v., rev.] Mr Gilling Withers Larkham and Atkins, were chosen for examiners by a considerable majority. Mr Larkham in their name reported that they were well satisfied in their orthodoxy and that their parts were competent. Dr May's Question: An Christus sit vere Deus? His Text. Eph. 2: 3. And were by nature, etc. Mr Lavington's: An Spiritus Sanctus sit Deus? His text John 3:2. Except a Man be born again. Mr Forse his Question: An Christus sit sacrificium propitiatorium? His text: Rom. 6:23. The Gift of God ... Mr Starr's question: An Supplicium Gehennae sit aeternum? His text: Heb. 12:14. And Holiness without which ... Orderd that Dr May's sermon and further trials be at Barnstable, the other Candidates at Exon in Whitsun week, the examiners & none else but ministers to be present.

Mr Stoddon. Mr Stoddon disappointed a Reference designd to be held at Topsham last Monday by Mr Edgley whom Bovey people chose and Mr Horsham whom he chose, upon the account of the death of his Mother-in-law: but he [fo. 37v., rev.] proposed to refer it to Ministers to have matters adjusted between this and next Assembly.

¹These words were deleted in MS.
²Blank in MS.
³A Memorandum on Stephen Towgood's ordination followed on here. The details have been transferred to a similar incomplete memorandum in the Minutes for May 1716, supra, p. 108.

Mr Enty complained that Plymouth Ministers were reflected on for not asking Mr [Fox][1] to preach. That they forbore in compliance with the order of the Assembly. That several ministers had broken that order. Mr Harding seconded Mr Enty and thought it hard they should be reflected on for keeping up order. The following letter to Mr [Fox[1]] drawn up by Mr Walrond, read:

Sir,[2] *Whereas we have always desired to act with the greatest uniformity and concord in the cases relating to the churches of Christ as becomes the ministers of peace, and accordingly have agreed by universal consent that no Candidates for the ministry be ordained to preach until they be 1st examined by some deputed by the Assembly and regularly licensed, we are willing to signify to you our concern to hear that you have preached in several congregations without such examination and license, and therefore [*3*] but since you devote yourself to the ministry of the Gospel you will present yourself to the Assembly [sic] to that purpose, not doubting that you will comply with public order which is so necessary to the welfare of the Church of Christ. Upon which account we cannot but approve of the conduct of the ministers at Plymouth in adhering to the minutes of the Assembly, and desire you will forgo preaching until you come in (at the right door) the right way, when we shall be glad of your society and the assistance of your good labours.*

[fo. 36v., rev.] Twas debated whether the letter should be sent, or the Assembly should depute some particular ministers to examine Mr [Fox] which Mr Edgley said, he would submit to. [Shorthand.] *Mr Sandercock proposed whether we should break the Articles for the sake of the rich and keep it with respect to the poor. Mr Enty said he could prove that Mr [Fox] said he would humble the Assembly; upon which the question being put whether the letter should be sent,* resolv'd that the letter be sent. The Assembly would not consent that Mr Colton should permit Mr [Fox] to preach in his pulpit next Lord's Day.

[Shorthand] *In the debate Mr Enty, Baron, Sandercock, were very warm, they submitted that they acted in this matter out of regard to the honour of the Assembly, and the interest of religion, that they had no prejudice against [Mr Fox], but if his preaching without examination be allowed others would think they might do the same, and thus could bring irregularities into our congregations; that if the Agreement of the Assembly with respect to this matter be a rule it ought to be insisted on; if a special person took upon himself to dispense with a rule of the Assembly, our Assembly signifieth nothing; if we make an order we bind ourselves. We must act agreeable to our order; if every one took a liberty to do as he pleases contrary to order, we come together for nothing. Mr Enty said 'twas better the congregations should be vacant than unexamin'd & unlicens'd candidates should preach.*

Thanks given to Mr Baron for preaching (on Feed the Flock of Christ) & Mr Brinley for praying. Orderd that Mr Jaspar How or Mr Huddy preach next Assembly: if they fail Mr Palk, that Mr Lissant pray, if he fail Mr Hancock. The Ministers din'd with Mr Henry Walrond, John Atkins, Pym, Vicary, Arnold, Brinley, Tozer.

---

[1]The Fox affair is dealt with in the Introduction, pp. xiv–xv. Fox's name was deleted in the MS.
[2]This and other shorthand passages in this sequence all occur in their correct positions in the MS.
[3]Blank in MS.

[fo. 35v., rev.]
EXETER, 1717, Sept. 3, 4. At the Meeting of the United Brethren of Devon.

[Present:] Mr Edgley Moderator, Mr Gilling, scribe; Mr Hallett, Horsham, Sandercock, Moor, Larkham, Withers, Evans, Ball, Jelinger Symonds, Enty, Peirce, Giles, Majendie, Atkins, Cox, Short, Wheeler, Wills, Sloly, Bartlett, Grigg, Powel, Lissant, Carkeet, Hancock, Flavel, Clark, Walker, Colton, Adams, Parr, Hallett junior, How, Towgood, Cock, Stephenson, Force. Mr Aaron Pitts of Somerset.
Candidates: Penuel Symonds, Hornabrook, Greby, Jacomb, Facey, Samuel Baker, Star, May, Thomas Lavington, Forse, Stogdon, Langdon, Whitty.

Brought to the Fund.

						£	s	d
By Mr Bartlett	...	...	...	...	...	7	17	0
Mr Wheeler	...	...	...	...	...	4	15	6
Mr Horsham	...	...	...	...	...	2	10	0
Mr Ball	...	...	...	...	...	1	16	0
Mr Short	...	...	...	...	...	1	10	0
From Mr Eveleigh	...	...	...	...	...	2	10	0
						20	18	6
Paid Mr Withers for Mr Arnold	...	...	...			5	0	0
Mr Bartlett for Mr Palk	...	...	...	...		2	0	0
for Mr P. Symonds	...	...	...			5	17	0
Mr Ball for Buckrel	...	...	...	...		1	16	0
To Mr Shapland	...	...	...	...	...	2	0	0

Mr Powel and Mr Cock promised to do somewhat for the Fund. And Mr Edgley promised to make a collection once a year if Mr Carkeet will. The Moderator at the motion of Mr Horsham recommended it to the Brethren to make a collection in their congregations for Mr Walker's Meeting House at Ford.

[fo. 34v., rev.] Examination of Candidates. [Mr John Fox of Plymouth][1] and Mr Thomas Elms of Tiverton propos'd themselves to be examin'd in order to be licens'd as candidates. They are both in communion, are of the age requir'd. Mr Hallett, senior [*said Mr Elms had read very little of*][2] Divinity. Twas said Mr Elms had been 2 years with Mr Hallett after Mr Moor had read Logick and Metaphysicks to him. Mr Edgley, Withers, Peirce, and Cox chosen examiners withdrew immediately to examine them. Mr Ball took the Moderators chair during his absence. Mr Aaron Pitts desir'd to be present at their examination. 'Twas said that it was not usual, he not being of our Assembly. However he went. The Examiners being return'd, the Moderator Mr

---

[1] The name and place were deleted in the MS.
[2] This phrase was written in shorthand. The sign preceding " Divinity " has not been identified. John Fox later described his fellow candidate as ' a very great blockhead '. *Trans. Devon. Assocn.*, 1896, xxviii, p. 145.

Edgley reported that they were fully satisfied as to their skill in all parts of learning, and that they were like to be very serviceable in the work of the Ministry.   Orderd that [Mr John Fox] preach at [Newton Abbot] before his examiners, or such of them as will come thither, & any other ministers, on Phillippians, [2:12.] Work out your own salvation with fear and trembling. And that he state and defend this question: An Separatio hominum ad munus pastorale sit a Christo instituta? That Mr Elms preach at Honiton before Mr Ball and the neighbouring ministers. His Text: [Phillippians 1:27.] Only let your conversation be as becometh the Gospel. His question: An anima Christi descendebat ad locum damnatorum?

Resolvd that when candidates preach their examiners take notice not only of the composure of their sermons, but of their motion, gesture, voice, and what else they think proper.

[fo. 33v., rev.] Mr Hallett senior (at the desire of the Assembly) preach'd, Mr Jaspar How, Mr Huddy, Mr Palk, who were appointed, all failing. Mr Lissant pray'd. Resolv'd that Mr How preach next Assembly, if he fail Mr Huddy, if he fail Mr Powel. [Shorthand.] *Some moved that Mr Powel might preach next Assembly; but 'twas carried against them as a breach of our orders, and that what might give offence if the Cornish ministers who were appointed should be set by. The Tuesday Mr How, Huddy, Palk, Wills were appointed, but Mr Powel was appointed the Wednesday morning.* Mr Gough to pray next Assembly; if he fail Mr Hancock or Mr Furse.

Ordinations. An account given that Mr Jones of Brampton was ordain'd in Wales about August, 1716. The Assembly was inform'd that Mr Newberry, Mr Greby, and Mr Cudmore have been preachers several years but not ordain'd. That Mr Enty hath pressd Mr Cudmore to be ordain'd, but he declined it without giving any reason. The Moderator press'd Mr Greby to be ordain'd. He said he did not understand that the people desir'd it. Twas said that 4 or 5 congregations depend on Mr Daniel Kellow to administer Sacraments. Resolv'd that the neighbouring Ministers ordain Mr Cudmore before the end of November next, and Mr Greby if Bodmyn people desire it; and that they appoint times, places, and exercises. The following letters drawn up, read, approv'd and order'd to be sent.

[Shorthand.] *To the Congregation of Dissenting Protestants at Bodmyn in Cornwall. Christian Brethren, Whereas a complaint has been made to this Assembly that Mr Greby has preached among you without being ordained,* [fo. 32v., rev.] *and being dealt with concerning the matter has alleg'd that you have not desired his ordination, we thought it proper by this letter to acquaint you with our judgment that every congregation that can should have a minister settled among them, that should statedly administer the ordinances of the Gospel. Subscribed in the name and by the order of the Assembly of the United Brethren of Devon and Cornwall now sitting at Exon this 4th of Sept., 1717. By T. Edgley, moderator, I. Gilling, scribe.*

To Mr Newberry, drawn up by Mr Hallett senior. Sir, The presence of all our Brethren at the stated times of meeting is very agreeable to us. Your non-attendance has occasion'd the writing of this to discover our concern for the delay of your ordination, which we are all agreed is your duty to submit to after so many years preaching as a probationer; the circumstances also of your congregation making

it requisite. We therefore request you to take this matter into your serious considera-
tion, and that you would no longer defer the putting yourself into a capacity of
exercising the whole work of a Gospel minister.

That which follows was added in the letter to Mr Cudmore.
[Shorthand.] *We have appointed the neighbour ministers to ordain you at a*
time and place when and where they and you shall agree provided *it be*
before the end of November, 1717. Viz. Plymouth ministers, Mr Sandercock,
D. Kellow & Martyn. His Question: An Sacra Scriptura sit divinitus
inspirata ?

Mr Stoddon. Two of Bovey people appeard before the Assembly
who said that Mr Stoddon had promis'd them a Reference to determine
the difference between them & him. Twas urg'd that he had not perform'd
his promise. Order'd that Mr Enty & Mr Hancock draw up a letter to
be sent to Mr Stoddon on this occasion. The following letter drawn up
and agreed to: Sir, There having been complaint made to us that you
have not complied with your promise to the last Assembly, in reference
to the affairs of Bovey: we are much concern'd that you should not have
the strictest regard thereto; but would believe that you have had some
material reason for your proceeding. [fo. 31v., rev.] We are again prest
that there may be a speedy conclusion put to this affair. We think your
own honour and the credit of religion do oblige you to comply with this
desire, and therefore do earnestly press you to put a suddain end to this
matter.

Mr Glanvill of Liscard. Resolv'd that 6 of the eldest Ministers in
age, viz. Messrs Ball, Horsham, Larkham, Powel, Moore, Withers, be a
Committee to inquire into that Brothers scandal. Mr Sandercock,
Harding, Enty, Baron, have heard it already. Mr Ball reported from the
Committee that Mr Glanvill had sinn'd grievously against the 7th
Commandment (tho' not by Fornication or Adultery) as was charg'd
upon him, and as he acknowledg'd. And they gave it as their opinion
that he should have 2 or 3 ministers with 7 or 8 of the people for him to
declare his repentance before them; and to have it order'd that he shall
desist from preaching for some time. The Assembly considerd this
report and came to the following Resolutions. (Out of Mr Edgley's
minutes.).

Introduction: Mr Glanvill professeth to several Ministers appointed by
the Assembly a deep repentance for some iniquities he hath fallen into.
But in as much as he hath given great scandal by these miscarriages of
his, the United Ministers came to the following resolutions. 1. Tis the
opinion of this Assembly that Mr Glanvill profess his repentance for his
great iniquity in the presence of the neighbouring ministers, and some of
the most serious of his congregation, at Liscard. [fo. 30v., rev.] 2. Tis
the desire of this Assembly that Mr Harding, Enty, Baron, and Daniel
Kellow be present when Mr Glanvill makes the foresaid profession of his
repentance. 3. Tis the opinion of this Assembly that Mr Glanvill desist
from the exercise of his Ministry from this time until the expiration of
3 months after his making the aforesaid profession of his repentance.
4. Tis the opinion of this Assembly that Mr Glanvill do not return to
the exercise of his ministry before the expiration of 3 months, until the
aforesaid ministers and any others they shall join with them declare their

approbation of it. 5. This Assembly request the Ministers of Plymouth to supply Liscard next Lord's Day, and that Mr Hornabrook & Mr Facey do supply 'em it for the future.

Mr Joseph Hallett, scribe, Wednesday afternoon.

APPENDIX A

MISCELLANEOUS SHORTHAND PASSAGES

[A Calendar of miscellaneous shorthand passages not included in the main text. These have been arranged chronologically as far as their order can be ascertained.]

1. [fo. 16v.] Certificate of ordination of William Yeo, M.A., aged about 27 years, under an Ordinance of Parliament of October 2nd, 1644, for the work at Brighthelmstone in Sussex as an assistant to the Pastor. Had satisfied his examiners of his election, had taken the National Covenant, was proficient in his studies and unblameable in conduct. Witnessed 24th April, 1645, by John Conant, Samuel Clark, Francis Roberts, Charity Offspring, Fulk Golley, Stanley Gower, George Walker. "Mr William Yeo was ordained in the Church of Butolph [sic] without Aldergate, London. Adoniram Byfield."

2. [fo. 8v.] Subscription that Aaron Pitts of Chard and Samuel Atkins of Exon were on May 18th, 1687 ordained by the Presbytery. Signed by George Mortimer, George Trosse, Benjamin Hooper.

3. [fo. 174r., reversed.] Call to Samuel Bartlet to be an assistant to Theophilus Polwhele at the Church of Christ in Tiverton. A comfortable subsistence promised. Dated July 2nd, 1688. Signed by Richard Prowse, Thomas Keen, Peter Bear, senior, Nicholas Hitchcock, Andrew Speed, John Sealy, Thomas Glover, George Martyn, John Hill, John Filmore, John Jarman, Peter Sharland, Humphry Tiller, Francis Bellamy, Richard Crudge, Alexander Johns, Thomas Glass, Matthew Wood, Simon Gale, Peter Carthew junior. Countersigned by Theophilus Polwheile. "Those of Mr Polwheile's society who clave to Mr Bartlet are 15 men and 28 women."

4. [fo. 174v., reversed.] January 29th, 1689. Pastors and messengers of neighbouring churches had been asked to advise on differences in the Church of Christ at Tiverton which had lately belonged to " Mr Polwheile and his Pastor ". They found Mr Keen and other members " destroying the peace of the Church ", breaking an agreement recently signed, and refusing to meet the present arbitrators. Mr Keen and his party were severely censured and the arbitrators stated they would " forbid to hold any communion with them till they repent and give satisfaction ". James Wood, Pastor at Bideford; Stephen Towgood, Pastor at Axminster; John Ashwood, Pastor of the Church at Exon; Samuel Jones, messenger from the Church at Bideford; Thomas Lane, Robert Brant, messengers from the Church at Axminster; Thomas Far, A. Watt, messengers from the Church at Ilfracombe; Nicholas Savory, Robert Tristram, messengers from the Church at Exon.

124 THE MINUTES OF THE ASSEMBLIES

5. [fo. 13v.] Exon, 13th August, 1691. Letter from Isaac Gilling to Mr Budley & Mr Plumleigh, at Dartmouth. Gilling thanked his friends for an invitation dated July 24th to succeed the late John Flavel at Dartmouth. He could not leave his people at Silverton unsettled with a pastor. Though " his circumstances as to the affairs of this vain world " required him to stay at Silverton, his affections strongly led him towards them. He desired his friends to apply themselves to others more suitable. Mr Edwards who he heard was to be with them " next Fast " might agree; if not, others might be found. Mr How was that day gone to Torrington.

6. [fos. 7v., 8v.] Copy of a document issued by London Ministers in an attempt to compose the dispute arising over the publication of Daniel Williams' book, *Gospel Truth*, in 1692. [The full text was printed in Stephen Lobb's *A Report of the present state of the differences in doctrinals, between some Dissenting Ministers in London; in a Letter.* London, 1697, pp. 11-15. There are several minor differences in wording between Gilling's shorthand copy and the later printed version: his copy of the paper must have been one of those circulated in manuscript before it was printed in 1697 by Stephen Lobb in his Report.]

7. [fos. 173v., 173r., reversed]. Isaac Gilling to Dr. Anth. Smith.[1] 7th December, 1692. Gilling was much of Mr W's[2] mind as to the points then controverted. There were about 40 ministers in London who approved of his book. He did not think it possible for Mr. W to declare his mind more clearly than in his Answer to Mr Chauncey's[3] piece. He declined uncharitable censures and personal reflections. He thought it incorrect that Mr Baxter had rested from writing when he wrote his *Saint's Everlasting Rest*, having seen the 22nd edition of his *Call to the Unconverted* which was written afterwards. Mr Troughton had dealt firmly with him in his *Lutherus Redivivus*.[4] He could easily show that Mr Hotchkiss[5] had done it very well, and the words cited by Dr Anth. Smith were none of Mr Baxter's nor agreeable to his opinions. Baxter held indeed that " Christ died for all, but not as the Arminians for all alike, and that he is the saviour of all men but especially of them that believe, tasted death for every man ... that the destruction of those who perish is not love of God but of themselves." That this was no new Arminian doctrine but as old as Christianity itself might be proved from the writings of the Evangelists and Apostles, and parts of Davenant, Usher, and Dallaei Apologia against Spanheimius.[6] Gilling believed Arminianism to be a dangerous error, yet judged charitably those who held Arminian tenets but lived Gospel lives. He abhorred the errors of " rank Arminians and ranting Antinomians ", the former as advancing his will and derogating from the freeness and efficacy of divine grace, the latter as "wresting the sceptre out of Christ's hands under a pretence

[1]This correspondent has not been identified. It is likely that he was a London layman. There was no Presbyterian minister of this name at the time.
[2]Daniel Williams, whose *Gospel Truth*, 1692, argued against the high Calvinist doctrines.
[3]Isaac Chauncey: *Neonomianism unmasked*, 1692.
[4]John Troughton: *Lutherus Redivivus*, 1677.
[5]Thomas Hotchkis: *An exercitation concerning the nature of foregiveness of sin*, 1655.
[6]Jean Daillé: *Apologia pro duabus Ecclesiarum in Gallia Protestantium Synodis Nationalibus adversus Spanheimium.* Amsterdam, 1635.

of setting the crown in his head." In particular he held "the doctrine of absolute Particular election of the certainty of the conversion, justification, perseverance and salvation of the Elect". Mr Charnock's judicious and elaborate works he prized but could not purchase.[1] The reflections which the very Reverend person was pleased to make upon him would make him more humble and watchful instead of hearkening to a carnal inclination which prompted him to pay him in his own coyn. What had been mentioned about the best Divines being of a different mind from Mr W's he could not help. Scripture and reason swayed him more than high names. He was living at the time of writing with Mr Nathaniel Strong, Apothecary in Exon. P.S. Dr Wallis[2] on the Christian Sabbath would give light on the present controversy.

8. [fo. 22r.] Request of the Assembly through James Wood as Moderator that Joseph Gilling, a student of Divinity, should consider becoming Pastor of the church at Okehampton, then three months without a minister. He was promised £10 from the Assembly's Fund to supplement the £20 offered by the Meeting itself.[3]

9. [fo. 171v., reversed.] Isaac Gilling to his Hearers at Silverton, Oct. 15, 1694. He desired answers to certain questions.

i. Which of his hearers were willing to join for communion in that place.

ii. He advised such as were willing to communicate at Silverton to obtain the approbation of the pastors and churches of which they were formerly members, and to gain the assistance of such pastors in the planting of a church there.

iii. From such church members as were desirous to have him settle there, Gilling expected a Call to the pastoral office in writing.

iv. He informed those of his hearers not already members of a church that the United Ministers of the county had agreed to admit " none but such as " were " knowing and sound in the fundamental doctrines of the Christian religion, persons of visible godliness and honesty." He asked for such to apply for admission to the church, or for further instruction.

v. In the trial of persons' qualifications for church fellowship and in other acts of government or discipline, he desired the advice of experienced Christians whom the society when formed should approve of.

vi. He expected that he should continue to have the stipend promised in August 1690, viz: £40 per annum and his diet, etc. He stated that on account of his wife it would be necessary to live at no great distance from the chapel.

10. [fo. 176v., reversed.] The Humble Address of some nonconformists of Devon Provincially assembled, to William III. It expressed gratitude for preservation of religion and civil liberties through the coming of William III to the throne. The petitioners pledged their loyalty and intention to

---

[1]Stephen Charnock: *Works*, 2 vols., 1684.
[2]John Wallis: *A defence of the Christian Sabbath*, 1692.
[3]The date is 1692. The minutes of the Assemblies for this year are wanting, but James Wood is not known to have been Moderator later. Joseph Gilling trained for the the Ministry but never entered it, greatly disappointing his father.

defend his right to the throne, against all other Pretenders, King James not excepted.[1]

11. [fo. 177r., reversed.] Mr James Wood's Association, May 6, 1696. A similar address to No. 10, more strongly worded.

12. [fo. 16v.] Certificate that Deborah Cary had been for several years a communicant at Bow Meeting in Exon and had carried herself well-becoming the ordinance of the Lord's Supper. John Hopping.

13. [fo. 16v.] Newton Abbot, Oct. 15, 1697. Certificate that Mrs Joan Saxon, formerly a Hearer of Bernard Star of Topsham, had for about 2 years constantly attended on his ministry, and joined in the Lord's Supper, and carried herself suitably to her position and relations. Isaac Gilling, minister in Newton.

14. [fo. 7r.] " We of the Congregation of [2] in the County [2] being desirous to have a gospel minister settled among us according to our bounden duty are resolved to give and allow to him a competent maintenance that he may follow his studies and be comfortably enabled to preach to us the Gospel of reconciliation and the word of grace. To which end we yearly subscribe as followeth. [2] Mr Hooper, Bow."[3]

15. [fo. 164r., reversed.] Petition by Dissenters of Hatherleigh, Devon. Their meeting house had been bequeathed to them for a certain number of years only, the period ending in the following February. The house had been sold to one of the opposite party, a Butcher. Neighbouring ministers had advised that a new meeting house should be built. This had been started on a suitable plot of land. Through poor circumstances, the cost was beyond the members' powers, and so an appeal was made to the Assembly for assistance. Signed by William Coombs, Edmund Edy, Richard Vogwell, William Beatty, Joseph Selden, James Collins, John Chubb. Countersigned by George Tross, Benjamin Hooper, Joseph Hallett, Samuel Hall, Isaac Gilling, John Walrond.

16. [fo. 164r., reversed.] Similar petition, in slightly variant language, signed by Isaac Gilling as Scribe of the Assembly, recommending the Petitioners as a fit object of charity.[4]

17. [fo. 22r.] Certificate that Rachel Bass had been for several years a communicant with Protestant Dissenters in Queen St., Ratcliffe, of unblameable conduct. April 12, 1707, John Mottershead, Pastor.

18. [fo. 122r., reversed.] Certificate dated Edinburgh the 21st day of June 1711, that Samuel Adams, student of Divinity, having come from the West of England, was at the University and had attended public lessons for 2 seasons of the sitting of the College. He was admitted to the Lord's Supper in the established Church of Scotland. Subscribed by William Hamilton, etc.[5]

[1] Undated, but probably issued at the same time as No. 11. James Wood was a Congregationalist, and his version may have been proposed on behalf of his colleagues. An attempt to assassinate William III had just failed.
[2] These spaces were left blank in MS.
[3] Benjamin Hooper succeeded Samuel Atkins at Bow Meeting, Exeter, in 1702.
[4] See also the Minutes of the May Assembly, 1716, *supra*, p. 107.
[5] See also Appendix B No. 5.

19.[1] [fo. 166v., reversed.] Questions discoursed.

1. Whether discipline be necessary to the well-being of the Church when Christianity is universally professed ? Aff.

2. Whether any communion, or how communion, may be kept with profane persons ?

3. Whether if magistrates neglect discipline it be in the power of ministers to set up a discipline in the Church ?

4. Whether the power of ordination be in one or more, and in whom ?

5. Whether all may promiscuously be admitted to the Lord's Supper.

6. Whether a single minister has power to admit or exclude ?

7. Whether ministers are warranted by scripture to search into the knowledge of the people ?

8. What is competent knowledge for a communicant ?

9. Whether notice being given to the minister, shortly before the time of communion, of some scandalous offence committed by a brother, the minister has warrant from the private notice and accusation to suspend the offender ?

10. Whether conscientious men, differing in something from this agreed way of discipline yet desiring Communion may be admitted ?

20. [fo. 178v., reversed.] A shorthand prayer for the opening of a meeting of the Assembly.

21. [fos. 170v., 170r., 169v., 169r., 168v., 167v., 167r., all reversed.] The Consent of several Ministers in Devon touching the administration of the Lord's Supper. The argument is long and involved and does not add to the general picture of the practice followed by Presbyterian societies in England at this time.

22. [fos. 178r., 177v., 177r., 176v., all reversed.] " A Double Scheme containing in the 1st Column the sins most incident to Particular Churches plainly forbidden in the word and for which God sets the mark of his displeasure on them, and in the 2nd the duties enjoined on them in the Scripture, in the conscientious discharge whereof they receive signal fruits of his favour." This has not been included.

[1]The whole of this passage has been transcribed in full.

APPENDIX B
MISCELLANEOUS LONGHAND PASSAGES

[Miscellaneous passages scattered through the notebook, partly in English, partly in Latin. Examples of each type of entry are given here, with notes of the remainder.]

1. [fo. 175v., reversed. The Fund Accounts for the years 1691–1695.]

		[INCOME.			OUTGOINGS.			BALANCE.]		
		£	s	d	£	s	d	£	s	d
1691.	Midsummer.	24	16	0	11	8	0			
	Michaelmas.	64	16	6	33	14	0			
	Christmas.	32	0	9	30	13	0			
		121	13	3	75	15	0	45	18	3
1692.	Lady Day.	57	18	6	30	11	0			
	Midsummer & Michaelmas	79	6	6	74	18	0			
	Christmas.	30	5	3	36	8	0			
		167	10	3	141	17	0	25	13	3
1693.	Lady Day.	33	2	9	39	13	0			
	Midsummer.	47	17	0	33	5	0			
	Michaelmas.	52	1	0	29	1	6			
	Christmas.	26	5	3	25	1	2			
		159	6	0	127	0	8	32	5	4
1694.	Lady Day.	52	14	3	28	6	0			
	Midsummer.	25	6	3	27	18	0			
	Michaelmas.	40	15	$4\frac{1}{2}$	47	6	0			
	Christmas.	24	10	3	38	10	6			
		143	6	$1\frac{1}{2}$	142	0	6	1	5	$7\frac{1}{2}$
1695.	Lady Day.	50	4	1	33	4	6			
	Midsummer.	24	15	3	48	9	6			
	Michaelmas.	54	16	3	52	15	6			
	Christmas.	24	2	0	42	9	6			
	Legacy from Mr. Harvey	25	0	0						
		178	18	0	176	19	0	1	19	0
	[Totals:]	770	13	$7\frac{1}{2}$	663	12	2	107	1	$5\frac{1}{2}$

2. [fo. 176r., reversed. Fragmentary note of income in the years 1698–1700.]

		£	s	d
1698.	Michaelmas.	38	0	2$\frac{1}{2}$
	Christmas.	20	10	2
1699.	Lady Day.	18	3	0
	Midsummer.	54	16	3
	Michaelmas.	32	11	3
	Christmas.	20	9	6
1700.	Lady Day.	17	19	6

3. [fo. 175r., reversed.] We whose names are underwritten do hereby testify upon our certain knowledge that Mr George Trosse of this City and County of Exeter is a Minister of Jesus Christ lawfully ordained by fasting and prayer and imposition of hands. Ames Short, Thomas Lye, William Ball, Robert Atkins, Joseph Alleine, John Kerridge.

4. [fo. 12r.] Hic jacet peccatorum maximus vates sanctorum minimus concionatorum indignissimus Georgius Trosse, huius civitatis indigena et incola qui huic maligno valedixit mundo undecimo die Januarii anno domini 1712/13 aetatis suae 82.

5. [fo. 20v.] Nos infra scripti S. S. Evangelii Ministri omnes hasce literas lecturos facimus certiores D. Samuelem Adams artium in academia Edinensi magistrum (examinatum prius ac probatum) ad sacrum Evangelii Ministerium fuisse admissum cum jejunio precibus et manuum impositione in conventu publico Chudleiae in agro Devon 18mo. Die Junii A.D. MDCCXIII. Benjamin Hooper, Joseph Hallett, Isaac Gilling, John Withers.

[On fo. 123r., reversed, there is a Latin certificate from Edinburgh University relative to the training of Samuel Adams there, and on fo. 122r. a similar testimonial to his character from one of his Edinburgh tutors, in English. Immediately following the Latin certificate of Adams' ordination, on fo. 20v., is a similar certificate for John Edmonds, ordained at the same time and place.]

6. [fo. 22v.] Nos infra scripti S. S. Evangelii Ministri, omnes hasce literas lecturos facimus certiores, Dm. Thomam Bishop, examinatum probatum, ac repertum talibus ornatum datibus, qualos sacrae vocationis dignitas necessario postulat (viz. eruditione, orthodoxia, morum probitate, et S. Scripturae scientia) cum jejunio, divini numinis invocatione et manuum Presbyterorum impositione, secundum verbi divini normam, ad Presbyterii functionum solemniter segregatum, et auctoritate praedicandi verbum, administrandi sacramenta, et fungendi toto evangelici ministri munere donatum fuisse, in conventu publico Topshamio, decimo nono die Decembris A.D. 1709, ex suffragio conventus Ministrorum Unitorum Agri Devoniensis, et Cornubiensis, Exoniae habiti, septimo die Septembris, 1709.

[On the same page are Latin certificates of ordination for Roger Beadon, at East Budleigh, July 21, 1709, and for Cornelius Bond, at Chudleigh, July 17, 1711.]

7. [fo. 171r., reversed.] Nos infra scripti, ecclesiarum pastores et evangelii ministri, omnes hasce literas lecturos certiores facimus, Johannem Munckley apud nos per aliquot annos studiis assidue et diligenter incubuisse, modeste et sobrie se semper gessisse, ac ad evangelii normam vitam suam formasse: atque post studiorum Academicorum curriculum, partim apud nos, partim in Belgio feliciter emensam, solemne per nos examen subiisse; in quo profectus sui in bonis literis, specialim in linguarum notitia, theologia, et aptitudine ad concionandum ac quirenda, egregia et laudanda edidit specimina. Qua propter idoneum illum censemus qui S. Ministerii Candidatus fiat, illique ad sacras literas interpretandas, et ad evangelium in publicis Christianorum conventibus praedicandum, cum ad id legitime vocatus fuerit, (secundam disciplinae nostrae normam) facultatem concedimus. Omnibus denique Christi servis fidelibus illum ex animo commendamus ut optimae spei juvenem, qui per dei gratiam futurus sit doctas at fidelis Domini Jesu Minister. Ad Dei itaque Gloriam et Ecclesiae aedificationem promovendam, omnis illi gratiae incrementam, piisque eius in Vinea Domini laboribus, uberem Jehovae benedictionem ardentibus votis apprecamur. Datum Londini, Julii 16, An. 1710. stylo Juliano. Richard Stretton, Gulielmus Lorimer, Joshua Oldfield, Matthaeus Henry, John Shower, Daniel Wilcox, Andreas Low.

[fo. 179r., reversed has similar, though shorter certificates relating to Walter Furse (London, 5 October, 1705) and Samuel Clark (London, 17 April, 1708).]

8. [fo. 179v., reversed.]

> Reader in Chrysostom's the second's Tomb,
> Flavel's whose lips dropt as the Honey Comb.
> Truth's champion pastor of most watchful eye,
> The oracle of Gospel mysteries.
> In love divine he wrought and suffered
> Christ's flock by word and pen he gently fed
> Fraternal strifes long grieved him which were ended
> Triumphing in their union he attended;
> The Synod's counsels he did moderate
> Thence fled with Angels to associate.
> O grave preserve with care his sacred dust
> Until the resurrection of the just.

[This epitaph for John Flavel is preceded on the same page by a Latin version by Samuel Tapper.]

9. [fo. 161v., reversed.] Nos infra scripti S. Evangelii ministri testamur D. Joannem Fox post studiorum Academicorum curriculum feliciter emensum, Fratrum Dissentientium Conventui, Exoniae habito, 3tio. die Septembris proximo elapso, testimonia de vita ad Christi normam acta, et S. Coena participata, exhibuisse et solemne ibidem examen subiisse in quo egregii in bonis literis Philosophicis et Theologicis profectus edidit specimina. Hisce accesserunt concio hodie in lingua vernacula coram nobis pronunciata et Thesis Theologica Latine explicata ac vindicata. Quum ergo haec exercitia summopere nobis omnibus arrisere illum idoneum censemus qui S. S. Ministerii Candidatus fieret, et Facultate S. Literas in publicis Christianorum coetibus interpretandi donaretur,

donec ad munus pastorale legitime vocatus fuerit. Newton Abbatis, 17o. Oct. 1717. Isaac Gilling, Jacobus Peirce, Thomas Edgley, Samuel Carkeet, Edward Colton, Samuel Adams, John Parr, John Force.
[fo. 164v., reversed, carries a similar license to preach for Joseph Hallett III, dated at Exeter, 6th May, 1713.]

10. [fo. 165v., and fo. 164v., both reversed. A list in English of the proposals put forward by the Provincial Association at Bristol on May 30, 1694. (See above p. 19–21.) The phrasing is slightly different but the sentiments and arguments are identical.]

APPENDIX C

BIOGRAPHIES OF MINISTERS

Abbreviations used.

B   Baptist.
b   born.
C   Congregationalist.
d   died.
Ej   Ejected or silenced.
ord.   ordained.
P   Presbyterian.

Sources of information.

MANUSCRIPT.

Evans, Dr John: List of Dissenting Congregations, 1715–29. [Dr Williams's Library MS. 34.4]

Manning, James: Account of Ministers settled in Devonshire from 1662 to the present time. [MS. dated 1794 inserted in the Minute Book of the Commonwealth Exeter Assembly, in the writing of James Manning, minister at George's Meeting, Exeter, 1777–1831. Deposited with other Assembly records at National Provincial Bank, Exeter.]

Gilling, Isaac: Lists made on certain leaves of the notebook now printed. They are:

fos. 24v., 25v. Deaths of Non. Cons. [Nonconformists], 1683/4 to 1717/18.

fos. 26v., 27v., 28v. United Brethren of Devon & Cornwall, Sept. 1715.

fos. 118r., 119r., and 118v., in that order. Ordained ministers in Devon, May 1701, and Candidates who preach in Devon, 1701.

fos. 161r., 160v., 160r., 159v., all reversed, in that order. List of Moderators, preachers, with texts, at Assemblies from 1691–1717.

fo. 21r. Ministers in the City & County of Exon and County of Devon, October 13, 1691.

PRINTED.

Calamy Revised . . . by A. G. Matthews. Clarendon Press, 1934.

Freedom after Ejection . . . ed. by Alexander Gordon. Manchester Univ. Press, 1917. [Contains list of ministers at work in 1691.]

Dictionary of National Biography.

Evans, G. E. *Vestiges of Protestant Dissent*, Liverpool, Gibbons, 1897.

Fox, John, " Memoirs ", *Trans. Devon. Assoc.* 1896–7, Vols. 28–9.

Murch, J.: *A history of the Presbyterian and General Baptist churches in the West of England.* London, R. Hunter, 1835.

Powicke, F. J.: "Arianism and the Exeter Assembly", *Trans. Congreg. Hist. Soc.*, vii, 1919, pp. 34–43.

ADAMS, Samuel. P. Studied Edinburgh Univ.
    ord. 18/6/1713 at Chudleigh, where he settled. d. July 1731.

ARCHER, John. From Tunbridge Wells, Kent. Attended May Assembly 1712. d. 1733.

ASHWOOD, John. C. Son of Bartholomew Ashwood of Axminster (See Calamy). Took part in Monmouth Rebellion of 1685. Castle Lane Meeting, Exeter. 1689(?)—1698. d. 22/9/1706. Scribe October 1693.

ATKINS, Henry. P. b. 28/12/1679. ord. 16/10/1701 at Crediton. May 1701 at Cofton. 1715 and 1719 at Puddington. Succeeded T. Edgley at Totnes 1722. d. December 1742.

ATKINS, Samuel. P. Baptized Exeter Cathedral 12/8/1660. Succeeded father Robert Atkins (See Calamy) 1685 at Bow Presbyterian Meeting, Exeter. d. 4/7/1702. Scribe June 1693, Moderator Sept. 1700.

AYCRIGG, Benjamin. P. Shepton Mallett 1710–16, then at Glastonbury.

BABB, Simon. Student Taunton Academy, Sept. 1691.

BACKALLER, Henry. P. Silenced at Newbury, Berks. 1662. Licensed Wootton Fitzpaine, 1672, still there 1685. Shobrooke 1690–1704. d. 20/2/1704. Moderator May 1699.

BAILY, BAYLISS, or BAILIES, Jacob. C. ord. 30/5/1693. At Independent Church, Bideford until d. 1719. Orthodox May 1719.

BAKER, John. (?). Attended as London minister, May 1712. Probably John Baker, at Brentford, Middlesex, in 1709. (See Calamy, E: *Life*, Vol. ii, p. 145.)

BAKER, Samuel. (1). C. Bridport 1687–1727.

BAKER, Samuel. (2). Candidate 1716 and 1717.

BALE, John. (?). Candidate May 1714 from outside Devon. Possibly the same who was at Auberry,[1] Wilts., near Marlborough in 1715 and left for Beckenham, Somerset 1728. (See Evans' List, op. cit.).

BALL, John. P. b. November 1654. ord. 20/1/1696. Honiton by May 1701, remained until d. 1745, aged 91. Moderator Sept. 1698, May 1712, Sept. 1716. Orthodox in 1719.

BALSTER, John. (1). P. At Uffculme 1691. Okehampton by May 1697. d. 1713. Moderator May 1697.

BALSTER, John. (2). P. Son of above. Student April 1695. Death reported Sept. 1695.

BANGER or BANJER, Bernard. P. Candidate from Somerset May 1709 and May 1710. Served Long Bredy in Dorset (Presbyterian Fund Minutes). Cerne, Dorset, 1723–30.

BARON, Peter. P. At Warren's Academy, Taunton, 1696. ord. 19/7/1704. Batter St., Plymouth, 1704–59. d. 1759. Orthodox 1719. Scribe May 1706.

BARTLETT, Samuel. C. Succeeded T. Polwheile, Tiverton, 1689. d. November 1705.

BARTLETT, William, II. C. Grandson of William Bartlett I, founder of Bideford Independent Church. b. 1678. Student in London, Sept. 1699. ord. 11/11/1702 Bideford. Co-pastor with J. Baily at Great Meeting, Bideford, until d. 28/9/1720. Orthodox 1719.

BATESBY, ... Somerset candidate, May, 1709.

BATSON or BADSON, Edmund. P. Trained at Warren's Academy, Taunton. Ilminster, 1693–7. Clapham, 1697–1706. Succeeded Warren at Paul's Meeting, Taunton, 1706. d. 1735.

[1]Sic, Presumably Avebury.

BATTEN, Robert. P. ord. 1715. Colleague of W. Youatt at Colyton, 1715–37. Then at Ottery St. Mary.

BEADON, Roger. P. ord. July 21, 1709. Budleigh 1708–18. Ej. November 1718 for suspected Arianism.

BEARNE, Edward. P. Student 1702–1707. Associated with Gilling and others in mid-Devon fraternal Sept. 1704. Attended May and Sept. 1715 as minister from " other counties ".

BENNET, John. Student on the Fund, 1699–1705.

BERRY, Benjamin. Student on the Fund, 1691–1700. At Edinburgh Univ. part of time. Examined for license Sept. 1700.

BERRY, Henry. P. Ej. Dulverton 1662. Torrington 1690–94. d. Aug. 1694.

BERRY, Humphrey. P. Son of John Berry (ej. East Down, 1662). Student, Edinburgh Univ., 1693–9. Ord. Launceston, August 1699, there until 1705. May 1711 at Wellington (probably succeeded Malachi Blake there in 1705.)

BERRY, James. Visiting Somerset minister May 1710.

BERRY, John. P. Ej. East Down, 1662. Licensed Barnstaple 1672. Barnstaple 1690–1704. Also reported Ilfracombe, May 1701, aged 71. d. Dec. 1704.

BILLINGSLEY, Nicholas. P. Ashwick, Somerset, 1699(?) to 1740. An avowed Arian.

BINDMORE, Richard. P. Ej. Woodleigh, Devon, 1662. Licensed 1672. On Gilling's list of ministers of 13/10/1691.

BIRDWOOD, James. P. Ej. St. Petrock's, Dartmouth, 1662. d. Dartmouth, 21/8/1693.

BISHOP, Edward. P. b. 6/2/1659. ord. 19/7/1688. Up-Ottery, May 1719. Orthodox May 1719, not present at Assembly.

BISHOP, Samuel. Candidate 1709.

BISHOP, Thomas. P. Student 1706–9. ord. 29/12/1709, Topsham. Settled at Shobrooke. Married Mary, daughter of Sir John Davy of Creedy, 1716, without father's consent. Moved Barnstaple 1720.

BLAKE, Malachi. P. Wellington, Somerset, where d. 18/6/1705.

BOND, Cornelius. P. Candidate May 1700 to July 1711. Licensed to preach May 1704. Sept. 1705–Sept. 1707 at Holsworthy. Sept. 1709 at Sandwick (sic) in Isle of Purbeck, but left within year. Censured Sept. 1710 by Assembly. Ord. 17/7/1711, settled Ashburton 1712. Last received grant there from Presbyterian Fund 1731. Orthodox 1719. See also Introduction, pp. x–xi.

BOWCHER, George. P. b. March 1678. Candidate June 1693 to May 1699. May 1700 to Plympton. Sept. 1700 to Truro. Ord. 16/10/1701 at Crediton. May 1701 until May 1707, at Bovey Tracey. 1707 until d. Jan. 1756, at Barnstaple. Orthodox 1719. Moderator May 1713.

BOWDON, Jonathan. C. Ej. Littleham St. Swithin, Devon. Joined William Bartlett I at Bideford ca. 1679. d. 18/3/1699.

BRETT, George. P. Candidate Sept. 1707 to Sept. 1715, not mentioned again. Sept. 1707 recommended to Shobrooke, Sept. 1709 at Lupton, promised to try Penzance.

BRETT, Henry. P. b. June 1679. Ord. Aug. 20, 1707. Assistant to N. Harding, Plymouth, 1707–23. d. Jan. 1724. Orthodox 1719.

BRIAL, ... A Huguenot pastor. Bideford Sept. 1708, given £3 by Assembly Ministers.

BRINLEY, Nicholas. P. Son of Benjamin Brinley (one of original members of Exeter Presbyterians' Committee of Thirteen 1687.) Candidate May 1697 to 1706. Ord. August 22, 1706. At Truro 1715–1725.

BROADMEAD, Samuel. Candidate May 1696 to May 1699. Ord. 1699 at Colyton, called to Beer. Unattached on Gilling's list of ministers of May 1701.

BROWN, Hugh. P. Candidate 1706–8. Sept. 1706–1708 at Bovey Tracey. Ord. 8/4/1708 Moretonhampstead. Sept. 1709 at Hatherly. 1710–1716 (at least) at Cofton, near Starcross. Orthodox 1719 when reported at Stoke. d. May 1748.

BROWN, Simon. Candidate from Somerset Sept. 1701.

BUSH, John. P. Ej. Huish with Langport, Somerset, 1662. Langport 1699–1706 (London Presbyterian Fund minutes). d. 9/3/1712.

BUSHROD, John. Candidate from Taunton May 1707, and May and Sept. 1708, whilst on probation at Hatherly.

CALAMY, Edmund, D. D. P. b. 5/4/1671, d. 3/6/1732. Son and grandson of ejected ministers. Known for his abridgement of the autobiography of Richard Baxter with an Account of the Ejected Ministers in Chapter IX. 1st. edn. 1702. 2nd edn. 1713 expanded the Account into separate volume. Continuation appeared 1727. May 1713 was envoy from London ministers advising on the call of James Peirce to Exeter. (See *Dictionary National Biography.*)

CAREL, Robert. P. Ej. Uplowman, 1660. Preached at Cullompton and Cofton during years of persecution. Settled Crediton 1689. d. 20/5/1702. Moderator April 1695.

CARKEET, Samuel. P. Candidate 1705–10. Licensed to preach Sept. 1705. 1707–1710 at Bodmin. Ord. 19/7/1710. Moved to Totnes May 1711, where d. 17/6/1746. Scribe May 1716. Refused the Trinitarian subscription in 1719.

CHANDLER, Henry. P. b. at Taunton. Ministered successively at Malmesbury, Wilts; Hungerford, Berks., and Coleford, Somerset; then at Frog Lane, Bath, for 19 years. d. 1719.

CHAPMAN, Thomas. Okehampton Oct. 1691. Dartmouth April 1693. Accused of false doctrine June 1693 but later judged orthodox. d. 10/9/1693.

CHAPPEL, Christopher. Candidate June 1693. Minister May 1698.

CHAPPEL, Edward. Candidate 1691–4. Licensed to preach 19/4/1693. To be ord. North Molton by order Sept. 1694.

CHORLEY, Josiah. Minister of Octagon Chapel, Norwich, Sept. 1691 to 1720.

CLARK, Isaac. Candidate 1709–11. Ord. 4/4/1711. At Sidbury 1711–21. d. 18/3/1721. Orthodox 1719.

CLARK, John. Of Buckerel. Received £3 from Fund, Jan. 1691.

CLIFFORD, ... Candidate Sept. 1699.

CLODE, Matthew. Devon candidate Sept. 1701. Sept. 1705 to Launceston on trial. From Dorset May 1707.

Cock, Nathaniel. C. Candidate 1713–16. Chulmleigh 1713–16. Ord. 24/10/1716. Succeeded J. Norman at Bideford "Little Meeting". d. 24/10/1760. A non-subscriber in 1719.

Collins or Collings, Robert. P. Ej. Talaton. Had estate at Ottery St. Mary where settled 1662 onwards. d. 6/3/1698. Moderator Sept. 1694.

Colton, Edward. P. Candidate 1708–11. Ord. 17/7/1711 Chudleigh. Promised to go to Bodmin Sept. 1712. Kingskerswell by 1716. d. there 17/1/1743. Orthodox 1719.

Copplestone, John. Candidate May 1706. Not ord. until 19/11/1718. Recommended Shobrooke Sept. 1707, South Molton Sept. 1708. To preach Penzance May 1709. Ordered to be ord. May 1710, not carried out. Orthodox 1719.

Cornish, James. Dulverton Sept. 1711.

Cox, John. P. b. 30/5/1671. At Warren's Academy, Taunton. Candidate 1699–1702. Ord. 6/8/1702. Settled Kingsbridge May 1701. Ej. 1719 for Arianism. d. 1754. Scribe Sept. 1704.

Crompton, William. P. b. 13/8/1633. Ej. Cullompton, 1662. Founder of Pound Square Meeting, Cullompton. d. July 1696.

Cudmore, John, I. On Gilling's List of ministers 13/10/1691. Chulmleigh May 1701. d. Oct. 1706.

Cudmore, John, II. Candidate 1711–1717. Licensed to preach May 1711. Sept. 1713 and 1719 at Looe. Orthodox 1719, but did not attend Assembly.

Darch, Robert. Candidate April 1693. Minister from Somerset May 1699. Tutor at Taunton Academy Sept. 1706. d. 31/1/1737, aged 65.

Darracot, Richard. Candidate May 1709 to Sept. 1710. Chulmleigh 1718–21. d. 1721.

Deacon, Baldwin. P. Ej. Wimborne Minster, Dorset, 1660. Broomfield, Somerset, 1672. In 1715 was minister at Stogursey and Stowey, then at Stogumber, Somerset. d. 1729.

Edgley, Thomas. P. b. 4/3/1675. Candidate May 1697 to June 1700. At Totnes 1698. Ord. 20/6/1700. d. 2/2/1722. Scribe Sept. 1705. May 1709, and May 1714 until Sept. 1715. Moderator May 1711 and Sept. 1717. Also scribe at crucial May 1719 Assembly, when he was orthodox.

Edmonds, John. Candidate May 1710 to June 1713. Ord. 18/6/1713 at Chudleigh. Plympton May 1710 until May 1719 at least. Orthodox 1719 but absent from Assembly.

Edwards, John. P. First regular minister of Honiton Presbyterians. At first under Malachi Blake of Wellington, but took affairs into own hands. Had violent temper, was ejected from meeting. Seceders built new chapel, but conduct did not improve. (See Assembly Minutes for May 1696, p. 28). Later conformed, became curate North Leigh, near Honiton.

Edwards, Stephen. From Chard. Candidate May 1705 to Sept. 1709.

Elms, Thomas. P. May 1716 at Hallett's Academy, Exeter. Examined and licensed Sept. 1717. Milborn Port, Somerset, 1722, when granted £7 from Presbyterian Fund on condition he settled there.

England, John. Candidate Sept. 1691 to Oct. 1693. Minister from Dorset May 1712. d. 1724 or 1725, Sherborne, Dorset. (Evans' List.)

ENTY, John. P. b. 4/3/1672. Ord. 11/5/1698. At Taunton Academy under Warren. Plymouth 1696–1720, at Batter St. from its building in 1708. Orthodox 1719. Replaced James Peirce at James' Meeting, Exeter, 1720. Wrote " Answer to Mr Peirce's Western Inquisition " 1721, as leader of Trinitarian majority. d. November 1743. Scribe Sept. 1700, Moderator Sept. 1709, May 1715.

EVANS, John. In list of ministers May 1716. Possibly mistake for Richard Evans.

EVANS, Richard. P. b. May 1672. Ord. 16/8/1694. After first ministry Staverton, nr. Ashburton, at Cullompton from April 10, 1698 until d. 22/7/1743. Scribe May 1698, Moderator Sept. 1710. Orthodox 1719.

EVELEIGH, Josiah. P. b. 29/3/1676. Candidate Sept. 1696 until ord. 6/8/1702. May 1700 to May 1701 at Little Meeting, Bideford. Sept. 1701 assistant Crediton, minister 1702 until d. 9/9/1736. Scribe Sept. 1703, May 1708. Orthodox 1719.

FACY, Mark. Candidate May 1713 until Sept. 1717. On Arian, non-subscribing side in 1719, probably never ordained.

FARWELL, William. Candidate in Devon, 1701.

FLAMANCK or FLAMMINCK, Henry. P. Ej. Lanivet, Cornwall, 1660. Licensed 1672 Goonrownson, St. Enoder. Abbey Chapel, Tavistock, 1688–1692. d. 1692. Younger brother of R. Flamanck.

FLAMANCK or FLAMMINCK, Roger. P. Ej. Sithney, Cornwall, 1660. Licensed St. Wendron, 1672. Replaced younger brother Henry at Goonrownson 1688 until d. Dec. 1708.

FLAVEL, Benjamin. Candidate 1709–10. Ord. Aug. 23, 1710 at South Molton. Holsworthy Sept. 1709 until May 1719 at least. Orthodox 1719.

FLAVEL, John. C. b. 1630. Ej. St. Clement's, Townstall, Dartmouth, 1662. Licensed Dartmouth 1672, where a Meeting house was built for him 1687. Key figure in recreation of Exeter Assembly 1691. d. 26/6/1691.

FORBES, James. C. b. 1630. Ej. Gloucester Cathedral 1660. Licensed 1672. Barton St. Chapel, Gloucester, built in 1699 until d. 31/5/1712.

FORCE, John, I. Student, to have £15 p.a. Sept. 1695.

FORCE, John, II. P. Candidate 1714–17. On probation at Aylesbeare before mid-1716, when exchanged with Samuel Stoddon II at Bovey Tracey. At Bovey May 1719, a non-subscriber. d. 27/7/1728.

FORSE, John. Candidate licensed to preach May 1717. Non-subscriber May 1719, still unordained.

FOX, John. See Introduction, pp. xiv–xv.

FURZE, Walter. P. Candidate May 1706–Aug. 1710. Ord. Aug. 23, 1710, pastor Chulmleigh 1710–18. Bristol, 1718–20. James's Meeting, Exeter, 1720–22. d. 1722.

GALPIN, John, I. P. Ej. Yarcombe, Devon, 1660, and Ashpriors, Somerset. 1662. During persecution was around Lydeard St. Lawrence, Somerset, Totnes 1689–98. d. 2/9/1698.

GALPIN, John, II. Staverton April 1693. Dartmouth, Oct. 1693 to May 1700. d. 24/11/1712 in London. Son of previous minister.

GARDNER, John. P. b. 1624. Ej. Staplegrove, Somerset, 1662. Licensed Bridgwater 1672. Yeovil 1691. Date of death unknown.

GATCHELL, Edward, I. B. Licensed as Baptist, Pitminster, Somerset. 1672. On Gilling's List of ministers in Devon 13/10/1691.

GATCHELL, Edward, II. Candidate May 1697. Probably son of previous minister.

GILES, William. P. b. 29/10/1673. Ord. 2/10/1700. Associate of Gilling in mid-Devon fraternal Sept. 1704. Modbury May 1719, when orthodox. Moderator Sept. 1711.

GILLARD or GILLET, Nicholas. Student with Hallett, Oct. 1693.

GILLARD or GAYLARD, Robert. Ej. Ide, 1662. Licensed Exeter 1672. One of founders of Bow Meeting, Exeter. d. 14/2/1697.

GILLING, Isaac. P. See Introduction, pp. viii, xv.

GILLING, Joseph. Son of Isaac Gilling. Grant from Fund Oct. 1691 and Jan. 1692. Educated Paris and Leyden. Did not enter ministry finally, to father's sorrow.

GLANVILL, Richard. P. Candidate 1702–5. Ord. 7/8/1705. Liskeard, Cornwall, 1705 until May 1719 at least. Suspended for immorality Sept. 1717. Orthodox 1719. d. March, 1748.

GOFFE, Hugh. Ord. July 1708 at St. Ives.

GOSWELL or GUSWILL, John. P. Son of Exeter merchant fined four times for non conformity (Exeter Sessions Records). Advised settle Honiton June 1691. On Gilling's List of ordained ministers 13/10/1691. Last attended Assembly Sept. 1698. Does not appear in settled pastorate.

GOUGH, Robert. Ord. 7/7/1708. St. Ives May 1719, when he was on orthodox side. d. June 1727.

GREBY or GROBY, John. Candidate Sept. 1710 to Sept. 1717. Sept. 1717 to be ord. Bodmin before November.

GRIGG, John. Candidate May & Sept. 1701.

GRIGG, Samuel. Candidate Sept. 1699 to June 1705. Ord. 6/6/1705, at Barnstaple. Kingskerswell May 1709. Regularly supported by the Fund throughout the period.

GROVE, Edward. Candidate Sept. 1696.

GROVE, Henry. P. Principal of the Taunton Academy after the death of Matthew Warren in 1706. d. 1738.

HADRIDGE, John or James. Ej. Halberton, 1662. Licensed 1672. On Gilling's list of 13/10/1691. Buried Halberton 12/2/1700.

HALL, Samuel. C. b. Feb. 1663. Ord. 23/1/1691. Scribe April 1695. At Pitt Meeting Tiverton. Controversy with Rector of Sandford, Sept. 1713. Orthodox May 1719. d. 23/1/1729.

HALLETT, George. Candidate examined and allowed to preach May 1709.

HALLETT, Joseph, II. P. b. 4/11/1656 (son of Joseph Hallett I, d. 1689, ej. Chiselborough, Somerset, 1660). Ord. 1683. Co-pastor at James's Meeting, Exeter, 1687–1719. Conducted Academy at Exeter for ministerial candidates 1690(?) to 1719. Moderator May 1700, May 1702, May 1704. A non-subscriber in May 1719, ej. from James's Meeting. From 1720 until d. Nov. 1722, at Mint Meeting, Exeter, with James Peirce.

HALLETT, Joseph, III. P. Son of the above. Candidate May 1713 to Sept. 1715. Introduced Arian ideas into father's Academy. Ord.

28/9/1715. A non-subscriber in May 1719. Minister at Mint Meeting, Exeter, 1722–44. d. 2/4/1744.

HALSEY, Joseph. P. b. 1626. Ej. St. Michael Penkevil, Cornwall. Licensed there 1672. Received grant from London Presbyterian Fund of £5 a year (increased to £6), 1690–1710, for Merther, Cornwall. d. 1/10/1711.

HAMLYN, ………. Candidate from Taunton, May 1712.

HANCOCK, Eliezer. Candidate Sept. 1705 to Aug. 1710. South Molton Sept. 1709 to 1728. Ord. Aug. 23, 1710. Orthodox May 1719. To Woodbury 1728.

HANCOCK, Thomas. P. Ej. St. Winnow, Cornwall, 1660. Licensed 1672 at Morval. From 1687 had congregation at East Looe, parish of St. Martin, until end of 1705. d. 1706?

HANMER, George. Licensed to preach May 1716. To Goonrownson May 1717. Ord. 1718 at Modbury. d. 1723. Not present May 1719.

HANMER, John. C. b. Bideford 1642. (Father Jonathan Hanmer ej. Bishops Tawton 1662, settled Barnstaple.) Ord. 1682, remained minister at Barnstaple until d. 19/7/1707. Co-pastor with Oliver Peard.

HARDING, Nathanael. P. b. 22/3/1665, in Ireland. Landed at Dartmouth 1688, protégé of J. Flavel, who recommended him to Presbyterian congregation in Plymouth, which later built Treville St. Meeting. Ord. 27/8/1690. Moderator May 1707, and also at crucial May 1719 Assembly. Strictly orthodox. d. 23/2/1744.

HARDING, Nicodemus. Candidate May 1716. Became Arian and disowned by father Nathanael.

HARFORD, Immanuel. P. b. 1641. Ej. Upton Noble, Somerset, 1662. Licensed 1672 at Stoke St. Mary, Somerset. 1687 co-pastor with Matthew Warren at Paul's Meeting, Taunton, and associated with Warren's Academy. d. 8/8/1706.

HART, Thomas. At Chulmleigh 1690 until d. 13/7/1694. Possibly a B.A. Pembroke College, Cambridge, 1640/1.

HENRY, Hugh. Sept. 1711, of " North Britain ". Asked for settlement in the county.

HENRY or HENERY, William. May 1708 considered for educating for minister. Knew Welsh. Helped again Sept. 1708, May 1709.

HERRING, John. At Taunton Sept. 1691. Possibly the J. Herring who matric. Oxford, New Inn Hall, 15/5/1662 age 18, but refused to conform 8/9/1662.

HEXT, Lawrence. Candidate from Staverton, Sept. 1706 to May 1711. d. 30/10/1711.

HOOPER, Benjamin. P. b. Exeter 1650. Thorverton June 1691. Silverton May 1701 (probably succeeded Gilling in 1697). At Bow Meeting, Exeter, 1702–1715. d. May 1715. Moderator May 1694, Sept. 1701, Sept. 1704, May 1714.

HOPPING, Charles. " Struck out of the Fund " Sept. 1700. Possibly a mistake for John Hopping II.

HOPPING, John, I. P. Fellow Exeter College, Oxford, 1652. Ej. 1662. Licensed Christow 1672. Moved to Exeter, suffered imprisonment, became one of founding ministers of Bow Meeting. d. 8/3/1705.

HOPPING, John, II. Candidate on Fund 1696 to 1699.

HORNABROOK, Thomas. Candidate Sept. 1709 to Sept. 1717. Appears, still a candidate, with non-subscribers in May 1719, at Liskeard, Cornwall.

HORSHAM, William. P. Ord. 24/11/1687. Stoke-in-Ham, April 1693. Topsham 1700, d. there 22/5/1725. Scribe May 1694, Moderator Sept. 1702. Orthodox May 1719.

How, James. Candidate 1714–5. Ord. 28/9/1715 in Exeter. A non-subscriber in 1719.

How, Jaspar, b. Dec. 1680. Candidate May 1702 to June 1704. Ord. June 1704. May 1710 at Falmouth. May 1719 at Penryn and Falmouth. Orthodox May 1719, but did not attend Assembly.

HUDDY or HODY, Matthew, P. Candidate May 1699 to 1704. Ord. 19/7/1704 at Plymouth. May 1710 had just left Plympton. Sept. 1712 Kingskerswell. By 1716 at Penzance. d. there 1738. A non-subscriber May 1719.

HUGHES, John. Candidate 1701. Ord. 6/10/1702. Dartmouth 1702–26. d. May 1726. Orthodox in 1719.

HUNT, Edward. P. Ej. Dunchideock, 1662. Licensed Exeter 1672. South Molton 1687 until d. some time in 1690s.

HURST, Edward. Only mentioned Oct. 1691. Probably E. Hunt was meant, as he spoke at this Assembly, but his name was not in the attendance list.

HUXHAM, John. b. Totnes 1692. Studied under Hallett at Exeter, then under Boerhaave at Leyden. Settled in Plymouth as doctor. Wrote several medical works of which most renowned was his " Treatise on Fevers ", 1739. d. 11/8/1768. (Moore, T. *History of Devon*, 1829–35, Vol. 2, pp. 690–5.)

JACOMB, George. Candidate Sept. 1716 until May 1719. A non-subscriber in 1719.

JAMES, Stephen. P. Studied at Warren's Taunton Academy 1692–6. Minister at Pitminster, Somerset. Succeeded Warren (1706) as Divinity Tutor at Taunton, with Henry Grove. d. early 1725, still under 50.

JAMES, ……… At Yeovil, May 1717.

JEWEL or JOOEL, or TOOELL. See TOOELL.

JILLARD, Nicholas. P. Minister from Kent, 1706. Presumably husband of Mrs Jillard mentioned May 1711, sister of Josiah Eveleigh, and mother of Peter Jillard, later minister at Crediton and Tavistock. Possibly the same as Nicholas Gillard mentioned above.

JONES, Thomas. Candidate from Sept. 1706 until August 1716. May 1711 to May 1716 preaching at Braunton, censured for delay in ordination. May 1717 at Tewkesbury. Sept. 1717 reported ordained in Wales that August.

KELLOW, Daniel. Ord. 23/8/1694. At Fowey, 1716. Orthodox in May 1719 but did not attend Assembly. d. 5/2/1721.

KELLOW, Peter. P. Ord. Oct. 1695. Succeeded Henry Berry at Torrington. Orthodox May 1719. d. Jan. 1731.

KELLOW, Thomas. Applied for ordination Sept. 1695. At Fowey Sept. 1696. Sept. 1706 called to South Molton. d. June 1708.

KERRIDGE, John. P. Ej. schoolmaster at Lyme. Licensed there 1672, associate with Ames Short. Minister at Colyton 1689–1705. d. 15/4/1705.

KNIGHT, John. P. Ej. Little Hempston, Devon, 1662, where he had been assistant to Thomas Friend, the Vicar. Licensed Crediton, 1672. 1691–1714 granted £6 a year from Presbyterian Fund for Abbotskerswell. Reported at Christow May 1701. d. Aug. 1715 at Exeter.

KNIGHT, Robert. At Crewkerne 1690–1738. On Gilling's List of ministers 13/10/1691. From Somerset Sept. 1699.

LANGDON, ... Candidate from Taunton May 1712, also in candidate's list Sept. 1717. (A Luke Langdon was at Maidstone 1717).

LARKHAM, Deliverance. C. b. 9/7/1658, son and grandson of ej. Congregationalists. Ord. Exeter 26/8/1691, settled at Launceston. Castle Lane Meeting, Exeter, 1698. Orthodox May 1719. d. March 1723. Scribe Sept. 1698, Moderator May 1703, Sept. 1705, May 1708.

LAVINGTON, John. P. Son of Exeter Presbyterian merchants. Ord. 28/9/1715. Co-pastor at Bow Meeting, Exeter, 1715–1759, when he died. The only one of the four Exeter Presbyterian ministers not suspected of Arianism. Orthodox in May 1719.

LAVINGTON, Thomas. Refused ordination Sept. 1713 because of youth (only 20). May 1717 examined for license to preach.

LENNET, ... Visitor from London May 1711. Suggested might supply Bodmin. Came with Mrs Jillard, Josiah Eveleigh's sister.

LEWIS, John. Ord. 26/8/1691 at Exeter. At Bovey June 1691. d. June 1692.

LIDDON, ... Candidate from Taunton May 1712.

LIGHT, Stephen. Present at Taunton Meeting, Sept. 1691.

LION, Monsieur de. Plymouth Huguenot nonconformist, in dispute with J. L. Violet of Exeter, May 1699.

LISSANT, George. b. Nov. 1680. On Fund 1691 to 1702. Ord. 24/8/1707. Hatherleigh by Sept. 1713. Successor there ordained 1729.

LOBB, ... Ord. July 1708 at St. Ives. Possibly son of Peter Lobb (d. 1718) and nephew of Stephen Lobb (d. June 1699), both Nonconformist ministers of Cornish origin.

LOBB, Theophilus. C. b. 1678, son of Stephen Lobb (d. 1699). At Guildford 1702, Shaftesbury 1706, Yeovil 1713, Witham, Essex, 1722, Haberdashers' Hall, London, 1732. Became M.D. of Glasgow University, and a London physician. d. 19/5/1768.

LOVERIDGE, Nathaniel. On Fund from May 1699 to May 1706. Protégé of Samuel Stoddon I.

MAJENDIE, Andrew. b. Sept. 1672. Ord. 8/9/1701. Huguenot nonconformist. Succeeded J. L. Violet at Exeter 1701. May 1712 asked assist Huguenots at Dartmouth. May 1719 transferred to Dartmouth. Orthodox 1719.

MANSTON, Joseph. P. Ord. 30/3/1703. Assistant to Samuel Tapper at Lympstone 1703, succeeded him 1708. Orthodox 1719. d. April 1720. Moderator May 1710.

MARSHAL, John. Of Staverton. Ord. 23/10/1700.

MARSHAL, Thomas. P. Licensed Ilminster 1672. d. there 1705.

MARTYN, Michael. P. b. 1670. Ord. Aug. 1694. Hatherly 1694. Orthdox 1719, when at Lympstone, succeed Manston there 1720. 1728 to Launceston. d. 9/8/1745.

MASTERS, ... Student receiving £8 in 1696.

MAY, ... A *doctor of physick* at a Scottish university examined and licensed in May 1717.

MEAD, John. From Chard. Ord. 16/8/1694 at Ashburton. Scribe Sept. 1695. Last mentioned Sept. 1701. Successor ord. 1702.

MERRYON, ... Sept. 1713 had moved to London from Looe.

MILFORD, ... Son of Richard M. of Thorverton. Not accepted for Fund in Sept. 1710.

MILLS, Benjamin. P. Ej. Chardstock Dorset. Preached there and at Bridport. d. about 1693.

MILNER, ... From Hallett's Academy, licensed to preach Sept. 1711, age 21. To supply Wrington in Somerset. Still candidate in Sept. 1715.

MOOR, John, I. P. b. 1642, Musbury. Educ. Colyton and Brasenose, Oxford. Vicar of Longburton, Dorset, resigned 1667. Licensed Presbyterian Ottery St. Mary 1672. To Bridgwater 1676. Founded Academy there 1688. d. 1717.

MOOR, John, II. P. Son of the above. b. 1673. Licensed 19/4/1693. Succeeded father in both Academy and church at Bridgwater. Adopted Arianism. d. 1747, and Academy ended also.

MOOR, John, III. P. Ord. 29/7/1691. Tiverton 1691–1730. Conducted small Academy. d. 25/8/1730. Moderator May 1705. Orthodox 1719.

MOOR, Philip. Received grant May 1708.

MOOR, Thomas. P. Son of John Moor I. Licensed 19/4/1693. Helped father and brother in Bridgwater until 1701. Then minister at Abingdon, till d. 1720.

MORTIMER, John. P. b. Exeter 1633(?). Ej. Sowton St. Michael, 1662. Licensed 1672 at Exeter. At Bow, 1691–2, when received grant from London Common Fund. d. Exeter 1696.

MUDGE, Zachary. b. Plymouth 1694. Educ. Hallett's Academy, Exeter, 1710–14. Headmaster Bideford Grammar School until his preferment to St. Andrew's Church, Plymouth in 1731, having previously conformed. d. 1769. (Worth, R. N. *History of Plymouth*, 1890, pp. 460–1.)

MULLINS, Samuel. Ord. 11/10/1699, Totnes. d. there 1710.

MUNCKLEY, John. P. Son of Exeter Presbyterian family. Pastor of Bartholomew Close Chapel, London, 1717–38. Trustee of Dr. Daniel Williams's Trust, 1733–8.

NEWBERRY, Samuel. Candidate Sept. 1715, preaching at Beer. Censured Sept. 1717 for failing to be ordained.

NOBLE, Isaac. C. Bapt. 30/1/1659. Ord. 28/5/1689, at Castle Green, Bristol. d. 1726/7.

NORMAN, John. C. b. March 1679. Ord. June 1703. At Little Meeting, Bideford, 1703–16. Portsmouth 1717–56.

ORCHARD, William. Candidate May 1702 to Sept. 1705. May 1704 joined with Gilling and 4 others in mid-Devon fraternal.

PALK, Thomas. P. b. Staverton 1636. Ej. Woodland, Devon, 1662. Licensed Ogwell 1672. d. Ashburton 18/6/1693.

PALK, William. P. b. 10/12/1681. Elder son of Thomas Palk. Trained at Warren's Academy, Taunton. Ord. 17/10/1705 at Appledore. May 1705 Chudleigh. By Sept. 1715 at Ilfracombe. At Sidmouth May 1719, when he was orthodox. To South Molton 1731. d. 1760.

PALMER, Anthony. P. b. 1613 Barnstaple. Ej. Bratton Fleming 1662. d. 10/9/1693.

PARDUE or PERDUE, Matthew. P. Licensed Oct. 1691. Ord. Bovey Tracey 10/5/1693. May 1701 at South Molton. d. April 1706.

PARR, Edward. P. Ej. Rew, 1662. Lived at Ottery afterwards. Preached there and particularly at Buckerel. d. 16/1/1701. Moderator October 1693.

PARR, John. Licensed, just under 22, May 1713. Ord. 20/7/1715, at Okehampton. A non-subscriber in May 1719.

PEARD, William. C. Son of Oliver Peard of Barnstaple. Succeeded John Hanmer there 1707. d. 1716.

PEIRCE, James, P. b. 1674(?). Ord. 1699. Minister at Cambridge 1701–6. Newbury 1706–13. James's Meeting, Exeter, 1713–19. Mint Meeting, Exeter, 1720–26. The key figure in the Arian Controversy, 1717–19, and leader of the non-subscribers in May 1719. d. 30/3/1726. Moderator Sept. 1714.

PIERSE, John. Candidate from Dorset, May 1713 and May 1714. Ordained minister from Dorset May 1717.

PITTS, Aaron. P. Ord. 18/5/1687. Succeeded Backaller at Chard, minister there 1715.

POLWHEILE, Theophilus. C. Ej. Tiverton 1660. Licensed Tiverton 1672. Meeting-house built for him 1687. Buried 3/4/1689.

POWELL, John, I. Candidate Oct. 1691. Ord. 13/5/1693. At Blandford, Dorset, May 1699.

POWELL, John, II. C. Ord. 1716. Succeeded William Peard at Barnstaple. Orthodox in 1719. d. 1721.

POWELL, Thomas. Welsh minister from Swansea. Appeal made on his behalf Sept. 1711.

PREW, John. Licensed to preach Sept. 1701. Admonished Sept. 1704. Disowned May 1706.

PYKE, ... Candidate May 1716.

PYM, John. Merchant of Exeter. Members of Exeter Presbyterians' Committee of Thirteen from beginning in 1687 until his death in 1727. Appointed Treasurer of Assembly Fund May 1709.

QUICK, John. P. b. 1636, Plymouth. Ej. Kingsbridge, 1660. Licensed 1672. In London from 1681, with meeting-house in Middlesex Court, Bartholomew Close, Smithfield. Wrote *Synodicon in Gallia Reformata*, 1692, 2 vols., giving the Acts and Canons of the French Reformed Church. d. 29/4/1706.

RABJENT, Samuel. Candidate Sept. 1696 to 1701. May 1710 and 1711 attended as a Minister from Somerset.

ROSSWELL or ROSEWELL, John. P. b. Nov. 1659. Ord. 31/12/1690. May 1701 at Colyton, assistant to John Kerridge. Succeded Kerridge 1705. 1711/1712 in dispute with congregation over provision of an assistant. Preached in own home in Colyton for some years. Last attended Assembly May 1716.

Rowe, Thomas. P. Son of Thomas Rowe (1631–80, ej. Lytchett Matravers, Dorset 1662). Studied at Utrecht 1691–2. Visited Assembly from London Sept. 1710, and possibly Sept. 1715. Minister at Poole, Dorset, as late as 1735.

Rutter, Henry. Candidate May 1706 to Sept. 1708. Failed to " rouse " congregation in South Molton in 1708 and decided to quit.

Sandercock, Jacob. P. b. Sept. 1664. Educ. at Warren's Academy, Taunton. Ord. 1/5/1688. At Tavistock until his death 24/12/1729. Moderator Sept. 1703, Sept. 1715. Orthodox May 1719.

Savage, ... Candidate from Lymptsone, May 1706 to Sept. 1709. (A Samuel Savage was minister at Bury St. Edmunds, 1714–18.)

Serle or Searle, John. P. b. 1613. Ej. Rattery, Devon. 1660, and Plympton St. Mary, 1662. Licensed Plympton 1672. Received grants from London Common Fund 1690–99. d. Oct. 1699.

Shapland, Angel. Candidate from Crediton May 1709 until after May 1717. d. 1748, age 57, as minister of Marshfield, Glos.

Sherwill, Nicholas. P. b. Plymouth, rich family, son of clergyman. Ord. 16/8/1660, at Oxford, without subscription or promise of obedience. Fined and imprisoned for nonconformity 1665–6. Licensed Plymouth 1672. Moderator Sept. 1695. d. 17/5/1696. His congregation became Congregationalist, and their present church is named after him.

Short, Ames. P. b. 1616. ej. Lyme Regis 1662. Licensed at Lyme, 1672. Held small Academy there c. 1682–97. d. 15/7/1697.

Short, John. Candidate May 1706 until May 1708.

Short, John, II. C. Son of Ames Short. b. 26/3/1649. Assisted father in school both at Lyme and at Colyton with John Kerridge, c. 1682–92. 1692–8 head of Academy at Bishop's Hall, Bethnal Green. 1698 succeeded Matthew Barker as minister of one of two Congregational Churches in joint occupancy of a meeting house in Miles' Lane, Cannon St. d. 1716/17.

Short, Samuel. b. June 1677. Candidate April 1695 to Sept. 1699. May 1701 at Bideford Little Meeting. Ord. 16/10/1701 at Crediton. At Ufculm 1701 until his death, April 1726. Orthodox May 1719. Scribe May 1705. Seems to have assisted at Colyton also at times between 1707 and 1719.

Simon, ... Candidate from Taunton, May 1712.

Sinclare, Alexander. P. b. 1658? at Belfast. Ord. 1686 Waterford. Assistant to John Weekes at Lewin's Mead, Bristol, c. 1690–2. Settled Dublin 1692–1722, when he died.

Slowly or Sloly, John. P. Candidate from Barnstaple, June 1693. On Fund, receiving special contributions from Tavistock, 1693–9. Student at Edinburgh, Sept. 1694. Ord. 6/8/1702 Crediton. Settled at Silverton 1702. Orthodox May 1719, still at Silverton. Later had pastorates at Chulmleigh and Newton Abbot. d. 23/5/1749. Scribe May 1704.

Smith, John. Delegate from Somerset May 1698.

Snowdon, Samuel. Candidate Sept. 1702.

Spark, Angel. P. Ord. 21/6/1692, Moretonhampstead. Orthodox May 1719, but absent from Assembly. d. Moreton Oct. 1721.

SPRINT, John. P. Minister at Wimborne, Dorset, 1685?, Stalbridge, 1687?, and Milbourne Port, Somerset 1700 until d. Jan. 1718.

STANDARD, ... Candidate of Somerset, Sept. 1708 and May 1709.

STARR, Bernard. P. Son of Exeter merchant, trained under Ames Short of Lyme. Ord. 25/8/1687. Topsham 1687–1700. Scribe June 1691. d. 28/11/1700.

STARR, John. Candidate May and Sept. 1717. Refused to subscribe Trinitarian declaration May 1719, still a candidate.

STEVENSON, Alexander. Refused admission to Sept. 1710 Assembly, as he had no certificate of introduction from Bristol, where his last pastorate took place. Ord. Manchester, a Scot by birth.

STEVENSON, Bennet. P. Candidate Sept. 1710–1717. A Doctor of Divinity. Ord. 25/4/1717. Sidmouth 1715–19. Bath, Trim St., 1719–56.

STODDON, John. Candidate at Warren's Academy, 1699–1706. Ord. 11/7/1706. Ashburton May 1708. d. 1712.

STODDON, Samuel, I. P. Sidmouth both in April 1693 and May 1701. Moderator May 1696. d. 3/3/1706 at Sidbury.

STODDON, Samuel, II. P. Son of above. Ord. 26/12/1706 at Ottery. Continued father's work at Sidbury & Sidmouth 1706–9. July 1711 at Bovey Tracey. May 1716 at Aylesbeare. May 1719 Budleigh. Orthodox 1719. d. 1755.

STOGDON, Hubert. P. Educ. Exeter Grammar School & Hallett's Academy. Chaplain to Sir John Davy of Creedy, 1715. Adopted Arianism and provoked controversy. N. Billingsley found him a refuge at Wokey near Ashwick in Somerset. Ord. 1718 Shepton Mallet. Later adopted Adult Baptism. d. 1728.

STRONG, James. May 1707 licensed to preach. May 1709 to Goonrown-son in Cornwall. Ord. 19/7/1710 Bodmin. May 1717 at Pitminster Somerset. Ilminster 1725–38.

SYMONDS, ... Candidate May 1711.

SYMONDS, Jelinger. P. b. 11/6/1672. Candidate 1691–95. Oct. 1693 at Staverton. Sept. 1694 preaching to seceders from Angel Spark at Moreton. July 1695 ord. at Bow. There until d. 28/4/1724. Orthodox May 1719.

SYMONDS, Penuel. Candidate June 1693. Ordination never ordered, but received grants from Fund between Sept. 1711 and Sept. 1717, when he appears to have become an ordained minister. d. 1733. Orthodox 1719.

SYMONDS, William. Candidate 1696 and again 1701.

TALBOT, John. Candidate from Somerset May 1707.

TAPPER, Samuel. P. b. 1636 Exeter. Ord. 5/8/1657. Ej. St. Merran, Cornwall, 1660. A moderate, who was esteemed by successive Bishops of Exeter despite Nonconformity. Settled at Lympstone 1687 until d. 3/3/1710. Moderator June 1693, May 1698.

TAYLOR, Christopher. P. b. Taunton, educ. Warren's Academy. Ord. 25/8/1687 at Lyme Regis. At Trim St., Bath, 1688–99 according to *Murch*, at Frog Lane, Bath, 1692–7, according to *Gordon*. Leather Lane, London, 1697 to d. 26/10/1723. Elected manager of London Presbyterian Fund, 25/10/1697.

TAYLOR, Ebenezer. Ord. Ashburton 6/7/1703. M.A. Glasgow, 1680. Sept. 1709 announced leaving Cofton for South Carolina. May 1710 letter received from him in Carolina.

TAYLOR, Michael. P. b. Silverton. Ej. Pyworthy, Devon, 1660. Licensed Holsworthy 1672. From 1687 had meeting-house at Holsworthy. d. 26/5/1705.

THOMPSON, ... Candidate of Devon 1701–2.

TINGCOMB, Theophilus. P. Silenced 1662, though not beneficed. Licensed Lostwithiel 1672. Callington 1689. Still preaching at Talvans, St. Germans, 1718. d. 1719. Reported orthodox 1719 but not present at May Assembly.

TOOELL, JOOEL or JEWEL, Richard. Ord. Lyme, Dorset, 25/8/1687. Succeeded Joseph Chadwick at Dulverton 1691, probably his assistant before then. Last mentioned at Assembly of April 1693.

TOUCHING. See TUTCHIN.

TOWGOOD, Stephen I. C. Son of Matthew Towgood (ej. Semley, Wilts., 1662). At Axminster as early as 29/1/1689, and still in 1715. Removed to Newport, IOW, in 1721. d. 1722. Moderator Sept. 1699. Did not attend Assembly after May 1707.

TOWGOOD, Stephen, II. P. Son of the former. Candidate May 1713. Ord. Axminster 4/7/1716. Topsham 1727–43. James's Meeting, Exeter, 1743–60. George's Meeting, 1760–77. d. 1777.

TROSSE, George. P. b. 25/10/1631, Exeter. Oxford, but no degree, 1657–64. Ord. 1666. Licensed 1672. Co-pastor James's Meeting, Exeter, 1687 until d. 11/1/1713. The leader of Devon Nonconformity during his life. Moderator Oct. 1691, April 1693, Sept. 1706, Sept. 1708.

TUCKER, Edmund. P. b. 1627 Milton Abbot. Ej. Halwell, Devon, 1662. Ord. 1654. Licensed West Alvington, 1672. Minister at Kingsbridge 1689. d. 5/7/1702.

TUTCHIN, or TOUCHING, John. P. Son of Robert Tutchin, Vicar of Newport, IOW. Ej. Fowey, 1662. Licensed 1672. Held Meeting at Fowey after 1687. Will proved 25/6/1697.

VIOLET, J. L. Minister to nonconforming Huguenots in Exeter from about 1686 until 1699. Invited join Assembly April 1693.

WALKER, Alexander. P. Candidate 1706–11. Ord. Chudleigh 17/7/1711. Sept. 1711 reported at North Molton for " 5 years past ". Still there 1716. Sept. 1717 collection for " Mr Walker's Meeting house at Ford ". Orthodox in May 1719, and moved to Kingsbridge where John Cox had been expelled for Arianism. d. 1/6/1750.

WALROND, John. P. b. 25/8/1673. Ord. 16/6/1698. At Ottery 1698–1729. Bow Meeting, Exeter, 1730–55. d. 4/10/1755. Moderator Sept. 1707, Sept. 1713. Leader of the Orthodox party in Assembly, 1717–19.

WALROND, John, II. P. Son of the above. Candidate 1716.

WALSH, John. On Gilling's list of ordained ministers, 13/10/1691. Possibly meant for the next.

WALSH, Thomas. P. b. 6/12/1668. Ord. 22/4/1690. Pitminster, April 1693. Stoke-in-Ham May 1701 until d. Nov. 1729. Orthodox 1719.

WARREN, Matthew. P. Ej. Downhead, Doulting, Somerset. Licensed Withypoole 1672. Co-pastor with Immanuel Harford at Paul's Meeting, Taunton, 1687. Conducted Academy at Taunton, earliest known pupil being John Shower, 1671. d. 14/6/1706.

WARREN, ... A " foreign " minister in May 1714.

WARREY, ... Devon candidate 1701.

WEBBER, Henry. Licensed to preach May 1709, at Hallett's Academy. May 1717 in list of Ministers from Somerset.

WEEKS, John. P. b. 1633. Ej. Buckland Newton, Dorset, 1662. Preached in Bristol area and Wiltshire 1662–72. Licensed Bristol, 1672. Lewin's Mead Meeting house built for him 1692–3. d. 22/11/1698.

WHEELER, Jonathan. C. Ord. 14/11/1705. Succeeded Samuel Bartlett with Tiverton Independents. Orthodox May 1719. d. 2/10/1723.

WHITTY, ... Candidate of other counties May 1715 and Sept. 1717.

WILCOX, Daniel. Candidate April 1695 to 1700. Ord. 23/10/1700.

WILLS, Benjamin. P. b. Jan. 1681. Ord. 17/10/1705 at Appledore, where he remained until d. 25/12/1747. Orthodox May 1719.

WITHERS John. P. b. 25/3/1669. Ord. 26/8/1691. Lupton June 1691. Modbury May 1701. Bow Meeting, Exeter, 1705 until d. 1729. Orthodox 1719 after suspicion of Arianism. Moderator May 1706, Sept. 1712.

WOOD, James. C. From Ireland. Co-pastor with Jonathan Bowden of Bideford Independents in mid-1680s. Seceded 1693 with portion of congregation. d. about 1697.

WOOD, Robert. P. Candidate 1699–1705. Ord. Honiton 9/8/1705. At Luppit 1705. Orthodox May 1719, still at Luppit.

WOOD, Samuel. P. Ord. 1/5/1688. North Molton 1693–7. Puddington May 1697. Halberton 1716. Hartinton (sic) 1719. Orthodox 1719. d. 5/5/1725.

WOOD, Thomas. Merchant of Exeter. Treasurer of the Fund 1696 until 1709. Member of Exeter Presbyterians Committee of Thirteen, 1689–1714.

WOODCOCK, Josiah. b. 1665. Ord. 25/8/1687, at Lyme.

WOOLCOMB, Robert. P. Bapt. 7/10/1632. Ord. Dartmouth 11/11/1657. Ej. Moretonhampstead 1662. Licensed Chudleigh 1672. Returned Moreton 1689. d. 29/4/1692.

YEO, Bartholomew. P. Bapt. Hatherleigh 25/5/1617. Ej. Merton, Devon, 1662. Licensed Hatherleigh 1672. Preaching there and Jacobstowe 1690–3. Buried 1/2/1694 (*Calamy*) but this must be 1693, as he was mentioned in April 1693 Assembly as already dead.

YEO, William. P. b. 1618. Ej. Wolborough, 1662. Licensed 1672 Newton Bushel. Preached there continuously until d. Nov. 1699. Succeeded by Isaac Gilling.

YOUAT, William. P. Candidate 1707–15. On Fund at Hallett's Academy 1707–11. Licensed to preach May 1711. Minister at Colyton 1715–45, when he died. Not present May 1719.

YOUNG, Samuel. b. 1648 Plymouth. At South Molton c. 1682. In London at time of Crispian controversy 1692. Attended Plymouth Assembly Sept. 1695. d. 1707.

INDEX

ABBOTSKERSWELL, 142.

Abingdon, 143.

Acleigh, William, 29.

Adams, Samuel, 87, 91-2, 94-5, 97, 101, 103-6, 114, 118, 126, 130, 132-3.

Agate, Mr., 77.

Ailsbear, *see* Aylesbeare.

Alleine, Joseph, 130.

Anabaptists, *see* Baptists.

Antinomianism, xii, xiii, 124.

Appledore, 58, 90, 115, 144, 148.

Archer, John, 87, 134.

Arianism, xiv, xv, 72, 101, 135, 137-40, 142-4, 146-8.

Arminianism, 17, 124.

Arnold, Mr., 107, 110, 115, 117-8.

Arscot, Mr., 36, 39, 45.

Ashburton, xi, 13, 18, 22, 53-4, 61, 69, 76, 90, 105-7, 111, 135, 138, 143, 146-7.

Ashpriors, 138.

Ashwick, 65, 135, 146.

Ashwood, Bartholomew, 134.

Ashwood, John, xi, xii, xiii, 4, 7, 10-1, 13-4, 16-8, 21, 24, 26, 29, 30, 32-6, 38, 123, 134.

Atkins, Henry, 47-55, 57-60, 62, 64, 67-8, 71, 74, 76, 78-80, 84, 87, 90-4, 97, 101-3, 105-7, 110, 114, 116, 118, 134.

Atkins, John, 72, 83, 95, 117.

Atkins, Robert, 130, 134.

Atkins, Samuel, 4, 7, 10-3, 16, 21, 28, 36, 39-40, 43, 45-50, 53, 123, 126, 134.

Audley, Mr., 34.

Avebury, 134.

Avery, Robert, 11.

Axminster, xi, xii, 108, 115, 123, 134, 147.

Aycrigg, Benjamin, 102, 134.

Ayers, Mr., 43.

Aylesbeare, 105, 108, 113, 138, 146.

BABB, SIMON, 7, 134.

Backaller, Henry, 4, 10-1, 13, 16, 19, 21, 24, 26, 28, 40-3, 47, 49-52, 134, 144.

Badcock, Samuel, xiii.

Badson, Edmund, 26, 97, 101, 134.

Baker, John, 87, 134.

Baker, Samuel, xi, 18, 29, 59, 62, 118, 134.

Bale, John, 101, 134.

Ball, John, 26, 28-30, 36, 38-43, 45-7, 49, 51, 53-7, 59-65, 67-9, 71-2, 74-82, 84, 87-94, 97-8, 101-11, 113-5, 118-20, 134.

Ball, William, 130.

Balster, John, 4-5, 7, 10-11, 16, 18, 21-4, 26-30, 36-41, 44-7, 49-50, 52-5, 57-60, 62-5, 67-8, 70-2, 74, 78-80, 82, 87, 92-3, 97, 102, 134.

Banger, *or* Banjer, Bernard, 71, 76, 134.

baptism, 7, 77-8, 91, 146.

Baptists, 7, 18, 20, 23, 36, 44, 77, 82, 133, 139.

Barker, Matthew, 145.

Barnstaple, xii, xiii, 17, 22, 45, 57, 60-1, 64, 86, 90, 97, 106-7, 115-6, 135, 139-40, 144-5.

Baron, Peter, 29, 37, 45, 49-50, 52, 55, 59-60, 67-8, 76-7, 87, 92-3, 101, 103,

105-8, 113-4, 117, 120, 134.

Bartlett, John, xiii.

Bartlett, Samuel, 1, 4, 6-8, 10-1, 13, 16, 40, 43-4, 47, 50, 55, 123, 134, 148.

Bartlett, William, I., xiii, 134, 135.

Bartlett, William, II, xiii, 42, 44-5, 48-55, 57-8, 60, 62, 67-70, 73-4, 78-81, 92-3, 102-3, 105-6, 110, 118, 134.

Barton, Thomas, 109-10.

Bass, Rachel, 126.

Bastard, Mr., 114.

Bates, William, xii.

Batesby, Mr., 71, 134.

Bath, 13, 26, 136, 146.

Batson, *see* Badson.

Batten, Robert, 87-8, 93, 101, 135.

Baxter, Richard, xii, 58, 124, 136.

Bayley, *or* Bailies, Jacob, xiii, xiv, 26, 28-9, 35-6, 38, 42, 44, 46-9, 51-2, 54, 57-8, 62-3, 67-8, 134.

Beadon, Roger, 62, 64, 68-9, 71-2, 74, 76, 80, 84, 87, 90, 92, 97-8, 101-6, 110-1, 114, 130, 135.

Beaminster, 65.

Bear, Peter, 123.

Bearne, Edward, 51-2, 54-5, 57-62, 103, 105, 135.

Beatty, William, 126.

Beckenham, 134.

Beer, 42, 66, 98, 111, 136, 143.

Belfast, 145.

Bennet, John, 41, 47, 49, 51-2, 57, 135.

Bellamy, Francis, 123.

Bere, Mr., 90.

Berry, Mr., 21-2, 26, 29, 40-1, 43, 45-8, 54, 57.

Berry, Mrs., 97.

Berry, Benjamin, 5, 11-2, 27, 37-8, 47-8, 135.

Berry, Henry, 13-4, 135, 141.

Berry, Humphry, 17, 19, 22, 27, 37, 40, 50-2, 58-60, 62, 64, 67, 69, 71, 74, 76, 80, 92, 114, 135.

Berry, James, 135.

Berry, John, 10, 13, 15, 18-9, 23, 27-9, 37, 40, 42-3, 45, 47, 49, 51, 53, 55, 135.

Berry, Thomas, 39.

Bethnal Green, 145.

Bideford, xii, xiii, xiv, 7, 14, 16, 19, 21-2, 24, 28-9, 34-5, 38, 41-2, 44, 46, 48-9, 51, 53-4, 63, 69, 76, 90-1, 106, 109-10, 113, 115, 123, 134-8, 140, 143, 145, 148.

Billingsly, Nicholas, 8, 65, 102, 135, 146.

Bindmore, Richard, 135.

Birdwood, James, 11-2, 135.

Bishop, Edward, 105-6, 111, 135.

Bishop, Samuel, 71, 73-4, 135.

Bishop, Thomas, 59-62, 64, 66-7, 69, 74-6, 78-80, 84, 87, 92-3, 97, 99, 101-3, 105-7, 110, 113-4, 130, 135.

Bishop's Tawton, 140.

Blake, Mr., 92, 101,

Blake, Malachi, 1, 4, 7-8, 10, 13, 16-8, 21, 29, 36, 39, 43, 50, 135, 137.

Blandford, 41-2, 144.

Bodmin, 8, 64, 72, 79, 83, 91, 93, 102, 112, 119, 136-7, 139, 142, 146.

149